An Introduction to Graphical User Interfaces with Java Swing

We work with leading authors to develop the strongest educational materials in computing, bringing cutting-edge thinking and best learning practice to a global market.

Under a range of well-known imprints, including Addison-Wesley, we craft high quality print and electronic publications which help readers to understand and apply their content, whether studying or at work.

To find out more about the complete range of our publishing, please visit us on the World Wide Web at: www.pearsoned.co.uk

An Introduction to Graphical User Interfaces with Java Swing

Paul Fischer

ADDISON-WESLEY

An imprint of Pearson Education

Harlow, England • London • New York • Boston • San Francisco • Toronto
Sydney • Tokyo • Singapore • Hong Kong • Seoul • Taipei • New Delhi
Cape Town • Madrid • Mexico City • Amsterdam • Munich • Paris • Milan

Pearson Education Limited
Edinburgh Gate
Harlow
Essex CM20 2JE
England

and Associated Companies throughout the world

Visit us on the World Wide Web at:
www.pearsoned.co.uk

First published 2005

ISBN 0321 22070 6

British Library Cataloguing-in-Publication Data
A catalogue record for this book is available from the British Library

Library of Congress Cataloguing-in-Publication Data
Fischer, Paul, 1956-
    Introduction to graphical user interfaces with Java Swing / Paul Fischer.
        p. cm.
    Includes bibliographical references and index.
    ISBN 0-321-22070-6
    1. Java (Computer program language)   2. Graphical user interfaces (Computer systems)
I. Title.
    QA76.73.J38F58   2005
    005.13′3 – dc22   2004062293

10 9 8 7 6 5 4 3 2 1
08 07 06 05

Typeset in 10/12pt Caslon and Frutiger by 59
Printed in Great Britain by Henry Ling Ltd, at the Dorset Press, Dorchester, Dorset

The publisher's policy is to use paper manufactured from sustainable forests.

Contents

Introduction

1

1.1 ■ General

Modern operating systems such as Microsoft's Windows, Apple's MacOS, and the different Unix-based versions such as Linux or Solaris use a graphical interface to communicate with the user. The communication consists of information displayed by programs and actions and commands issued by the user. This book is an introduction to graphic programming in Java. It is assumed that the reader knows the basic concepts of Java such as object-orientation, inheritance, interfaces, exceptions and use of packages.

There are two libraries for graphics components in Java: the *Abstract Windowing Toolkit* (AWT) and *Swing*. The first is the older one. It contains all the components needed to design graphical user interfaces. However, using AWT is not easy and the library is not free of bugs. The components of the Swing library are easier to work with and are much better implemented. Some Swing components need classes from the AWT library. To make these classes available we have to import them by

```
import java.awt.*;
import javax.swing.*;
```

Sometimes it is advisable not to include the whole library by using * (because it is so large) but only the classes needed.

Here we introduce the fundamental graphical components of the Swing library. The aim is to enable the reader to design an interactive graphical interface. This includes displaying graphics and text, making buttons react and the use of the mouse. We present only the most important graphical components and control concepts in this book. There are many more components that are not considered. Only the essential features of the components are described. Information on additional components features can be found in the Java documentation.

Important facts and sources of frequent errors are marked by a '!' in the margin. **!**

The example programs are designed independent of a development environment. They can be compiled and run from the command line. All programs are contained in the main package its for 'Introduction to Swing'. This package contains further (sub-)packages, each of which contains the programs for a specific topic. Packages correspond to directories/folders. The directory structure looks like this:

```
Unix/Linux: its/[subPackageName]/[sourceFileName].java
MS-Windows: its\[subPackageName]\[sourceFileName].java
```

where you have to insert the appropriate names for `[subPackageName]` and `[sourceFileName]`.

To compile and then run a program go to the super-directory of `its` and issue the following commands:

```
javac its\[subPackageName]\[sourceFileName].java java
its.[subPackageName].[sourceFileName]
```

Note that dots are used instead of the slashes in the `java` command. The file path separators are different on different operating systems. Look at Section B.5 in Appendix B for solutions to some common problems.

The `its`-package can be downloaded as a ZIP-file from the book's home page (`http://www.imm.dtu.dk/swingbook/`). It is in Windows file format so if you are on Linux or Unix you might see a CR or an <M> at the end of every line. Use `dos2unix` to get rid of it.

The correct directory structure is reconstructed when the ZIP-file is reconstructed. To test it, go to the super-directory of `its` and type commands:

```
javac its\Test\Test.java
java its.Test.Test
```

You should get the picture in Figure 1.1. If you get error messages, see Section B.5.

The example programs follow the paradigm of object-orientation in that we define a class for every customized component. Most applications are started from a separate start class (driver). The names of the start classes end with `Driver`. All the example programs are **very** simple because we want to concentrate on the graphical concepts. This means that we also omit tests that check for safety and plausibility. For example, if the size of a graphical component is set to certain values we do not check whether the values are positive, neither do we check

Figure 1.1 Result of the test program

whether a file we want to open really exists. **If writing an application for serious purposes, you have to insert these tests.** Also, exceptions are not used to cope with errors; for some errors a message will be displayed on the console. When writing a larger application, it is advisable to make use of Java's exception mechanism.

The author is grateful for any corrections and suggestions. Please do not hesitate to report typographical errors or to point out parts that appear unclear. Also tell me if you would like to see an example of something specific or if there are any problems concerning the example programs. If the reader is looking for a special component or a feature of a component that is not explained in the book, you should first consult the Java documentation. Answers to frequently asked questions and program updates will also be placed on the book's home page. The author's address is

Paul Fischer
IMM, Technical University of Denmark
Building 322
DK-2800 Kgs. Lyngby
Denmark

email `paf@imm.dtu.dk`

1.2 ■ How graphical interfaces work

Programs with graphical user interfaces (GUIs) are *event driven*. This means that the program reacts to actions of the user; these actions are called *events*. Examples of events are pressing a key, moving the mouse, pressing a button and selecting a menu item.

A program with a GUI has a (short) start-up phase in which the GUI is constructed but not yet displayed. Some other preparations (not related to graphics) are also performed. This phase is not event driven and user interaction is not possible. After this phase the GUI is displayed on the screen and the program is now controlled by events.

Of course, we want the program to react only to a few types of event, not all. The programmer has to specify those events to which the program has to react and, of course, what the reaction should be. In Java this is done by implementing so-called *listeners* which wait for specific kinds of events to occur. Once the programmer has implemented a listener for a specific type of event, the runtime system will automatically inform the listener when such an event occurs. The listener then performs the desired action. Events are processed in the order of their occurrence.

There are many types of event in Java, associated with the different event sources, such as buttons, menus or the mouse. Events contain information on what has happened, e.g. what triggered the event (a button, a menu) and where it occurred (the coordinates of the mouse). This information is then exploited by the listener.

1.3 ■ A note on code formatting

The following notational conventions are used to address frequent questions from attendants of courses which the author gave on Swing programming. Some frequently occurring problems are addressed in Appendix B.

In the code listings we sometimes use comments to make the block structure appear more clearly. Comments are added after the closing braces. This is not always done but is used if many blocks are nested or there is a lengthy code segment in a block. Here is an example:

```
for(int i =0; i < N; i++){
 for(int j =0; j < N; j++){
  if(j < i){

  // many statements

  }//if
 }//for j
}//for i
```

When calling a method of a graphic component we sometimes unnecessarily add the key word `this` to make clear to which component the method belongs. Here is an example:

```
public MyPanel(){                    // constructor of graphical component
    JLabel myLabel = new JLabel("Test"); // another component
    this.add(myLabel);               // add the label to this panel
    this.setSize(200,200);           // set the size of this panel
                                     // not of the label

}
```

1.4 ■ A note for teachers

This book is based on material that the author has used in various courses on graphical interfaces. Students are assumed to know the basic concepts of Java, such as classes, inheritance and range of variables. The courses are usually run before the first large programming project is to be performed. Using a model–view–control approach has greatly improved the quality of the resulting programs.

For a three-day intensive course Chapters 2 to 8 are appropriate. If additional features are needed in a follow-up project, the students can easily find them in the remaining chapters. In a one-week intensive course one can cover Chapters 10 to 14 in addition or include some chapters on more elaborate topics if needed.

1.5 ■ Some books on Swing and related topics

The following list is a very individual selection on material and books on Swing:

- *Java Software Solutions* by J. Lewis and W. Loftus, Addison-Wesley, 2003. Sound introduction to (mainly) non-graphical Java.

- *Java 2 SDK, Standard Edition Documentation* is essential. You can download it from the Java site at SUN `http://java.sun.com/`.

- *Core Java,* Volume 1 by C. Horstmann and G. Cornell, Sun Microsystems Press/Prentice Hall, 2002. Is mainly an introduction to non-graphical Java but also addresses the basics of Swing.

- *Graphic Java*, Volume 2: *Swing* by D. Geary, Sun Microsystems Press/Prentice Hall, 2001; 1680 pages. Explains most Swing components in much detail and covers a number of advanced techniques.

- *UML Distilled*, Second Edition by M. Fowler and K. Scott, Addison-Wesley, 2000. A compact hands-on introduction to the Unified Modelling Language.

■ Acknowledgements

The author would like to thank Anne Haxthausen, Jens Thyge Kristensen, Hans Henrik Løvengreen and Jørgen Steensgaard-Madsen for suggesting many important improvements. A special thanks to Thyge for his thorough proof-reading of the lecture notes on which this book is based.

PART I

Basics

Frames, panels and layouts

2

The basic element of any graphical operating system is a 'window'. In this chapter we shall first learn how to create a window and how to display it on the screen. Then we shall see how one can embed other graphical objects into the window and how they can be arranged in different ways.

2.1 ■ Frames

The main components of graphical applications are the so-called *windows*. These are rectangular areas in which text, pictures or other information can be displayed. Windows may also contain elements for user interaction, such as menus, buttons or areas for text input. Most other graphical components discussed in this book cannot be displayed alone but have to be placed inside a window. The actual appearance of a window depends on the operating system, especially the width and type of the border around a window. The position and colour of buttons might vary.

In Java, the term *frame* is used for what is generally called a 'window' and we shall henceforth stick to that notation[1]. In Swing, frames are realized by the class JFrame. A frame is a rectangular area with a *title bar* on top. The title bar also contains buttons for closing, maximizing or making an icon of the frame. As mentioned above, the type and position of these buttons depend on the platform (Windows, MacOS, Linux, Solaris, etc.). Below the title bar is an area into which further graphical components can be embedded. This area is divided into two parts: a space for a *menu bar* at the upper edge and the *content pane* below. The content pane may have further graphical components embedded. If no menu bar is added then the content pane is extended upwards. Usually there is a small border around the frame to separate it from the background. The basic functions such as resizing or moving the frame with the mouse are automatically supplied and do not have to be implemented by the programmer. Figure 2.1 shows the structure of a frame.

---

[1] There is actually a component called 'window' in the Swing library. It is frameless, i.e. it does not have a title bar, a border or additional buttons.

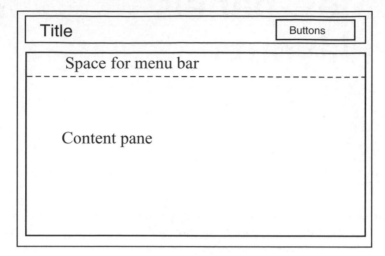

Figure 2.1 Structure of a frame. The title text can be set. The position and appearance of the buttons depend on the operating system. Further graphical components can be embedded into the content pane

We now present the constructor, list some methods of JFrame and explain their behaviour:

```
JFrame()

setVisible(boolean b)
setTitle(String title)
setSize(int width, int height)
setLocation(int horizontal, int vertical)
pack()
setDefaultCloseOperation(int operation)
```

JFrame() is the default constructor. It generates an untitled frame. 'Generate' here means that the information for drawing the frame is provided. The frame is, however, not shown on the screen. This is done by calling the method setVisible, explained below.

setVisible(boolean b) makes the frame appear on the screen if b = true. If a frame is visible then setVisible(false) makes it disappear but does not destroy the information for drawing it. So, calling setVisible(true) on this frame another time will make it visible again; we do not have to use the constructor a second time.

setTitle(String title) sets the title appearing in the title bar to title.

setSize(int width, int height) sets the width of the frame to width and the height to height. These are outer measures in screen pixels.

setLocation(int horizontal, int vertical) moves the frame, so that its upper left corner is at position (horizontal,vertical). See also Figure 2.2.

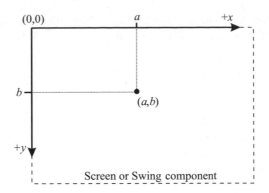

Figure 2.2 The Java coordinate system is upside down. The origin (0,0) is the upper left corner of the screen. The positive *x*-axis points right, the positive *y*-axis points *downwards*. If embedding components into another one, e.g. into the content pane of a frame, then the origin is the upper left corner of the parent component

`pack()` resizes the frame so that it tightly fits around components embedded into its content pane.

`setDefaultCloseOperation(int operation)` determines what happens if the 'close' button of the frame is clicked. See the comments below.

Let us briefly discuss method `setDefaultCloseOperation`. By default, the frame becomes invisible when its 'close' button is clicked. The application that made it visible is, however, still running, i.e. the program is **not** terminated. There are some predefined constants in the class `JFrame` which can be used for `operation`. We shall use `JFrame.EXIT_ON_CLOSE`.

```
setDefaultCloseOperation(JFrame.EXIT_ON_CLOSE)
```

Then the whole application is automatically terminated when the 'close' button is clicked. Not adding this line would result in the following problem. Suppose an application is started over and over again – as happens in the test phase of a new program – and every time displays a new frame. Though the frames are all made invisible by clicking the 'close' buttons, the applications are still running and consuming resources. If many applications run in parallel and share the processor, each of them is slowed down. Problems might also arise if all the free memory were consumed.

Simply terminating an application by clicking the 'close' button is not always a good idea. In general some cleaning up would be performed before exiting the program. For example, one would save changes made to files, store data computed or received while the program was running, etc. We shall see later in Section 9.3 how this can be achieved.

Let us apply our knowledge and create a first frame and display it. We shall derive our own frame class from `JFrame` and add some new functions. Our class is called `SimpleFrame`. As it is derived from Swing class `JFrame`, it inherits its functionality. The constructor of a `SimpleFrame` is extended: it sets the size and location of the frame and also ensures proper termination as explained above. We now list the program and explain it in detail.

File: `its/SimpleFrame/SimpleFrame.java`

```
1. package its.SimpleFrame;
2.
3. import javax.swing.JFrame;
4.
5. public class SimpleFrame extends JFrame
6. {
7.   public SimpleFrame()
8.   {
9.       this.setSize(200,200);
10.      this.setLocation(200,200);
11.      this.setDefaultCloseOperation(JFrame.EXIT_ON_CLOSE);
12.   }
13.
14.   // Makes the frame visible.
15.   public void showIt(){
16.      this.setVisible(true);
17.   }
18.
19.   // Makes the frame visible and sets the title text.
20.   public void showIt(String title){
21.      this.setTitle(title);
22.      this.setVisible(true);
23.   }
24.
25.   // Makes the frame visible and sets the title text
26.   // and the position of the window.
27.
28.   public void showIt(String title,int x, int y){
29.      this.setTitle(title);
30.      this.setLocation(x,y);
31.      this.setVisible(true);
32.   }
33.
34.   // Makes the frame invisible.
35.   public void hideIt(){
36.      this.setVisible(false);
37.   }
38.}
```

Let us look at the code: the class `SimpleFrame` is defined in a package of its own which is also called `SimpleFrame`. It is a sub-package of the `its` package. We have to specify `[package].[subpackage]`, in our case `package its.SimpleFrame`. Next, we import class `JFrame` from the `javax.swing` library, so it becomes accessible in our program (`import javax.swing.JFrame;`). We then specify the class name `SimpleFrame` and that this class is derived from `JFrame`:

```
public class SimpleFrame extends JFrame
```

The constructor and the methods of `SimpleFrame` are now described in more detail:

```
public SimpleFrame()

public void showIt()
public void showIt(String title)
public void showIt(String title,int x, int y)
public void hideIt()
```

`SimpleFrame()` augments the constructor of `JFrame` and sets the size to 200×200 pixels by calling `setSize(200,200)` in Line 9. Otherwise one would see only the title bar because the content pane does not now contain anything. We also set the position of the upper left corner of the frame to 200 pixels below the upper edge of the screen and 200 pixels to the right. This is done by calling `setLocation(200,200)` in Line 10. Note that the Java coordinate system is upside-down: the positive y-axis points down; see also Figure 2.2. Finally the constructor calls method `setDefaultCloseOperation` in Line 11 to guarantee correct termination as described above. Note that keyword `this` in Lines 9 to 11 can be omitted. As mentioned in the introduction, we added it to make clear that these statements refer to this frame.

`showIt()` makes the frame appear on the screen by calling `setVisible` with argument `true`.

`showIt(String title)` sets the title in the title bar to `title` and makes the frame appear on the screen.

`showIt(String title,int x,int y)` sets the title in the title bar to `title`, changes the location to x, y, and makes the frame appear on the screen.

`hideIt()` makes the frame disappear from the screen by calling `setVisible` with argument `false`. The frame is not destroyed by this command. The graphical information is preserved and the frame can be made visible again without calling a constructor.

To test the class `SimpleFrame` we use a *driver program*. We might have defined a `main`-method in `SimpleFrame` for this purpose but we did not because we shall use `SimpleFrame` as the basis for further applications. The driver class is `SimpleFrameDriver`. It generates two frames in Lines 7 and 8. The first frame receives a title and is made visible in Line 9. The second one is in addition moved

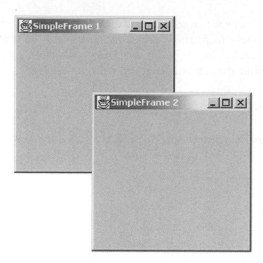

Figure 2.3 Result of the program `SimpleFrameDriver`

to position (300, 300) in Line 10. Both frames are empty, i.e. there is nothing in their content panes.

File: `its/SimpleFrame/SimpleFrameDriver.java`

```
1. package its.SimpleFrame;
2.
3. public class SimpleFrameDriver
4. {
5.   public static void main(String[] args)
6.   {
7.     SimpleFrame sFrame1 = new SimpleFrame();
8.     SimpleFrame sFrame2 = new SimpleFrame();
9.     sFrame1.showIt("SimpleFrame 1");
10.    sFrame2.showIt("SimpleFrame 2",300,300);
11.  }
12. }
```

The result should look like Figure 2.3. This picture is taken under WindowsXP; it might appear slightly different on other platforms. As mentioned above, the frame can be resized and moved with the mouse. These basic functions are automatically supplied.

2.2 ■ Panels and layouts

We will now embed other graphical components into a frame. The components used are called *panels*. These are rectangular components, which serve two main purposes: they can be used as a *canvas* that one draws on or they can be used as *containers* to embed further graphical components.

In Swing the class `JPanel` implements panels. We list the constructor and some methods and then present an example program that demonstrates the use of the methods:

```
JPanel()

setBackground(Color c)
setPreferredSize(Dimension d)
```

`JPanel()` is the constructor. The size of panel is set to default values, 10 by 10 pixel on most systems.

`setBackground(Color c)` sets the background colour of the panel. The class `Color` is from the AWT library. There, some colours are predefined, e.g. red by `Color.red`. By default the background colour is grey.

`setPreferredSize(Dimension d)` sets the size of the panel. The class `Dimension` is from the AWT library. The constructor has the syntax `Dimension(int width, int height)`. Both `width` and `height` are in pixels. It is important to remember that these values are only **recommendations** for the size of a component. Depending on the size of other components, the runtime system might choose different values! The values actually used are determined by a `LayoutManager` at runtime. This flexibility is important for Java to be platform-independent. We describe layout managers later in this chapter.

We now want to embed some panels into a frame. To make them visible and distinguishable we colour them differently. As mentioned in the introduction, we shall derive our own class for every non-trivial concept. It might look like some kind of overkill here, where only the colour of the panel is set. However, we want to follow the paradigm of object-orientation right from the beginning.

In the following listing we derive our own class `ColorPanel` from `JPanel`. Its two constructors allow a panel to be constructed, each with a given background colour, and given width and height.

File: `its/SimpleFrameWithPanels/ColorPanel.java`

```
package its.SimpleFrameWithPanels;                          1.
                                                            2.
import java.awt.*;                                          3.
import javax.swing.JPanel;                                  4.
                                                            5.
public class ColorPanel extends JPanel                      6.
{                                                           7.
  // Generate a JPanel with background color col.           8.
  public ColorPanel(Color col)                              9.
  {                                                        10.
```

```
11.        this.setBackground(col);
12.    }
13.
14.    // Generate a JPanel with background color col,
15.    //   width width, and height height
16.    public ColorPanel(Color col, int width, int height)
17.    {
18.        this.setPreferredSize(new Dimension(width,height));
19.        this.setBackground(col);
20.    }
21.
22. }
```

We embed the `ColorPanel`s into a `SimplePanelFrame` which is derived from `Sim-pleFrame`. Thus a `SimplePanelFrame` inherits the functions of a `SimpleFrame`; in particular an application will be terminated if the frame is closed. We generate five `ColorPanel`s in white, red, yellow, green and blue. The white one has a width of 50 pixels and a height of 20 pixels. For the others no size is specified, so they will have the default size. The panels are then embedded into the frame.

Graphical components are embedded into others as follows. Let us call the component into which we want to embed the *parent component* and the component to be embedded the *child component*. Those Swing components into which others can be embedded have a method `add`. Then, to embed a component `childComp` into another component `parentComp`, the syntax is

    parentComp.add(childComp)

The `add`-method might have more arguments which, for example, specify alignments or positions. There is a difference when embedding into a frame. Here we have to specify that we want to embed into the content pane. Besides the content pane a `JFrame` has more panes which we do not discuss here. It can be referred to by using method `getContentPane` of `JFrame`. Then the syntax to embed a component `childComp` into a frame `parentFrame` is:

    parentFrame.getContentPane().add(childComp)

Let us now specify how the components are to be arranged in the content pane. In order to have platform-independence the designers of Java have given some flexibility to the graphic system. The programmer only specifies the structure of the arrangement of the components, **not** their absolute positions. For example, one specifies that 'component A is to the right of component B' instead of requiring that 'component A is at position (x, y)'. At runtime, the positions of the components are determined. This is done by the so-called *layout manager* which is associated with the parent component. There are different predefined layout managers, some of which we describe here. The programmer can define individual ones.

A `JFrame` has by default a `BorderLayout`, more precisely the content pane has a layout manager of type `BorderLayout`. It allows the user to place one (big) central component and up to four components at the borders. The positions are

Figure 2.4 A frame generated by `SimplePanelFrameDriver` with a border layout. Note that the panel at 'West' has been constructed with width 50 and height 20. While the width is obeyed, the height has changed to fill the available space

specified by the constants `CENTER`, `NORTH`, `SOUTH`, `EAST` and `WEST`. These constants are defined in class `BorderLayout`; see Figure 2.5a). If a border component is not present, then the central component extends in that direction. The central component usually contains the main information. The border components contain additional information such as a status bar in the 'South'-component. To insert a component `childComp` into the content pane at location `pos` we use method

```
this.getContentPane().add(childComp,pos)
```

where `pos` is one of the constants `BorderLayout.CENTER`, `BorderLayout.NORTH`, `BorderLayout.SOUTH`, `BorderLayout.EAST` or `BorderLayout.WEST`.

The code for class `SimplePanelFrame` and the listing for the driver class `SimplePanelFrameDriver` follow. The first class is derived from `SimpleFrame`. The five panels are created in its constructor and then embedded into the content pane. The driver class generates a `SimplePanelFrame` and makes it visible. The result is shown in Figure 2.4. There one can see that all the border panels are sized to span the entire width or height of the content pane. The other dimensions are the default width and height, which are 10 on most platforms. The white panel `CPWest` at 'West' has width 50 as specified in its constructor. The height specification of 20 is ignored in the layout; the height of panel `CPWest` is extended to fill the available height inside the frame. The central component is also extended to fill all the space in the middle.

File: `its/SimpleFrameWithPanels/SimplePanelFrame.java`

```
package its.SimpleFrameWithPanels;                              1.
                                                                2.
import java.awt.*;                                              3.
import javax.swing.JFrame;                                      4.
import its.SimpleFrame.SimpleFrame;                             5.
                                                                6.
```

```
 7. public class SimplePanelFrame extends SimpleFrame
 8. {
 9.   public SimplePanelFrame()
10.   {
11.     ColorPanel CPWest = new ColorPanel(Color.white,50,20);
12.     ColorPanel CPEast = new ColorPanel(Color.red);
13.     ColorPanel CPNorth = new ColorPanel(Color.yellow);
14.     ColorPanel CPSouth = new ColorPanel(Color.green);
15.     ColorPanel CPCenter = new ColorPanel(Color.blue);
16.     this.getContentPane().add(CPWest,BorderLayout.WEST);
17.     this.getContentPane().add(CPEast,BorderLayout.EAST);
18.     this.getContentPane().add(CPNorth,BorderLayout.NORTH);
19.     this.getContentPane().add(CPSouth,BorderLayout.SOUTH);
20.     this.getContentPane().add(CPCenter,BorderLayout.CENTER);
21.   }
22. }
```

File: `its/SimpleFrameWithPanels/SimplePanelFrameDriver.java`

```
 1. package its.SimpleFrameWithPanels;
 2.
 3. public class SimplePanelFrameDriver
 4. {
 5.   public static void main(String[] args)
 6.   {
 7.     SimplePanelFrame spFrame = new SimplePanelFrame();
 8.     spFrame.showIt("Simple Panel Frame");
 9.   }
10. }
```

We now introduce two more layout managers: *flow layout manager* (`FlowLayout`) and *grid layout manager* (`GridLayout`). Both classes as well as `BorderLayout` implement the interface `LayoutManager`. Layouts are not restricted to frames. Every Swing component into which other components can be embedded (a so-called *container*) has a layout. The default layout is a border layout. In order to change the layout of a parent component `parentComp` to another layout `newLayout` one uses the command

```
parentComp.setLayout(newLayout)
```

If a component has a flow layout then the embedded components are placed row-wise from left to right. If a row is full, the next one is started. Row layout (mostly) respects the dimensions of the embedded components. The order of the calls `parentComp.add(child)` determines the order of the embedded components in the parent component. The height of a row is determined at

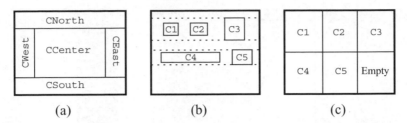

Figure 2.5 Three layout managers. (a) The arrangement of the components in a border layout. (b) The row-wise arrangement of the embedded components. The dashed lines indicate the upper and lower boundaries of the rows. The height of each row is individually determined by the height of the tallest component in it. The spacing between the components and between the rows can be modified. (c) A 2 × 3 grid layout into which five components are embedded. All columns and rows are equally wide and high.

runtime by checking all components in the row. See Figure 2.5b. Here are some constructors of `FlowLayout`:

```
FlowLayout()
Flowlayout(int align)
Flowlayout(int align, int hdist, int vdist)
```

The first constructor generates a layout which by default has five pixels between the components in a row and five pixels between the rows. In addition, the second constructor specifies the alignment of the components, where `align` is one of

```
FlowLayout.RIGHT, FlowLayout.LEFT, FlowLayout.CENTER
```

This determines whether the components in every row are 'packed' to the right, the left or whether they are centred. The third constructor also specifies the horizontal distance `hdist` between the components in a row and the vertical distance `vdist` between rows. Program `LayoutDriver` shows some examples. The size of the components for which we did not define dimensions are set to default minimum values; these are 10 × 10 on most systems.

The layout manager for a component `comp` recomputes the layout every time the component `comp` is redrawn, especially after a resizing of `comp`. If after resizing more or fewer components fit into a row then they are newly arranged. Try it in `LayoutDriver`. See also Figure 2.5.

The third layout manager described here is the `GridLayout` which orders the components in a grid. The parent component (the content pane in our example) is divided into $r \times c$ rectangular *cells*, where c is the number of cells per row and r is the number of rows. All cells have the same size. The components are embedded into the cells row-wise from left to right. If there are more cells than embedded components the layout manager tries to fill all rows as far as possible and might generate fewer than c columns! If there are fewer cells than components then **columns** are added. Basically the grid layout manager ignores the column number. In order to have a fixed number $c > 0$ of columns, the row number must be set to $r = 0$ and the column number to c. Then there will always be c columns and the

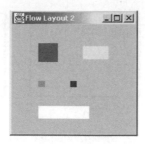

Figure 2.6 Output of `LayoutDriver`. Standard flow layout; flow layout with bigger spacing; grid layout

row number is adjusted depending on the number of embedded components. In program `LayoutFrame` we generate a 2 × 4 grid for five components. The layout manager then generates a 2 × 3 grid, where only one cell is empty. Sometimes one embeds *dummy components* into a grid layout. These are Swing components, usually labels, with no function other than to fill certain cells. They can be used to produce an 'empty' cell between two other cells. Chapter 6 contains an example. The dimensions of the embedded components are basically ignored by the grid layout; the components completely fill the cells. See also Figure 2.5c.

Below we list the constructor and some methods for grid layouts. The number of rows r and columns c and also the width of the gaps can be passed between the columns (`hdist`) and rows (`vdist`):

```
GridLayout(int r, int c);
setHgap(int hdist);
setVgap(int vdist);
```

The following listings `LayoutFrame` and `LayoutDriver` show examples for the layouts. The first defines a frame for which the layout can be selected by passing a `LayoutManager` in the constructor.

Program `LayoutDriver` generates three `LayoutFrame`s and makes them visible. The first one is given a standard flow layout. The second one receives a flow layout with specified distances between rows/columns and left alignment. The third frame is given a 2 × 4 grid layout. The locations in the `showIt` instructions are set in such a way that the three frames appear side by side. Figure 2.6 shows the result.

File: `its/Layouts/LayoutFrame.java`

```
1. package its.Layouts;
2.
3. import java.awt.LayoutManager;
4. import its.SimpleFrameWithPanels.ColorPanel;
5. import java.awt.Color;
6. import its.SimpleFrame.*;
7.
```

```
public class LayoutFrame extends SimpleFrame          8.
{                                                     9.
  public LayoutFrame(LayoutManager layout)            10.
  {                                                    11.
    this.getContentPane().setLayout(layout);           12.
                                                       13.
    ColorPanel CP1 = new ColorPanel(Color.red,30,30);  14.
    ColorPanel CP2 = new ColorPanel(Color.yellow,40,20); 15.
    ColorPanel CP3 = new ColorPanel(Color.green);      16.
    ColorPanel CP4 = new ColorPanel(Color.blue);       17.
    ColorPanel CP5 = new ColorPanel(Color.white,80,20); 18.
    this.getContentPane().add(CP1);                    19.
    this.getContentPane().add(CP2);                    20.
    this.getContentPane().add(CP3);                    21.
    this.getContentPane().add(CP4);                    22.
    this.getContentPane().add(CP5);                    23.
  }                                                    24.
}                                                      25.
```

File: its/Layouts/LayoutDriver.java

```
package its.Layouts;                                   1.
                                                       2.
import java.awt.FlowLayout;                            3.
import java.awt.GridLayout;                            4.
                                                       5.
public class LayoutDriver                              6.
{                                                      7.
  public static void main(String[] args)               8.
  {                                                    9.
    FlowLayout  flowLayout1 = new FlowLayout();        10.
    LayoutFrame flow1Frame  = new LayoutFrame(flowLayout1); 11.
    flow1Frame.showIt("Flow Layout 1",60,60);          12.
                                                       13.
    FlowLayout  flowLayout2 = new FlowLayout(FlowLayout.LEFT,40,30); 14.
    LayoutFrame flow2Frame  = new LayoutFrame(flowLayout2); 15.
    flow2Frame.showIt("Flow Layout 2",300,60);         16.
                                                       17.
    GridLayout  gridLayout  = new GridLayout(2,4);     18.
    LayoutFrame gridFrame   = new LayoutFrame(gridLayout); 19.
    gridFrame.showIt("Grid Layout",540,60);            20.
  }                                                    21.
}                                                      22.
```

Exercises

2.1 What happens if you click on the 'close' button of one of the windows? Explain the observed behaviour. Then remove the line.

```
setDefaultCloseOperation(JFrame.EXIT_ON_CLOSE);
```

from the constructor of `SimpleFrame`. Add the following code at the beginning of the `main`-method in class `SimpleFrameDriver`:

```
int k = 0;
while(true){
  System.out.println("SimpleFrameDriver: Still running! "+k);
  k++;
}
```

This will print lines to the console as long as the application is running. Then compile and start the application and click on the 'close' buttons of the windows. Observe what has changed and explain it.

2.2 Check what happens if the central component in a border layout of a frame is not present. Add different combinations of border components, e.g. 'East' and 'South'.

2.3 Play around with layouts to get a feeling of what the layout managers do. Resize the frames, change the parameters in the layouts (distances, row/column numbers), etc.

A first GUI

3

The purpose of graphical interfaces is to display data and to allow a communication between the user and a program at runtime. In this chapter we shall learn how to design such graphical interfaces. In this example the user can communicate with the program by pressing buttons. The program updates the display in reaction to that.

In this chapter we shall see the first example of a real *GUI* (*graphical user interface*). 'Real' here means that we have a user–program interaction. The interaction is realized using buttons in the graphical display. Although the program is very simple we would like to introduce the concept of a *model–view–control* approach at this point. The (non-graphical) *model* part of the program deals with storing, maintaining or manipulating the data. The graphical *view* part displays the data and provides the components for user interaction, e.g. buttons. The (again non-graphical) *control* part ensures that the user actions result in the desired responses by the program. The control part is the bridge between the model and view parts.

The separation of the model, view and control structures is often the crucial concept to a successful save and fast implementation. It also helps beginners to better recognize the essential concepts and their interplay. In Java such a separation is easily possible by using object-orientation, i.e. different classes or at least different methods for the different parts. In complex applications separate packages might be used for the different parts.

In the following we start by specifying the GUI we want to implement. Then we construct the non-graphical model and test that it works correctly. This is followed by the design of the graphical display. Finally we implement the control structure, i.e. the user–program interaction.

3.1 ■ The specification of the application

We want to implement a *counter*. It is specified as an abstract data structure. The counter has a variable *value* which is an integer. Initially the value is 0. The counter allows four *operations* (of course, more operations might be useful in some applications):

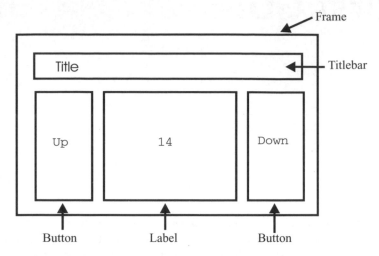

Figure 3.1 The specification of the layout for the counter GUI

- `increment` – increments the value of the counter by 1.
- `decrement` – decrements the value of the counter by 1.
- `reset` – sets the value of the counter to 0.
- `getValue` – returns the current value of the counter.

Next, we specify what the graphics should look like and how it is to work. The GUI we have in mind should display the current value of the counter and allow the user to increment or decrement it. To this end the GUI has two *buttons*. Pressing the first one (labelled 'Up'), e.g. clicking it with the mouse, will increment the counter. Pressing the other one (labelled 'Down') will decrement the counter. Figure 3.1 shows how we want this GUI to look. This concludes the specification of the GUI's functionality and layout.

3.2 ■ The counter model

We now implement a counter in the non-graphical class `CounterModel`. A counter has only one integer variable `value` which is initialized to 0 in the constructor as required by the specification. The variable `value` is `private` so that other classes can only manipulate it through the methods of `CounterModel`. We implemented the four operations requested by the specification in four methods with obvious names: `increment()`, `decrement()`, `reset()` and `getValue()`. Here is the listing of the class:

File: `its/CounterGUI/CounterModel.java`

```
1. package its.CounterGUI;
2. public class CounterModel {
3.    private int value;
4.
```

```
// The constructor initializes the counter to 0          5.
  public CounterModel() {                                 6.
    value = 0;                                            7.
  }                                                       8.
                                                          9.
  public void increment(){                               10.
    value++;                                             11.
  }                                                       12.
                                                         13.
  public void decrement(){                               14.
    value--;                                             15.
  }                                                       16.
                                                         17.
  public void reset(){                                   18.
    value = 0;                                           19.
  }                                                       20.
                                                         21.
  public int getValue(){                                 22.
    return(value);                                       23.
  }                                                       24.
}                                                        25.
```

A counter is such a simple object that we can immediately 'see' that our implementation is correct, i.e. meets the specifications. For slightly more complicated entities, however, one can easily overlook a mistake. The problem of checking whether a program meets its specifications is hard to solve, in fact it is in general unsolvable. Therefore one has to rely on *empirical tests*. This means that one sets up a *test plan*. This contains a (large) number of possible inputs to the program and the correct responses of the program. The plan should activate all parts of the program, e.g. all methods of all classes. Then one checks whether the observed and expected responses coincide. Of course, such a plan is no guarantee that the program is indeed correct because it might not contain an existing input that causes an error. However, a good test plan often does discover mistakes in the program.

To give an idea of what a test plan can look like we add the listing of class CounterModelTest which implements a test plan for the counter model. It addresses all methods at least once and compares the expected and observed results. The comparison is done by method checkValue(a,b), which compares a and b and prints the result of the comparison to the screen.

File: its/CounterGUI/CounterModelTest.java

```
package its.CounterGUI;                                   1.
                                                          2.
                                                          3.
public class CounterModelTest {                           4.
```

```
5.
6.    private static  boolean passed = true;
7.
8.    public static void main(String[] args) {
9.        CounterModel cm = new CounterModel();
10.
11.       checkValue(0,cm.getValue());
12.       cm.increment();
13.       checkValue(1,cm.getValue());
14.       cm.decrement();
15.       checkValue(0,cm.getValue());
16.       for (int i = 0; i < 37; i++) {
17.          cm.increment();
18.       }
19.       checkValue(37,cm.getValue());
20.       for (int i = 0; i < 21; i++) {
21.          cm.decrement();
22.        }
23.       checkValue(16,cm.getValue());
24.       cm.reset();
25.       checkValue(0,cm.getValue());
26.
27.       if(passed){
28.          System.out.println("Test passed.");
29.       }
30.       else{
31.          System.out.println("Test NOT passed.");
32.       }
33.    }
34.
35.    private static void checkValue(int expectedValue, int observedValue){
36.      if(expectedValue == observedValue){
37.        System.out.println("Values are both equal to "+expectedValue);
38.      }
39.      else{
40.         System.out.println("ERROR expected value "+expectedValue+
41.                            " and observed value "+observedValue+" differ!");
42.        passed = false;
43.      }
44.    }
45. }
```

The following is the result of a run of `CounterModelTest`:

```
Values are both equal to 0
Values are both equal to 1
```

```
Values are both equal to 0
Values are both equal to 37
Values are both equal to 16
Values are both equal to 0
Test passed.
```

3.3 ■ The counter view

To implement the graphical part of the counter application we use two new graphical components from the Swing library, *labels* and *buttons*.

3.3.1 □ Labels

A *label* is a rectangular component which displays text that cannot be edited by the user (but might be changed by the program). Class `JLabel` realizes labels in Swing. Here we present a constructor and a few methods.

```
public JLabel(String text)
public JLabel(ImageIcon picture)

public String getText()
public void setText(String text)
public void setText(String text, int alignment)

public void setForeground(Color c)
public void setBackground(Color c)
public void setOpaque(boolean b)
```

`JLabel(String text)` constructs a label which displays the `text`.

`JLabel(ImageIcon picture)` constructs a label which displays the image `picture`. For details on using images see Chapter 15.

`getText()` returns the text currently displayed in the label as a `String`.

`setText(String text)` replaces the text currently displayed in the label by `text`. The new text is instantly displayed in the label.

`setText(String text, int alignment)` replaces the text currently displayed in the label by `text`. It also sets the alignment of the text, left, right or centre. The possible values of `alignment` can be found in the class `SwingConstants`, e.g. use `SwingConstants.CENTER` to centre the text in the label.

`setForeground(Color c)` sets the text colour to `c`.

`setBackground(Color c)` sets the background colour to `c`. Note that labels are transparent by default and their background colour is not visible. One sees the background colour of the parent component shining through. To change the

!

background colour of a label one has to first make it opaque (non-transparent) using the method `setOpaque`.

`setOpaque(boolean b)` makes the label transparent if `b` is `false` and non-transparent if `b` is `true`.

3.3.2 ☐ Buttons

Buttons are rectangular areas (usually with a line around) which – like labels – can display text. They differ from labels in the fact that they can trigger *events*. An event occurs whenever a button is pressed. The Java runtime system monitors buttons and recognizes when such an event occurs. Note that a button is not necessarily pressed by clicking the mouse, it might also be a finger on a touch screen monitor. Therefore, buttons are treated separately from the mouse.

In Section 3.4 we shall learn in detail how the runtime system informs our program that an event has occurred. For now, the following explanation should suffice: in order to notice when a button is pressed, something has to keep an eye on the button. This is done by a *listener*, a (non-graphical) component from the AWT library. The listener has to be *assigned* to the button in order to monitor it. If an event occurs at that button the runtime system informs the listener. The listener can then analyse the event and initiate a certain action.

Class `JButton` implements buttons in Swing. We only present the constructor and the method to assign a listener to the button.

```
public JButton(String text);
```

```
public void addActionListener(ActionListener listener);
```

3.3.3 ☐ Constructing the graphics

We use two buttons to change the value of the counter and a label to display its value. There are many ways to arrange these components. One would be to 'glue' the buttons and the label directly into the content pane of the frame. We use a different approach here: an intermediate panel into which the buttons and the label are embedded. The corresponding class is called `CounterPanel`. Then a `CounterPanel` is glued into the frame; see Figure 3.2. The advantage of this approach is that one can reuse the `CounterPanel` as a ready-made module in other applications.

We first have to decide which layout manager supports the intended GUI. In our case, a border layout is appropriate for both the panel and the frame. We glue the buttons into the west and east positions of the panel and glue the label into the central one. Actually, panels have a border layout by default. We nevertheless set the layout to make clear that this is one step of a GUI implementation.

Every `CounterPanel` holds its own instance of `CounterModel` in the variable `counter`. This variable is private so that the counter cannot be manipulated directly from outside the class `CounterPanel`. Instead `CounterPanel` offers two methods, `increment()` and `decrement()`, which simply call the respective methods of counter model `counter`.

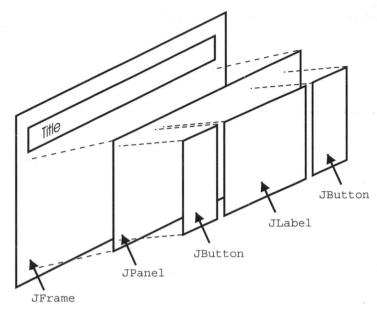

Figure 3.2 The construction of the counter GUI. The intermediate `JPanel` is introduced to guarantee modularity. The panel can be reused in other applications

The frame of our counter application is implemented in the class `Counter Frame`. This class is derived from `SimpleFrame` so that the application is terminated when the frame is closed. A `CounterFrame` has a `CounterPanel` embedded into the central position of its content pane. We list the code of the classes `CounterPanel`, `CounterFrame` and the driver class `CounterDriver` below.

When the application is started, the frame appears. We can press the buttons and see that their colour changes for a short period in response. This function is automatically supplied. The application does not, however, change the value of the counter in the label. It cannot do this at this point because we have not yet 'told' the application to do this. The control part introduced in Section 3.4 will be responsible for that. In the listing of `CounterPanel`; Lines 29 to 31 will later be used to enable the listener. Currently they are comments, so do not have any effect.

File: `its/CounterGUI/CounterPanel.java`

```
package its.CounterGUI;                          1.
                                                 2.
import javax.swing.JPanel;                       3.
import javax.swing.JButton;                      4.
import javax.swing.JLabel;                        5.
import java.awt.BorderLayout;                    6.
import javax.swing.SwingConstants;               7.
                                                 8.
```

```
 9. public class CounterPanel extends JPanel {
10.
11.    private CounterModel counter;
12.    private JLabel valueLabel;
13.
14.    public CounterPanel() {
15.        counter = new CounterModel();
16.
17.        BorderLayout bordLay = new BorderLayout();
18.        this.setLayout(bordLay);
19.
20.        JButton upButton   = new JButton("Up");
21.        JButton downButton = new JButton("Down");
22.        valueLabel = new JLabel(""+counter.getValue(),SwingConstants.CENTER);
23.
24.        this.add(upButton,BorderLayout.WEST);
25.        this.add(downButton,BorderLayout.EAST);
26.        this.add(valueLabel,BorderLayout.CENTER);
27.
28.        // The next three lines will later be used to incorporate
           //the listener.
29.        // CounterListener countList = new CounterListener(this);
30.        // upButton.addActionListener(countList);
31.        // downButton.addActionListener(countList);
32.    }
33.
34.    public void increment(){
35.       counter.increment();
36.       valueLabel.setText(""+counter.getValue());
37.    }
38.
39.    public void decrement(){
40.       counter.decrement();
41.       valueLabel.setText(""+counter.getValue());
42.    }
43. }
```

File: its/CounterGUI/CounterFrame.java

```
1. package its.CounterGUI;
2.
3. import javax.swing.JFrame;
4. import java.awt.BorderLayout;
5. import its.SimpleFrame.SimpleFrame;
6.
```

```
public class CounterFrame extends SimpleFrame {          7.
                                                          8.
  public CounterFrame() {                                 9.
    CounterPanel counterPane = new CounterPanel();        10.
    this.getContentPane().add(counterPane,BorderLayout.CENTER);  11.
  }                                                       12.
}                                                         13.
```

File: `its/CounterGUI/CounterDriver.java`

```
package its.CounterGUI;                                   1.
                                                          2.
public class CounterDriver {                              3.
  public static void main(String[] args) {                4.
    CounterFrame cfr = new CounterFrame();                5.
    cfr.showIt("Counter");                                6.
  }                                                       7.
}                                                         8.
```

3.4 ■ The counter control (listeners and events)

The link between the user actions like pressing a button and the application is established by listeners. These are non-graphical components supplied by the AWT library `java.awt.events.*`. There are different listeners for different types of events (pressing a button, moving the mouse, etc.). Listeners are, in general, interfaces not classes. We will, however, first treat listeners in much the same way as classes. Experience has shown that this is much easier for inexperienced programmers to understand. Later we will describe how to make use of the interface mechanism.

We proceed by describing how the concept of a listener works in general. Some components of Swing can trigger *events*. For example a button can be pressed or a menu item can be selected. Such events are automatically noticed by the Java runtime system. Now, the programmer can implement a listener and *assign* it to the graphical component, say a button. The listener then 'waits' until the button is pressed and takes action if this happens. The runtime system automatically notifies the listener if the button is pressed. The notification is done by calling a specific method of the listener. The name of this method is predefined in the listener's interface. The programmer must implement this method by inserting the code that should be executed in response to the button being pressed.

In our counter application the counter has to be incremented or decremented in response to pressing the respective button. The listener is thus assigned to both buttons, i.e. it monitors both. If a button is pressed the listener is informed. In order to take the appropriate action it has to know which button has been pressed. This information is provided by the runtime system in the form of an object of type

ActionEvent. This class is also found in the AWT library (in java.awt.events). An object of type ActionEvent contains information about the event noticed by the runtime system.

For our counter application we implement a listener in the class CounterListener. A CounterListener implements the Java *interface* ActionListener. The implementation requires the definition of only one method actionPerformed:

> **public void** actionPerformed(ActionEvent evt)

This is the method called by the runtime system whenever the button is pressed. You do not have to call this method yourself, and you should not do this. The runtime system also generates an action event evt and passes it to the method actionPerformed. The programmer puts the code into the body of method actionPerformed[1]. This code is then executed in response to pressing the button. The information contained in the action event can be used to gather further information on what triggered the event.

The code for the class CounterListener is listed below. We shall explain it after the listing.

File: its/CounterGUI/CounterListener.java

```
1. package its.CounterGUI;
2.
3. import java.awt.event.ActionListener;
4. import java.awt.event.ActionEvent;
5.
6. public class CounterListener implements ActionListener{
7.
8.    private CounterPanel countPane;
9.
10.   public CounterListener(CounterPanel counp) {
11.      countPane = counp;
12.   }
13.
14. // This method is called by the runtime system.
15. // The programmer has to add the code to be executed
16. // as a response to the event.
17.   public void actionPerformed(ActionEvent evt){
18.   // Beginning of own code
19.   String actionCommand = evt.getActionCommand();
20.   if(actionCommand.equals("Up")){
21.       countPane.increment();
22.   }
23.   else if(actionCommand.equals("Down")){
24.       countPane.decrement();
```

---

[1] This formulation has to be taken with a grain of salt. Some of the code might actually be in other methods which are then called from inside actionPerformed.

```
    }                                                            25.
  else{                                                          26.
     System.out.println("ERROR: Unexpected ActionCommand");      27.
  }                                                              28.
  // End of own code                                            29.
 }                                                              30.
}                                                              31.
```

In the code for the class `CounterListener` we find the word `implements` instead of `extends`. This is due to the fact that `ActionListener` is an interface and not a class. The constructor receives a `CounterPanel` as an argument. The listener then 'knows' which counter panel it has to update. Check Section B.4 for more details on this.

The heart of class `CounterListener` is the implementation of the method `actionPerformed`. We first determine which of the two buttons had been pressed. This is done by inspecting the action event object `evt` that the method `actionPerformed` received from the runtime system. The line

```
String actionCommand = evt.getActionCommand();
```

extracts the *action command* out of the event object `evt`. The action command is usually the text of the button which has been pressed. In our case it can only be 'Up' or 'Down'. We use an if–then–else structure to check which one it was[2]. Depending on the outcome of the test we call the method `increment` or `decrement` of the counter panel. At this point we see why the listener is given a reference to a `CounterPanel` in the constructor. The listener thereby knows which panel it has to update in response to the event.

In the listing of `CounterPanel` the comment signs at Lines 29 to 31 are removed. These lines are

```
CounterListener countList = new CounterListener(this);
upButton.addActionListener(countList);
downButton.addActionListener(countList);
```

The first one creates an instance of `CounterListener`. The listener receives a reference (`this`) to the panel in the constructor. The next two lines associate the listener to both buttons of the GUI. This completes the implementation of our GUI. Figure 3.3 shows what the application looks like. The structure of the its.`CounterGUI` package can be found in Figure 3.4 as an UML-like diagram[3].

---

[2] The last case can only be reached if the action command is neither 'Up' nor 'Down'. We added this case to make sure that we become aware of an error that could be due, for example, to changing the text of the buttons in the counter panel.

[3] UML stands for 'Unified Modelling Language'. UML is used to specify the structure of object-oriented programs also by using graphical representations by the class structure. For more details see the book by Fowler and Scott in Section 1.5.

Figure 3.3 The counter application

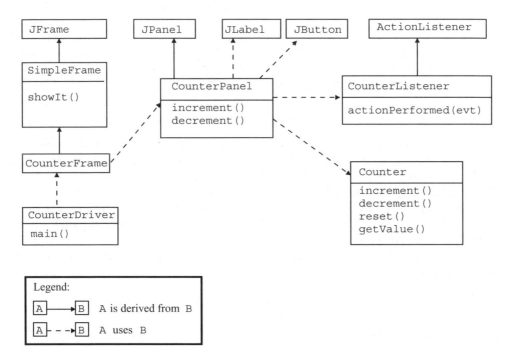

Figure 3.4 The class diagram for the `its.CounterGUI` package. The test class `CounterTest` has been omitted

3.5 ■ Summary

In order to develop an interactive GUI the following steps are necessary:

1. Implement and test the model.

2. Implement the view, especially:

   (a) Decide which graphical components to use.
   (b) Decide how to arrange them.
   (c) Decide which layout manager(s) to use.

3. Create an action listener, especially:

   (a) Define in method `actionPerformed` what has to happen in response to an event.
   (b) Use the `ActionEvent` object to get information about the type of event that occurred.

4. Assign the action listener to the relevant graphical components of the view.

The user–program interaction then works as follows:

■ The user presses a button.

■ The runtime system detects the user action and creates an event object which contains information about the action.

■ The runtime system calls method `actionPerformed` of the listener which is assigned to the button. The event object is passed to `actionPerformed` as an argument.

■ The code in method `actionPerformed` is executed.

Exercises

3.1 Add a third button to the `CounterPanel`. It should be located at the bottom and labelled 'Reset'. When pressing this button, the counter should be reset to 0. Then write an application that displays the new panel as in Figure 3.5.

3.2 Write an application that displays two counters as shown in Figure 3.6. Try to 'recycle' components already defined, e.g. `CounterPanel`.

3.3 Write an application that displays four buttons labelled '1', '2', '3' and '4' and a label. Arrange the components as shown in Figure 3.7. The label initially displays the text 'No button pushed'. When one of the four buttons is pushed the text in the label changes to 'Last button pushed was no. X', where X is the number of the button.

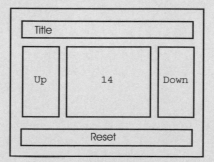

Figure 3.5 Layout for the GUI in Exercise 3.1

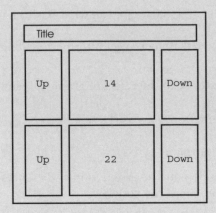

Figure 3.6 Layout for the GUI in Exercise 3.2

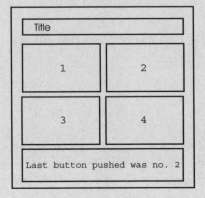

Figure 3.7 Layout for the GUI in Exercise 3.3

A second GUI

4

In this chapter we construct another graphical interface. The purpose of this one is to pass text to a running application.

4.1 ■ The specification of the application

The application is to perform an extremely simple text analysis. The appearance and functionality of the GUI should look like Figure 4.1. To the right of the text 'Enter text:' is an editable area where the user can enter or change text. If one clicks on the button 'Analyse' then a small analysis of the text is performed and the result is displayed in the following way. The text is converted to capital letters and copied into the area to the right of 'Current text:'. The number of occurrences of the letter 'E' in upper or lower case is displayed to the right of 'No. of Es in current text:'. At the same time the content of the user editable area is erased.

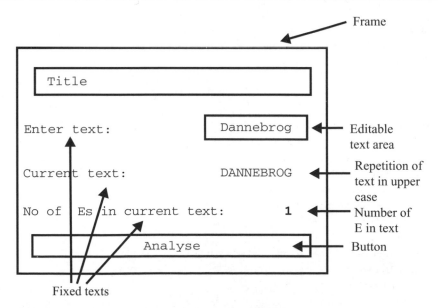

Figure 4.1 The specification of the GUI for text analysis

4.2 ■ The model part

The model is implemented in class `TextAnalysisModel` which is listed below. The class uses the string variable `currentText` to store the text to be analysed in upper-case letters. The integer variable `currentNumberOfEs` is used to store the number of 'E's in the current text. The two other variables `totalNumberOfEs` and `totalNumberOfTexts` will only be used in the exercises to this chapter.

The actual analysis is performed by method `analyse(String str)`. This converts the string `str` to upper case and stores the result in `currentText`. Then the number of occurrences of the letter 'E' in `currentText` is computed by looking at every character in the string. The last two lines of `analyse` update the variables to be used in the exercises. The four `get`-methods return the respective values of the variables.

File: `its/TextAnalysisGUI/TextAnalysisModel.java`

```
1.   package its.TextAnalysisGUI;
2.
3.   public class TextAnalysisModel {
4.
5.     private int totalNumberOfEs;
6.     private int currentNumberOfEs;
7.     private int totalNumberOfTexts;
8.     private String currentText;
9.
10.    public TextAnalysisModel() {
11.      totalNumberOfEs = 0;
12.      totalNumberOfTexts = 0;
13.      currentText = "";
14.    }
15.
16.    public void analyse(String str){
17.      currentText = str.toUpperCase();
18.      currentNumberOfEs = 0;
19.      for (int i = 0; i < currentText.length(); i++) {
20.        if(currentText.charAt(i) == 'E'){
21.          currentNumberOfEs++;
22.        }//if
23.      }//for i
24.      totalNumberOfEs += currentNumberOfEs;
25.      totalNumberOfTexts++;
26.    }// analyse
27.
28.    public int getCurrentNumberOfEs(){
```

```
      return(currentNumberOfEs);                          29.
    }                                                      30.
                                                           31.
    public String getCurrentText(){                        32.
      return(currentText);                                 33.
    }                                                      34.
                                                           35.
    public int getTotalNumberOfEs(){                       36.
      return(totalNumberOfEs);                             37.
    }                                                      38.
                                                           39.
    public int getTotalNumberOfTexts(){                    40.
      return(totalNumberOfTexts);                          41.
    }                                                      42.
}                                                          43.
```

We do not list the test class here but it should be obvious which functions it has to check.

4.3 ■ The view part

We use one new Swing component to construct this GUI, described below.

4.3.1 □ Text fields

Text fields display a single line of text. The text can be edited by the user. The class JTextField realizes text fields in Java. To edit a text, click inside the text field and a cursor will appear. The text field automatically scrolls horizontally if the text gets long. This functionality is built in. Text fields are non-transparent and have a white background and black text by default.

```
public JTextField(String text);

public String getText();
public void setText(String text);

public void setForeground(Color c);
public void setBackground(Color c);
```

JTextField(String text) constructs a text field which displays the text.

setText(String text) replaces the text currently displayed in the text field by text.

getText() returns the text currently displayed in the text field as a String.

setForeground(Color c) sets the text colour to c.

setBackground(Color c) sets the background colour to c.

4.3.2 ☐ **Constructing the view**

We now describe how to construct the GUI. Figure 4.2 shows the structure. We take a frame with border layout. The class is called TextAnalysisFrame and is derived from SimpleFrame. At the bottom (South) we 'glue' a JButton into the frame. In the middle (centre) we glue a panel of type TextAnalysisPanel. This panel is defined to take the text components. It has a 3 × 2 grid layout. The grid contains – in this order – a label, a text field and four more labels. The components are coloured to make them easier to distinguish and the gap between rows and columns is increased. Through these gaps we can see the yellow background of the panel.

Other ways of constructing the GUI are possible. One could use another panel that contains the 'Analyse' button and the text analysis panel. In this case the listener should be instantiated in the new panel.

To achieve the desired functionality, we define the method startAnalysisAnd-DisplayResult in TextAnalysisPanel. This method reads the text from text field inputField and passes it to the text analysis model by calling method analyse of TextAnalysisModel. The panel itself does not know how the text is analysed. The

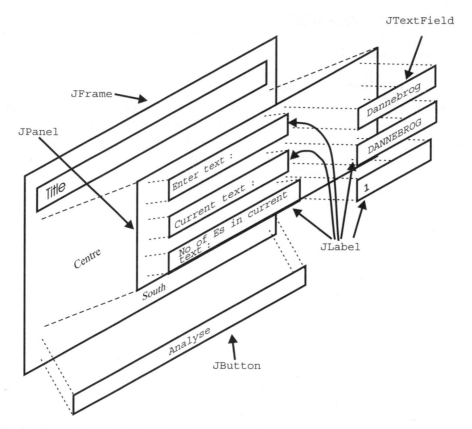

Figure 4.2 The blueprint for our GUI

result of the analysis (the text in upper case and the number of 'E's in it) is then acquired from the text analysis model by calling the appropriate `get`-methods of the `TextAnalysisModel`. The results are displayed and the text in the text field is erased, i.e. replaced by the empty string.

We now list the two classes defining the view.

File: its/TextAnalysisGUI/TextAnalysisFrame.java

```
package its.TextAnalysisGUI;                                              1.
                                                                         2.
import its.SimpleFrame.SimpleFrame;                                      3.
import java.awt.*;                                                       4.
import javax.swing.JButton;                                             5.
                                                                         6.
public class TextAnalysisFrame  extends SimpleFrame                      7.
{                                                                        8.
  public TextAnalysisFrame()                                            9.
  {                                                                     10.
    this.setSize(300,150);                                             11.
    TextAnalysisPanel taPanel = new TextAnalysisPanel();               12.
    this.getContentPane().add(taPanel,BorderLayout.CENTER);            13.
    JButton analyseButton = new JButton("Analyse");                    14.
    analyseButton.setBackground(Color.blue);                           15.
    analyseButton.setForeground(Color.yellow);                         16.
    this.getContentPane().add(analyseButton,BorderLayout.SOUTH);       17.
                                                                        18.
    TextAnalysisListener taList = new TextAnalysisListener(taPanel);   19.
                                                                        20.
    analyseButton.addActionListener(taList);                           21.
    }                                                                  22.
                                                                        23.
  }                                                                    24.
```

File: its/TextAnalysisGUI/TextAnalysisPanel.java

```
package its.TextAnalysisGUI;                                              1.
                                                                         2.
import java.awt.Color;                                                   3.
import java.awt.GridLayout;                                              4.
import javax.swing.JLabel;                                               5.
import javax.swing.JPanel;                                               6.
import javax.swing.JTextField;                                           7.
```

```
8.
9.   public class TextAnalysisPanel extends JPanel
10.  {
11.     private JLabel lastTextLabel;
12.     private JLabel numberOfEsLabel;
13.     private JLabel numberOfTextsLabel;
14.     private JTextField inputField;
15.     private TextAnalysisModel analysisModel;
16.
17.     public TextAnalysisPanel()
18.     {
19.        analysisModel = new TextAnalysisModel();
20.
21.        this.setBackground(Color.yellow);
22.        this.setLayout(new GridLayout(3,2,10,10));
23.        JLabel questionLabel   = new JLabel("Enter text:");
24.        JLabel replyLabel      = new JLabel("Current text:");
25.        JLabel numberTextLabel = new JLabel("No. of Es in current text:");
26.        lastTextLabel          = new JLabel("");
27.        numberOfEsLabel        = new JLabel("--");
28.        inputField             = new JTextField("");
29.
30.        questionLabel.setOpaque(true);
31.        questionLabel.setBackground(Color.black);
32.        questionLabel.setForeground(Color.white);
33.
34.        replyLabel.setOpaque(true);
35.        replyLabel.setBackground(Color.black);
36.        replyLabel.setForeground(Color.white);
37.
38.        numberTextLabel.setOpaque(true);
39.        numberTextLabel.setBackground(Color.black);
40.        numberTextLabel.setForeground(Color.white);
41.
42.        numberOfEsLabel.setOpaque(true);
43.        numberOfEsLabel.setBackground(Color.red);
44.        numberOfEsLabel.setForeground(Color.white);
45.
46.        lastTextLabel.setOpaque(true);
47.        lastTextLabel.setBackground(Color.red);
48.        lastTextLabel.setForeground(Color.white);
49.
50.        this.add(questionLabel);
51.        this.add(inputField);
52.        this.add(replyLabel);
53.        this.add(lastTextLabel);
```

```
  this.add(numberTextLabel);                                          54.
  this.add(numberOfEsLabel);                                          55.
  }                                                                   56.
                                                                      57.
  public void startAnalysisAndDisplayResult()                         58.
    {                                                                 59.
      String text = inputField.getText();                            60.
      analysisModel.analyse(text);                                    61.
      lastTextLabel.setText(analysisModel.getCurrentText());          62.
      int noOfEs = analysisModel.getCurrentNumberOfEs();              63.
      numberOfEsLabel.setText(Integer.toString(noOfEs));              64.
      inputField.setText("");                                         65.
    }                                                                 66.
                                                                      67.
  }                                                                   68.
```

4.4 ■ The control part

Class `TextAnalysisListener` implements the interface `ActionListener`. It is required to implement method `actionPerformed`. Here `actionPerformed` calls the method `startAnalysisAndDisplayResult` of `TextAnalysisPanel`. To this end the `TextAnalysisListener` has to know the `TextAnalysisPanel`. This is achieved by passing (a reference) to `TextAnalysisPanel` in the constructor of `TextAnalysisListener`.

```
public TextAnalysisListener(TextAnalysisPanel taPanel)
```

Class `TextAnalysisFrame` generates an instance of `TextAnalysisListener` and assigns it to the button labelled 'Analyse'.

```
TextAnalysisListener taList = new TextAnalysisListener(taPanel);
analyseButton.addActionListener(taList);
```

Below are the listings of the class `TextAnalysisListener.java` and the driver class `testanalysisTest.java`. Figure 4.3 shows the result.

Figure 4.3 The appearance of the text analysis GUI

File: its/TextAnalysisGUI/TextAnalysisListener.java

```
1.  package its.TextAnalysisGUI;
2.
3.  import java.awt.event.ActionEvent;
4.  import java.awt.event.ActionListener;
5.
6.  public class TextAnalysisListener implements ActionListener
7.  {
8.    private TextAnalysisPanel taPanel;
9.
10.    public TextAnalysisListener(TextAnalysisPanel t)
11.    {
12.      taPanel = t;
13.    }
14.
15.    public void actionPerformed(ActionEvent evt)
16.    {
17.          taPanel.startAnalysisAndDisplayResult();
18.    }
19.  }
```

File: its/TextAnalysisGUI/TextAnalysisDriver.java

```
1.  package its.TextAnalysisGUI;
2.
3.  public class TextAnalysisDriver
4.  {
5.    public static void main(String[] args)
6.    {
7.      TextAnalysisFrame taFrame = new TextAnalysisFrame();
8.        taFrame.showIt("Text analysis");
9.    }
10.  }
```

4.5 ■ The embedding structure

Both the GUI in this chapter and the counter GUI of Chapter 3 were constructed by a *hierarchical embedding*. This means that some components are first embedded into a parent component and then the parent component is embedded into a grandparent component. Hierarchical embeddings can span even more generations.

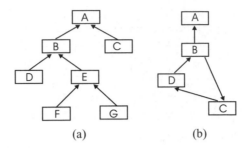

(a)   (b)

Figure 4.4 (a) A legal and (b) an illegal embedding structure. The illegal structure contains a cycle consisting of components B, C and D. The arrow from component B to component A means that B is embedded in A

The important rule to obey with hierarchical embeddings is that they have to be *cycle-free*. This means that there is no cyclic embedding such as component A into component B, and component B into component C and then component C into component A. Formally, the embedding structure has to form a *rooted tree*; see also Figure 4.4. A cyclic embedding will result in a runtime error.

Exercises

4.1 Augment the text analysis application in two steps:

(1) Add two more rows to the `TextAnalysisPanel` which display the number of all texts analysed so far and total number of 'E's seen in these texts. The model supplies this information.

(2) Add another button labelled 'Reset'. When this button is pushed the total number of texts and the total number of 'E's seen are set to 0. This also requires a change of the model part.

4.3 Construct a traffic light GUI. At the bottom there is a button. Clicking the button makes the traffic light go to the next phase, i.e. 'red', 'red-yellow', 'green', 'yellow', and back to 'red'. Above, the current lights should be shown as colours or text; see Figure 4.5.

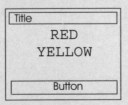

Figure 4.5 Sketch for the traffic light in Exercise 4.2

4.4 Design a GUI, with three buttons and one panel. The buttons are labelled 'red', 'blue' and 'yellow'. When clicking on a button the panel should show the corresponding colour; see Figure 4.6.

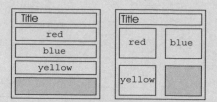

Figure 4.6 Sketch for Exercise 4.3

4.5 Construct an application where you can enter texts one after the other. After entering a new text the application tells you whether this text has been entered before or not.

Displaying a drawing

5

In this chapter we shall learn how a program can display a drawing in a panel. For now, the drawing is predefined and cannot be altered by the user.

To display graphics we use panels as canvases. The whole rectangular area of a panel can be used to draw on, no matter whether it is currently visible or not. The central means for drawing is method `paintComponent` of class `JPanel`. This method redraws the panel. It is automatically called by the runtime system when necessary; for example, when the GUI is resized. All the commands to draw something into the panel should therefore be put into that method. More precisely we override `paintComponent` to add our own commands.

It is important **never** to call `paintComponent` directly in order to initiate a redrawing. To do that, one calls the `repaint()`-method of the panel. This is done to avoid conflicts between redrawing and other operations of the runtime system. A call to `repaint` does not immediately repaint a component. Instead it tells the runtime system that one would like the component to be redrawn. The system calls `paintComponent` after other pending actions have been completed; see also Chapter 20.

5.1 ■ Method `paintComponent`

Method `paintComponent` of class `JPanel` has the following syntax:

```
public void paintComponent(Graphics g)
```

It receives a parameter g of type `Graphics`. This is an abstract class from the AWT library. A `Graphics` object connects the Java drawing commands to the actual drawing mechanism of the current computer. The class `Graphics` also provides methods to draw into a panel. As we will never call `paintComponent` directly, we do not have to construct a `Graphics` object; this is done by the operating system.

To add our own drawings to a panel we extend `paintComponent` by adding graphics commands. To this end we *override* `paintComponent`. Of course we do

!

not want to lose the original function of paintComponent, namely to draw the panel itself, especially its background. Hence we call the original method using the super command. This has to be the **first** command in our implementation of paintComponent. Then our own graphic commands follow. Hence we have the following generic structure:

```
public void paintComponent(Graphics g)  {
    super.paintComponent(g);
    // Own graphics command
    // which draws on the panel.
}
```

We are then sure that first the empty panel is drawn, and then our drawing is displayed. In particular, any existing old drawing is erased before our drawing is begun.

5.2 ■ The graphics commands

The class Graphics supplies a number of commands for drawing. We present only a few – further commands can be found in the Java documentation.

```
drawLine(int xstart, int ystart, int xend, int yend)
drawRect(int xleft, int ytop, int width, int height)
drawOval(int xleft, int ytop, int width, int height)
drawString(String text, int xleft, int ybottom)
fillRect(int xleft, int ytop, int width, int height)
fillOval(int xleft, int ytop, int width, int height)
setColor(Color col)
```

We explain the commands below; see also Figure 5.1. The coordinates are in pixels in the Java coordinate system. The shapes are drawn in the order in which the graphic commands are executed. If shapes overlap, the one drawn later covers those drawn previously.

drawLine(xstart,ystart,xend,yend) draws a line segment between the points with coordinates (*xstart*, *ystart*) and (*xend*, *yend*).

drawRect(xleft,ytop,width,height) draws the contour of an axes-aligned rectangle. The upper left corner of the rectangle is at *(xleft, ytop)*. It is *width* pixels wide and *height* pixels tall.

drawOval(xleft,ytop,width,height) draws the contour of an ellipse. The axes of the ellipse are parallel to the coordinate axes. The upper left corner of the bounding rectangle of the ellipse is at *(xleft, ytop)* and is called the *reference point*. The horizontal axis of the ellipse has length *width*, the vertical one *height*.

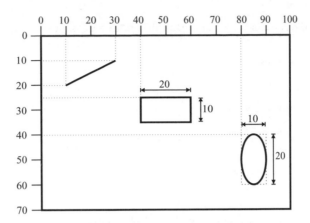

Figure 5.1 The effect of the commands `drawLine(10,20,30,10)`, `drawRect(40,25,` `20,10)` and `drawOval(80,40,10,20)`. The dotted lines and the dimensions do not appear in the graphic. The bounding rectangle for the oval is shown as a dotted line

`drawString(text,xleft,ybottom)` draws the string `text`. The lower left corner of the bounding rectangle of the text is at (*xleft*, *ybottom*). This is the *reference point*.

`fillRect` draws a filled rectangle using the current colour, otherwise like `drawRect`.

`fillOval` draws a filled ellipse using the current colour, otherwise like `drawOval`.

`setColor(col)` sets the colour of the drawing to `col`. This colour is used until the `setColor` command is used again.

5.3 ■ A simple graphical application

Our application is only to demonstrate the use of the graphic commands inside `paintComponent`. As there is no user interaction that changes the drawing, we do not need a model or control part. In the example we derive a class `SimpleGraphicsPanel` from `JPanel`. In the constructor we set the background to white (it is normally grey) and set the size to 300 × 300 pixels. Then method `paintComponent` is overridden. As explained above, we first make a call to the original `paintComponent` method. Then follow a number of graphics commands which set the drawing colour and draw various shapes and a string. The commands are provided by the `Graphics` class of AWT and thus have the syntax `g.drawSomething` where `g` is an instance of `Graphics`. Now whenever the panel is redrawn these commands are executed and the graphical objects are displayed. Note that drawing a filled object with the background colour makes parts of other objects 'disappear'. In the example a white oval partly covers a cyan coloured one.

File: its/SimpleGraphics/SimpleGraphicsPanel.java

```
1.  package its.SimpleGraphics;
2.
3.  import java.awt.*;
4.  import javax.swing.JPanel;
5.
6.  public class SimpleGraphicsPanel extends JPanel
7.  {
8.      public SimpleGraphicsPanel()
9.      {
10.         this.setBackground(Color.white);
11.         this.setPreferredSize(new Dimension(300,300));
12.     }
13.
14.     public void paintComponent(Graphics g)
15.     {
16.         super.paintComponent(g);
17.         g.setColor(Color.black);
18.         g.drawLine(10,10,100,100);
19.         g.setColor(Color.red);
20.         g.drawLine(10,100,100,10);
21.         g.setColor(Color.green);
22.         g.drawOval(120,60,70,40);
23.         g.setColor(Color.yellow);
24.         g.fillOval(230,150,30,30);
25.         g.setColor(Color.red);
26.         g.fillOval(245,150,30,30);
27.         g.setColor(Color.black);
28.         g.fillOval(238,160,30,30);
29.         g.setColor(Color.cyan);
30.         g.fillOval(10,120,100,60);
31.         g.setColor(this.getBackground());
32.         g.fillOval(50,140,100,60);
33.         g.setColor(Color.blue);
34.         g.drawString("Swing is nice.",100,200);
35.     }
36. }
```

The next two listings define class SimpleGraphicsFrame and SimpleGraphics-Driver. In the constructor of SimpleGraphicsFrame a SimpleGraphicsPanel is created and glued into the frames content pane. The pack() command ensures that the frame is packed around the embedded panel and the latter is visible in its full size. Class SimpleGraphicsDriver is the driver class. Figure 5.2 shows the result.

Figure 5.2 Result of `SimpleGraphicsFrame`. The covering of shapes occurs in the order in which the graphic commands are processed

File: `its/SimpleGraphics/SimpleGraphicsFrame.java`

```
package its.SimpleGraphics;                                          1.
                                                                     2.
import its.SimpleFrame.SimpleFrame;                                  3.
import java.awt.BorderLayout;                                        4.
                                                                     5.
public class SimpleGraphicsFrame extends SimpleFrame                 6.
{                                                                    7.
                                                                     8.
  public SimpleGraphicsFrame()                                       9.
  {                                                                  10.
   this.setTitle("Simple Graphics");                                11.
                                                                     12.
    SimpleGraphicsPanel SGP = new SimpleGraphicsPanel();            13.
    this.getContentPane().add(SGP,BorderLayout.CENTER);            14.
                                                                     15.
    pack();                                                          16.
  }                                                                  17.
}                                                                    18.
```

File: `its/SimpleGraphics/SimpleGraphicsDriver.java`

```
package its.SimpleGraphics;                                          1.
                                                                     2.
public class SimpleGraphicsDriver                                    3.
{                                                                    4.
                                                                     5.
```

```
 6.  public SimpleGraphicsDriver()
 7.  {
 8.    SimpleGraphicsFrame SGF = new SimpleGraphicsFrame();
 9.    SGF.showIt();
10.  }
11.  public static void main(String[] args)
12.  {
13.    SimpleGraphicsDriver sgt = new SimpleGraphicsDriver();
14.  }
15. }
```

Exercises

5.1 Check and explain what happens if one omits the super-command in paint-Component or if it is put at the end of paintComponent.

5.2 Add further graphic commands to paintComponent. Test what happens if you draw outside the currently visible area. Resize the window.

5.3 A repaint of the GUI is initiated by the runtime system quite frequently. We would like to see how often this occurs. To this end, define an integer variable noOfRepaints in SimpleGraphicsPanel and set it to zero in the constructor. Increment this variable in method paintComponent. Then its current value is the number of calls to paintComponent. Add a command to paint-Component which draws the value of noOfRepaints into the panel with some explanation, for example, 'The number of redraws is'. Move and resize the panel to see how many repaints are actually performed.

Adding the mouse

6

In this chapter we learn how the mouse is integrated into an application. We shall see how the mouse motion and the use of buttons can be monitored and used by an application.

In this chapter we describe how to use the mouse[1] in a Swing component. In previous chapters we used the mouse indirectly as a means of pressing buttons. As buttons can be pressed in other ways (by a finger on a touch screen), these applications reacted to buttons but they did not react to the mouse itself.

In order to directly integrate the mouse into an application we have to add a *mouse listener* to some component. The listener then keeps an eye on the mouse and starts user-defined actions if certain events occur. Such events can be clicking a mouse button, the mouse leaving or entering the component, a change of the mouse position while inside the component, etc. Note that the listener is assigned to a component not to the mouse itself. It tracks the mouse only while it is inside the component.

Often one is interested in the mouse buttons or in the mouse motion but not both. Therefore there are two listeners defined by the interfaces `MouseListener` and `MouseMotionListener` in the AWT library `java.awt.event`. The first is for handling the mouse buttons while the latter monitors the motion. To add a mouse listener to a Swing component `comp` use

```
comp.addMouseListener(MouseListener mouseListener);
comp.addMouseMotionListener(MouseMotionListener motionListener);
```

In Chapters 3 and 4 we introduced the `ActionListener` and the corresponding `ActionEvent`. The implementation of an `ActionListener` requires the implementation of only a single method, `actionPerformed`. Mouse listeners have more methods which correspond to different mouse actions. There is also a special event, the `MouseEvent`. This is discussed in the following sections.

---

[1] We use the term 'mouse' also to denote the reference point (hot spot) of the mouse pointer icon.

6.1 ■ The mouse listener

Interface `MouseListener` allows us to react to the use of the mouse buttons and to entering or leaving the component to which the mouse listener is assigned. Whenever the mouse enters or leaves the component or a mouse button is used inside that component then the runtime system generates a `MouseEvent` and informs the listener. Depending on the event, different methods of the listener are called. The event object is passed as an argument to the method. The event object contains information on the event; see Section 6.3 below. Interface `MouseListener` has five such methods, *all* of which have to be implemented:

```
void mouseClicked(MouseEvent mevt)
void mouseEntered(MouseEvent mevt)
void mouseExited(MouseEvent mevt)
void mousePressed(MouseEvent mevt)
void mouseReleased(MouseEvent mevt)
```

`mouseClicked(MouseEvent mevt)` is automatically called by the runtime system when a mouse button is clicked[2]. To find out which button was clicked one has to look at the `MouseEvent` object `mevt`, see Section 6.3.

`mouseEntered(MouseEvent mevt)` is automatically called by the runtime system if the mouse enters the component to which the listener is associated.

`mouseExited(MouseEvent mevt)` is automatically called by the runtime system if the mouse leaves the component to which the listener is associated.

`mousePressed(MouseEvent mevt)` is automatically called by the runtime system if a mouse button is pressed. To find out which button was pressed one has to look at the `MouseEvent` object `mevt`, see Section 6.3.

`mouseReleased(MouseEvent mevt)` is automatically called by the runtime system if a mouse button is released. To find out which button was released one has to look at the `MouseEvent` object `mevt`, see Section 6.3.

A click results in calling three methods, `mousePressed`, `mouseReleased` and `mouseClicked`.

6.2 ■ The mouse motion listener

Interface `MouseMotionListener` supplies methods to track the mouse. If a `MouseMotionListener` is assigned to a Swing component and the mouse is moved while inside this component then the runtime system generates a `MouseEvent` and

---

[2] In most operating systems 'clicking' is equivalent to 'press and release'.

informs the listener. Depending on whether the mouse was moved or dragged[3], different methods of the listener are called. The event object is passed as an argument to the method. A `MouseMotionListener` has two methods; *both* of which have to be implemented:

```
void mouseMoved(MouseEvent mevt)
void mouseDragged(MouseEvent mevt)
```

`mouseMoved(MouseEvent mevt)` is automatically called if the mouse is moved while it is in a component that the listener is associated to. The new mouse position can be found by analysing the event object `mevt`. The mouse is 'moved' if the runtime system receives a signal from the mouse. Usually this results in a change of the position of the mouse pointer on the screen by at least one pixel.

`mouseDragged(MouseEvent mevt)` is automatically called if the mouse is moved while a mouse button is pressed.

6.3 ■ Mouse events

The methods described above all receive a (`MouseEvent`) as a parameter. This object contains information on what triggered the listener. The following methods from the class `MouseEvent` show where the event occurred. The *x*- and *y*-coordinates are in pixels in the coordinate system of the component to which the listener is assigned:

```
int getX()
int getY()
```

To find out which button was used we can use the following methods from class `SwingUtilities`. They return `true` if the button appearing in the method name is used, and `false` otherwise:

```
boolean SwingUtilities.isLeftMouseButton(MouseEvent me)
boolean SwingUtilities.isMiddleMouseButton(MouseEvent me)
boolean SwingUtilities.isRightMouseButton(MouseEvent me)
```

Java does not (yet) support *double clicks*. One can use method

```
int getClickCount()
```

to determine the number of clicks in a short period. The length of this period depends on the platform and can usually be set using utilities of the operating system. Then a double click can be checked by using `if(mevt.getClickCount() == 2)`.

---

[3] Dragging means moving the mouse with a button pressed.

6.4 ■ A first mouse application

6.4.1 □ Specification of the application

Let us specify the application that demonstrates the mouse listeners. The component to which the mouse listeners are associated will be a 300 × 300 panel that is centrally placed in a frame. Below that is another panel which displays information about the mouse. We would like to display the current mouse position, the number of clicks of the mouse button and whether the mouse is inside or outside the 300 × 300 panel. The information is continuously updated. The intended layout can be seen in Figure 6.1. We describe the implementation of the view and control parts; a model part is not implemented because there is hardly any data to be handled.

6.4.2 □ The view part

For the implementation we define the class `MouseEventPanel`. The panel (now) has no methods of its own; it serves only as a playground for the mouse. It will be the central component in a frame of type `MouseEventFrame` which we also define. The mouse listeners will be assigned to this panel. They will then track the mouse while it is in the panel.

Below the mouse event panel (South) we add another panel to the frame. This is of type `StatusPanel` and will be used to display information on the mouse.

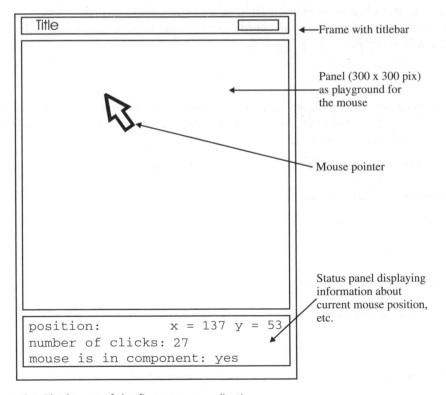

Figure 6.1 The layout of the first mouse application

A `StatusPanel` has a 3 × 3 grid layout, containing nine labels. The first one in every row contains a fixed text, e.g. 'Position', the second and third are used to display varying information, e.g. the current *x*- and *y*-coordinates of the mouse. Two labels are 'dummies' placed at unused positions in the grid. A `StatusPanel` has methods to set the coordinate values, the click count and the information whether the mouse is in or out. Figure 6.2 shows how the components are arranged. The listings of the classes are given below. In `MouseEventFrame` instances of `My-MouseListener` and `MyMousePositionsListener` are created and are both assigned to the `MouseEventPanel`. This demonstrates that more than one can be assigned to a single component.

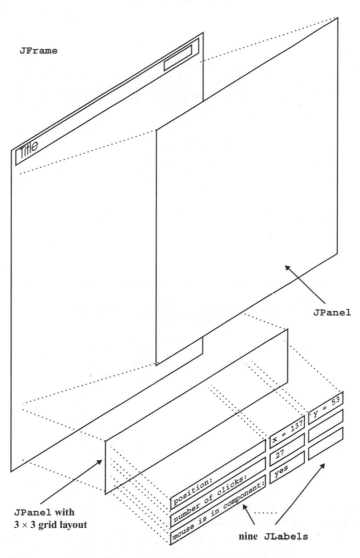

Figure 6.2 A blueprint for the view part of the mouse application

File: its/MouseEvents/MouseEventFrame.java

```
1. package its.MouseEvents;
2.
3. import its.SimpleFrame.SimpleFrame;
4. import java.awt.BorderLayout;
5.
6. public class MouseEventFrame extends SimpleFrame
7. {
8.    MouseEventPanel mePanel = new MouseEventPanel();
9.    StatusPanel     stPanel = new StatusPanel();
10.
11.   public MouseEventFrame()
12.   {
13.      this.setTitle("Mouse application");
14.      this.getContentPane().add(mePanel,BorderLayout.CENTER);
15.      this.getContentPane().add(stPanel,BorderLayout.SOUTH);
16.      pack();
17.
18.      MyMousePositionsListener mPosAdpt =
                 new MyMousePositionsListener(stPanel);
19.      mePanel.addMouseMotionListener(mPosAdpt);
20.
21.      MyMouseListener MAdpt = new MyMouseListener(stPanel);
22.      mePanel.addMouseListener(MAdpt);
23.
24.   }
25. }
```

File: its/MouseEvents/MouseEventPanel.java

```
1. package its.MouseEvents;
2.
3. import java.awt.Color;
4. import java.awt.Dimension;
5. import javax.swing.JPanel;
6.
7. public class MouseEventPanel extends JPanel
8. {
9.    public MouseEventPanel()
10.   {
11.        this.setBackground(Color.white);
12.        this.setPreferredSize(new Dimension(300,300));
13.   }
14. }
```

File: its/MouseEvents/StatusPanel.java

```
package its.MouseEvents;                                              1.
                                                                     2.
import java.awt.GridLayout;                                          3.
import javax.swing.JLabel;                                           4.
import javax.swing.JPanel;                                           5.
                                                                     6.
public class StatusPanel extends JPanel                              7.
{                                                                    8.
  private JLabel posText    = new JLabel("position:");               9.
  private JLabel XCoord      = new JLabel("0", JLabel.RIGHT);        10.
  private JLabel YCoord      = new JLabel("0", JLabel.RIGHT);        11.
  private JLabel countText  = new JLabel("no. of clicks");          12.
  private JLabel counts      = new JLabel("0", JLabel.RIGHT);        13.
  private JLabel dummy1      = new JLabel();                         14.
  private JLabel inOutText  = new JLabel("mouse is in comp.");      15.
  private JLabel inOut       = new JLabel("no", JLabel.RIGHT);       16.
  private JLabel dummy2      = new JLabel();                         17.
  private int clickCount = 0;                                       18.
                                                                    19.
  public StatusPanel()                                              20.
  {                                                                 21.
    this.setLayout(new GridLayout(3,3));                            22.
    this.add(posText);                                              23.
    this.add(XCoord);                                               24.
    this.add(YCoord);                                               25.
    this.add(countText);                                            26.
    this.add(counts);                                               27.
    this.add(dummy1);                                               28.
    this.add(inOutText);                                            29.
    this.add(inOut);                                                30.
    this.add(dummy2);                                               31.
  }                                                                 32.
// Updates the displayed coordinates of the mouse position.        33.
  public void setCoordinates(int x, int y)                          34.
  {                                                                 35.
   XCoord.setText(Integer.toString(x));                            36.
   YCoord.setText(Integer.toString(y));                            37.
  }                                                                 38.
// Sets the information whether the mouse is in or out.             39.
  public void setInOut(String str)                                  40.
  {                                                                 41.
   inOut.setText(str);                                             42.
  }                                                                 43.
// Increments the click count and displays it.                     44.
```

```
45.    public void incrementClickCount(){
46.       clickCount++;
47.       counts.setText(Integer.toString(clickCount));
48.    }
49. }
```

6.4.3 ☐ The control part

The control part has to implement the following functionality:

■ If the mouse is in the MouseEventPanel the StatusPanel displays the current mouse coordinates and a 'yes'.

■ If the mouse is not in the MouseEventPanel, the StatusPanel displays the coordinates $(-1, -1)$ and a 'no'.

■ When a mouse button is clicked the click count is increased by one.

■ Whenever the mouse is moved or a button is clicked, the information in the status panel is updated.

■ The initial values to the coordinates and click count are all zero, and 'no' is displayed.

To implement the first function we derive class MyMousePositionsListener from MouseMotionListener. The listener is assigned to the MouseEventPanel. We override method mouseMoved in such a way that it sets the current coordinates in the status panel. In order for the MyMousePositionsListener to have access to the status panel it receives a reference to the panel in the constructor. As the method mouseMoved is executed every time the mouse is moved (in the panel) we always display the current coordinates. Method mouseDragged is implemented with empty body because we have not specified any reaction to dragging.

The second, third and fourth functions are realized by a mouse listener, namely the class MyMouseListener derived from MouseListener. There we implement the methods mouseEntered and mouseExited such that they set the text of the inOut label in the status panel and also the coordinates to $(-1, -1)$ when exiting MouseEventPanel. For the fourth function, method mouseClicked in MyMouseListener is implemented to call incrementClickCount() of MouseEventPanel. In order for MyMouseListener to have access to the status panel it receives a reference to the panel in the constructor. Methods Mouse-Pressed and MouseReleased are not needed and therefore implemented with no functions, i.e. with empty bodies.

This completes the application (see Figure 6.3); the listings of the two listener classes and the driver class MouseEventDriver are given below.

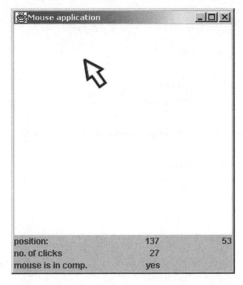

Figure 6.3 The first mouse application

File: its/MouseEvents/MyMousePositionsListener.java

```
package its.MouseEvents;                                              1.
                                                                     2.
import java.awt.event.MouseEvent;                                     3.
import java.awt.event.MouseMotionListener;                            4.
                                                                     5.
public class MyMousePositionsListener implements MouseMotionListener  6.
{                                                                    7.
  private StatusPanel statusPane;                                    8.
                                                                     9.
  public MyMousePositionsListener(StatusPanel s)                    10.
  {                                                                 11.
    statusPane = s;                                                 12.
  }                                                                 13.
                                                                    14.
  public void mouseMoved(MouseEvent evt)                            15.
   {                                                                16.
   statusPane.setCoordinates(evt.getX(),evt.getY());               17.
   }                                                                18.
                                                                    19.
  public void mouseDragged(MouseEvent evt)                          20.
   {                                                                21.
     // implemented with empty body                                22.
   }                                                                23.
}                                                                   24.
```

File: `its/MouseEvents/MyMouseListener.java`

```java
1. package its.MouseEvents;
2.
3. import java.awt.event.MouseEvent;
4. import java.awt.event.MouseListener;
5.
6. public class MyMouseListener implements MouseListener
7. {
8. private StatusPanel statusPane;
9.
10.    public MyMouseListener(StatusPanel s)
11.    {
12.       statusPane = s;
13.    }
14.
15.    public void mouseEntered(MouseEvent e)
16.     {
17.        statusPane.setInOut("yes");
18.     }
19.
20.    public void mouseExited(MouseEvent e)
21.     {
22.        statusPane.setInOut("no");
23.        statusPane.setCoordinates(-1,-1);
24.     }
25.
26.    public void mouseClicked(MouseEvent e)
27.     {
28.        statusPane.incrementClickCount();
29.     }
30.
31.    public void mousePressed(MouseEvent e)
32.     {
33.      //implemented with empty body
34.     }
35.
36.    public void mouseReleased(MouseEvent e)
37.     {
38.      //implemented with empty body
39.     }
40.
41. }
```

File: its/MouseEvents/MouseEventDriver.java

```
package its.MouseEvents;                                        1.
                                                               2.
public class MouseEventDriver                                   3.
{                                                              4.
  public static void main(String[] args)                       5.
  {                                                            6.
    MouseEventFrame MEF = new MouseEventFrame();               7.
    MEF.showIt();                                              8.
  }                                                            9.
}                                                             10.
```

Exercises

6.1 Change the status panel such that instead of the number of all clicks, the number of clicks of the right and left buttons are displayed separately. Augment the mouse listener such that these functions work. Recall that the class SwingUtilites provides methods to check which button was used.

6.2 Add the following function to the application described in Section 6.4. If the mouse is in the 'upper left corner' of the MouseEventPanel then the colour of this panel changes to yellow. By the upper left corner we mean the *x*- and *y*-coordinates of the click position are both less than 50. If the mouse is inside of the MouseEventPanel but outside the upper left corner then the colour is white.

Hint: Find out which listeners have to be modified. If necessary, pass more references to the listeners in their constructors. To change the colour of a panel use the following two commands:

```
this.setBackground(Color.yellow);
this.repaint();
```

6.3 Remove the status panel from the application and display the information in the MouseEventPanel. Do not embed any components into that panel, use paintComponent.

Interactive graphics 7

In Chapter 5 we saw how an application can display predefined graphics. In Chapter 6 the mouse was embedded into an application. We shall now see how to combine these two things so that one can interactively generate and manipulate graphics.

We extend the application from Chapter 6 by an interactive part. This will enable you to generate and alter a drawing using the mouse. The drawing consists of circles that are added to or removed by mouse clicks. The resulting application has a model, a view and a control part. The model part consists of a class defining a circle and a class defining a data structure which stores the circles currently in the graphic and which also supplies methods to add a circle or remove one. The view part is mostly like the application in Chapter 6. The class `MouseEventPanel` of Chapter 6 is augmented by overriding its `paintComponent` method as described in Chapter 5. The control part is implemented by extending the listeners from Chapter 6.

7.1 ■ Specification of the GUI

The layout is very much like that in Figure 6.1. We therefore specify only the additional functions:

- If clicking the left mouse button inside the 300×300 panel, a small filled black circle appears at the current mouse position.

- If clicking the right mouse button the circle closest to the current mouse position is removed, but only if the distance is less than 30 pixels. Distances are in the Euclidean metric of $\mathbb{R}^2$. If more than one circle has the same distance to the click position, choose an arbitrary one.

- The status panel now also displays the current number of circles.

7.2 ■ The model part

In this section we describe two classes that form the model part of our application: `Circle` and `CircleAdministration`. The first is an *abstract* representation of a circle and the second is used to administer the circles currently in the drawing. Here 'abstract' means that a `Circle` is independent of its graphical representation. A circle is specified by defining two quantities: the location of the centre and its radius. As we do not want to restrict ourselves to pixel coordinates, we use `double` variables. The class has methods to compute the distance of the centre to a given point. The class `CircleAdministration` stores the circles that are currently in the graphic. It also supplies methods to add a circle or to remove one.

7.2.1 ☐ Circles

Class `Circle` has three double fields, `x`, `y` and `radius`, which contain the co-ordinates of the centre of the circle and its radius, respectively. Following the object-oriented paradigm of Java, only the class `Circle` knows how to draw a circle. Therefore, `Circle` provides a method `draw` which contains the graphics commands to draw the circle. These commands need a graphics reference (`Graphics`) which is given as an argument to `draw`. Note that the `draw`-method of class `Circle` actually is a view part method. Thus, the distinction of view and model part in this case is not only *between* classes but also *inside* a single class: some methods handle 'view' aspects and others 'model' aspects.

The data on the centre and radius of the circle are stored as double; the draw method, however, needs integers. We convert double to integers by simply rounding to the nearest integer. We shall learn about a better and more flexible way of converting to pixel coordinates in Section 13.3. The `fillOval`-method expects the upper right corner of the bounding box and the width and height of the box as parameters. The coordinates are found by subtracting the radius from the co-ordinates of the centre of the circle. By multiplying the radius by two we find the width and height. To keep the code short we do not check whether the values are plausible, e.g. that the radius or the pixel coordinates are non-negative.

Class `Circle` also supplies the method `distance(double x1, double y1)` which computes the Euclidean distance between the circle's centre and the point (x_1, y_1). This method is used to determine which circle is closest to the location of a mouse click and has to be deleted.

File: `its/InteractiveGraphic/Circle.java`

```
package its.InteractiveGraphic;          1.
                                          2.
import java.awt.Graphics;                 3.
                                          4.
public class Circle                       5.
{                                         6.
                                          7.
```

```
8.    private double x,y,radius;
9.
10.   public Circle(double xx, double yy, double rad)
11.   {
12.     x      = xx;
13.     y      = yy;
14.     radius = rad;
15.   }
16.
17.   // Draws the circle
18.   public void draw(Graphics g)
19.   {
20.     g.fillOval((int)Math.round(x-radius),(int)Math.round(y-radius),
21.               (int)Math.round(2.0*radius),(int)Math.round(2.0*radius));
22.   }
23.
24.   // Computes the distance between the circle's
25.   // centre and the point (x1,y1).
26.   public double distanceTo(double x1, double y1)
27.   {
28.     return(Math.sqrt(Math.pow(x-x1,2)+Math.pow(y-y1,2) ));
29.   }
30. }
```

7.2.2 □ A data structure to administer circles

Class `CircleAdministration` does most of the work. The heart of it is an object of type `Vector`. This is a class predefined in Java; one can think of it as an array with flexible length. Vectors can store arbitrary objects. If a vector contains n objects then they are indexed from 0 to $n - 1$. The vector `circles` used in `Circle-Administration` stores the `Circle` objects currently in our graphic. To access the ith object one uses the method `get(i)`. The method returns an `Object` and thus one has to *cast* it to the correct data type, a `Circle` in our case[1]. The syntax for this is:

```
(Circle)(circles.get(i))
```

Besides the constructor, the class `CircleAdministration` has the following methods:

```
void addCircle(Circle circ)
void removeNearestCircle(int x1, int y1)
void drawAll(Graphics g)
int getNoOfCircles()
```

---

[1] Version 1.5 of the Java SDK (software development kit) allows *typed vectors* to be defined. These can only store objects from a single class, e.g. only `Circles`. This avoids casting.

`addCircle(circ)` adds circle `circ` to vector `circles`.

`removeNearestCircle(x1,y1)` determines a circle stored in vector `circles` whose centre has minimum distance to the point (x, y). If the distance is at most 30 (pixel), then the circle is removed from `circles`.

`drawAll(g)` draws all circles currently stored in `circles`. This is done by calling the `draw`-method of each of them. The `Graphics` object g is passed on.

`getNoOfCircles()` returns the number of circles currently stored in vector `circles`.

In method `removeNearestCircle(x1,y1)` the circle to be removed is found by computing the distances of the point (x_1, y_1) to the centre of all circles. This is not the most effective way of doing this but we choose it to keep the code short.

File: `its/InteractiveGraphic/CircleAdministration.java`

```
package its.InteractiveGraphic;                              1.
                                                            2.
import java.awt.Graphics;                                    3.
import java.util.Vector;                                     4.
                                                            5.
public class CircleAdministration                            6.
{                                                            7.
  private Vector circles;                                    8.
                                                            9.
  public CircleAdministration()                             10.
  {                                                         11.
   circles = new Vector();                                  12.
  }                                                         13.
                                                           14.
  public void addCircle(Circle circ)                        15.
   {                                                        16.
      circles.add(circ);                                    17.
   }                                                        18.
                                                           19.
  public void removeNearestCircle(int x1, int y1)           20.
   {                                                        21.
     Circle circ;                                           22.
     double minDist = Double.MAX_VALUE;                     23.
     int    minDistIndex = -1;                              24.
     for (int i=0 ; i < circles.size() ; i++)               25.
     {                                                      26.
       circ = (Circle)(circles.get(i));                     27.
       if(circ.distanceTo(x1,y1) < minDist)                 28.
```

```
29.        {
30.          minDist = circ.distanceTo(x1,y1);
31.          minDistIndex = i;
32.        }// if
33.      }//for i
34.      if ((minDistIndex >= 0) && (minDist < 30))
35.        {
36.          circles.removeElementAt(minDistIndex);
37.        }//if
38.    }//method
39.
40.    public void drawAll(Graphics g)
41.    {
42.      Circle currentCircle;
43.      for (int i=0 ; i < circles.size() ; i++)
44.      {
45.          currentCircle = (Circle)(circles.get(i));
46.          currentCircle.draw(g);
47.      }//for i
48.    }//method
49.
50.    public int getNoOfCircles(){
51.      return(circles.size());
52.    }//method
53. }
```

7.3 ■ The view part

The view is much like that in Chapter 6. The frame class `InteractiveFrame` is just a renamed copy of class `MouseEventFrame` from Chapter 6.

The panel `InteractivePanel` is extended with respect to class `MouseEvent-Panel` from Chapter 6. It now contains a field of type `CircleAdministration` and methods `addCircle` and `removeNearestCircle` for adding and deleting a circle to the circle administration. These methods just pass the mouse positions to those methods of `CircleAdministration` with the same name and then call `repaint`. It is important to call the `repaint` method of the panel after every deletion and insertion of a circle! Otherwise a circle would only be added to or deleted from the circle administration – the display would not be updated.

The `paintComponent` method of `JPanel` has to be overridden to draw the circles. The panel itself knows neither which circles are currently present nor how to draw them. This is known only by the `CircleAdministration`. Thus the only drawing command in `paintComponent` is a call of the method `drawAll` of `CircleAdministration`.

File: its/InteractiveGraphic/InteractivePanel.java

```java
package its.InteractiveGraphic;                              1.
                                                            2.
import java.awt.Color;                                      3.
import java.awt.Dimension;                                  4.
import java.awt.Graphics;                                   5.
import javax.swing.JPanel;                                  6.
                                                            7.
public class InteractivePanel extends JPanel               8.
{                                                           9.
                                                            10.
private CircleAdministration circleAdm;                     11.
private double radius = 6.0;                                12.
                                                            13.
public InteractivePanel()                                   14.
  {                                                         15.
    circleAdm = new CircleAdministration();                 16.
    this.setBackground(Color.white);                        17.
    this.setPreferredSize(new Dimension(300,300));          18.
  }                                                         19.
                                                            20.
public  void paintComponent(Graphics g)                    21.
  {                                                         22.
    super.paintComponent(g);                                23.
    circleAdm.drawAll(g);                                   24.
  }                                                         25.
                                                            26.
public void addCircle(int x, int y)                        27.
  {                                                         28.
    circleAdm.addCircle(new Circle(x,y,radius));            29.
    repaint();                                              30.
  }                                                         31.
                                                            32.
public void removeNearestCircle(int x, int y)             33.
  {                                                         34.
    circleAdm.removeNearestCircle(x,y);                     35.
    repaint();                                              36.
  }                                                         37.
                                                            38.
public int getNoOfCircles()                                 39.
  {                                                         40.
    return(circleAdm.getNoOfCircles());                     41.
  }                                                         42.
}                                                           43.
```

The status panel has to display the number circles. We change class `StatusPanel` from Chapter 6 as follows. We now use a 4 × 3 grid layout and three more labels. The additional labels contain the text 'No. of circles', the number of circles, and a dummy to fill the grid. We add a method `setNoOfCircles(int n)` to set the number of circles.

File: `its/InteractiveGraphic/StatusPanel.java`

```
1. package its.InteractiveGraphic;
2.
3. import java.awt.GridLayout;
4. import javax.swing.JLabel;
5. import javax.swing.JPanel;
6.
7. public class StatusPanel extends JPanel
8. {
9.     private JLabel posText    = new JLabel("position:");
10.    private JLabel XCoord     = new JLabel("0", JLabel.RIGHT);
11.    private JLabel YCoord     = new JLabel("0", JLabel.RIGHT);
12.    private JLabel countText  = new JLabel("no. of clicks");
13.    private JLabel counts     = new JLabel("0", JLabel.RIGHT);
14.    private JLabel dummy1     = new JLabel();
15.    private JLabel circleText = new JLabel("no. of circles");
16.    private JLabel noOfCirc   = new JLabel("0", JLabel.RIGHT);
17.    private JLabel dummy2     = new JLabel();
18.    private JLabel inOutText  = new JLabel("mouse is in comp.");
19.    private JLabel inOut      = new JLabel("no", JLabel.RIGHT);
20.    private JLabel dummy3     = new JLabel();
21.
22.    private int clickCount = 0;
23.
24.    public StatusPanel()    {
25.      this.setLayout(new GridLayout(4,3));
26.      this.add(posText);
27.      this.add(XCoord);
28.      this.add(YCoord);
29.      this.add(countText);
30.      this.add(counts);
31.      this.add(dummy1);
32.      this.add(circleText);
33.      this.add(noOfCirc);
34.      this.add(dummy2);
35.      this.add(inOutText);
36.      this.add(inOut);
37.      this.add(dummy3);
38.    }
39.
```

```
public void setCoordinates(int x, int y){      40.
  XCoord.setText(""+x);                         41.
  YCoord.setText(""+y);                         42.
}                                               43.
                                                44.
public void setInOut(String str){               45.
  inOut.setText(str);                           46.
}                                               47.
                                                48.
public void incrementClickCount(){              49.
  clickCount++;                                 50.
  counts.setText(Integer.toString(clickCount)); 51.
}                                               52.
                                                53.
public void setNoOfCircles(int n){              54.
  noOfCirc.setText(Integer.toString(n));        55.
}                                               56.
}                                               57.
```

7.4 ■ The control part

Of the two listeners only `MyMouseListener` is changed by adding more commands to method `mouseClicked`. Depending on whether the left or right button was pressed a circle is added using the methods `addCircle(e.getX(),e.getY())` or deleted using `removeNearestCircle(e.getX(),e.getY())` of class `Interactive Panel`. The information about which mouse button was clicked is extracted from the `MouseEvent` object e using methods from the class `SwingUtilities`. If a mouse has three or more buttons, any button that is not the left one is considered as a right button. In any case the number of circles is updated using

```
[StatusPanel].setNoOfCircles([InteractivePanel].getNoOfCircles())
```

The texts in brackets have to be replaced by the appropriate variable names without brackets. In order for the listener to have access to that panel the constructor of `MyMouseListener` now receives a reference to the interactive panel.

File: `its/InteractiveGraphic/MyMouseListener.java`

```
package its.InteractiveGraphic;                 1.
                                                2.
import java.awt.event.MouseEvent;               3.
import java.awt.event.MouseListener;            4.
import javax.swing.SwingUtilities;              5.
                                                6.
```

```
 7.  public class MyMouseListener implements MouseListener
 8.  {
 9.  private StatusPanel statusPane;
10.  private InteractivePanel interactivePane;
11.
12.    public MyMouseListener(StatusPanel s,InteractivePanel i)
13.    {
14.      statusPane = s;
15.      interactivePane = i;
16.    }
17.
18.    public void mouseEntered(MouseEvent e)
19.    {
20.      statusPane.setInOut("yes");
21.    }
22.
23.    public void mouseExited(MouseEvent e)
24.    {
25.        statusPane.setInOut("no");
26.        statusPane.setCoordinates(-1,-1);
27.    }
28.
29.    public void mouseClicked(MouseEvent e)
30.    {
31.        statusPane.incrementClickCount();
32.        if(SwingUtilities.isLeftMouseButton(e)) //left mouse button
33.        {
34.          interactivePane.addCircle(e.getX(),e.getY());
35.        }
36.        else // any other mouse button
37.        {
38.          interactivePane.removeNearestCircle(e.getX(),e.getY());
39.        }
40.      statusPane.setNoOfCircles(interactivePane.getNoOfCircles());
41.    }
42.
43.    public void mousePressed(MouseEvent e)
44.    {
45.      //implemented with empty body
46.    }
47.
48.    public void mouseReleased(MouseEvent e)
49.    {
50.      //implemented with empty body
51.    }
52. }
```

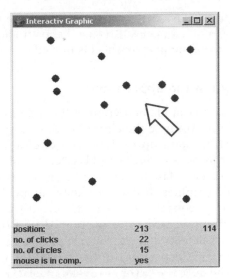

Figure 7.1 The interactive application. Only 14 circles are shown, rather than the 15 given on the status panel, as 2 occupy the same location

7.5 ■ Running the application

Our interactive application is now complete. The result is shown in Figure 7.1. Note that more than one circle can be at the same coordinates in which case one 'sees' fewer circles than there actually are. The number of circles displayed in the status panel is always correct. Some circles might also be invisible because the frame was resized and they are now outside the visible area.

7.6 ■ Summary and remarks

7.6.1 □ Mouse listeners

We have seen how the two mouse listeners work. A `MouseListener` becomes active when the mouse buttons are used or the mouse leaves or enters the component to which the listener is assigned. A `MouseMotionListener` becomes active whenever the mouse is moved. The mouse event object generated by the runtime system contains information on the type of event and the location where it occurred.

The following steps are necessary to implement mouse listeners:

1. Determine inside which component the mouse should be tracked.

2. Create a mouse (motion) listener. That is, define in method `mouseClicked`, etc. what has to happen in response to an event.

3. Assign the action listener to the relevant component.

Since version 1.4 of the Java SDK (software development kit) there is a third listener for the mouse: a MouseWheelListener keeps tracks of the mouse wheel and is activated every time the mouse wheel is moved.

7.6.2 ☐ The design of the application

Let us again summarize the implementation of the model–view–control concept of this application. In this example the class CircleAdministration does all the work to keep the abstract data up to date. The circles are stored in Circle-Administration and this class deletes or adds circles. Only this class knows how many circles there are. The class InteractivePanel, on the other hand, does the work to display the graphics. It does not know about the circles. In order to draw the graphic it has to consult CircleAdministration. It does so by calling the drawAll method of CircleAdministration. Also, if the listener associated with InteractivePanel detects a click, InteractivePanel only knows whether to add or delete a circle and the position. It then passes the work to CircleAdmin-istration by calling the addCircle (or removeNearestCircle) method. After an update (add or delete) has been completed by CircleAdministration, Inter-activePanel updates the display. To this end it calls its method repaint, which causes the runtime system to call paintComponent at an appropriate time.

Exercises

7.1 Change the application as follows. Add a field color to class Circle as an instance of java.awt.Color. Define a second constructor for Circle which allows it to pass a colour in addition. Then modify CircleAdministration in such a way that the circles in turn receive the colours red, blue, green, red, etc.

7.2 Modify the application in the following way. Add a line to the status panel which displays the coordinates of the centre of that circle that is currently closest to the mouse pointer. Note that this might change with every move of the mouse. Make sure that the application can handle the situation where no circle is present.

7.3 Change the application to display line segments instead of circles. A line is added by two consecutive clicks of the left mouse button. The location of the first click is one end point of the line, the location of the second click is the other end point. A click of the right button removes a line nearest to the click location. There are various ways to define 'nearest', for example one can take the distance to the first end point, to the middle of the line or the geometrical distance.

Menus

8

In this chapter we learn how to add menus to a frame and how to integrate them into our application.

Menus are most often used as subcomponents of frames. They are hierarchically organized. The topmost component is the *menu bar*. This is a rectangular area located below the title bar of a frame and above the content pane. The intermediate components are the *menus*. A menu appears as text in the menu bar. When one clicks on such a text the actual menu will roll out. It contains the *menu items*, which are lowest in the hierarchy. Figure 8.1 illustrates the structure. The menu items are the components that trigger actions. They can be considered as a special kind of button. In fact, like buttons, one uses an action listener to monitor them. It sometimes is necessary to *disable* certain menu items for some of the time. A disabled menu item does not trigger any action when clicked on. On most platforms the text of a disabled menu item is shown lighter than that of enabled ones. One situation where disabling a menu item makes sense is the following: assume data are loaded from a file, and a menu item is then clicked on to start extensive calculations on the data. It would make no sense to repeat these extensive calculations on the same data if the result is always the same. Thus one disables the menu item that starts the calculations. It is enabled again only when new data are present.

We shall now implement a small GUI that demonstrates the use of menus in Swing. As it does not handle any other data we do not implement a model part.

8.1 ■ Specification of the GUI

The GUI consists of a frame with a label embedded into the content pane. It has a menu bar with two menus entitled 'Menu 1' and 'Menu 2'. The first has three items entitled 'Item 1', 'Test' and 'Exit'. The second menu has two items entitled 'Enable Test' and 'Disable Test'. Initially all items are enabled.

When a menu item is selected, the label displays a text 'Item XXXX selected'. The two items in the second menu do something in addition. Whenever 'Disable Test' is clicked on, the item 'Test' in the first menu is disabled; if it was disabled before, nothing changes. Whenever 'Enable Test' is clicked on, the item 'Test' in the first menu is enabled; if it was enabled before, nothing changes.

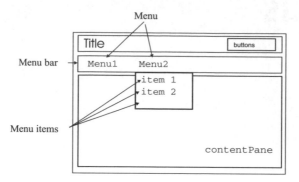

Figure 8.1 The structure of an application with menus. The second menu is rolled out and its entries can be selected

8.2 ■ The view part

We need the following three Swing components to implement menus. First, a menu bar realized by class `JMenuBar`. This is added to a frame between the title bar and the content pane. Second, we need a menu realized by `JMenu`, which adds a menu to the menu bar by displaying its title. Finally, we need menu items realized in class `JMenuItem`, which defines the menu items on which the user can click. The basic functions are automatically supplied: a menu rolls out if one clicks on the title and it closes if one clicks somewhere else.

8.2.1 ☐ Menu bars

From `JMenuBar` we only need the constructor and the method to add a menu:

```
JMenuBar()
add(JMenu menu)
```

Menus are added to the menu bar from left to right in the order of the `add` commands. To add a menu bar to a frame we use the following method from class `JFrame`:

```
setJMenuBar(JMenuBar menuBar)
```

Note that there are distinct methods `setJMenuBar` and `setMenuBar` for adding a `JMenuBar` (Swing) and a `MenuBar` (AWT).

8.2.2 ☐ Menus

From class `JMenu` we need the constructor which receives the menu title in a string and methods to add menu items or *separators* (horizontal lines) to the menu:

```
JMenu(String menuTitle)
add(JMenuItem menuItem)
addSeparator()
```

In a menu, the items or separators are added from top to bottom in the order of the `add` commands.

8.2.3 □ Menu items

From `JMenuItem` we need the constructor which receives the item title in a string and a method to assign an action listener to the menu item. Menu items behave much like buttons. In particular, the action listener is automatically informed when the item is clicked on. The listener then starts the desired actions. Finally we need a method to enable or disable a menu item:

```
JMenuItem(String itemText)
addActionListener(ActionListener listener)
setEnabled(boolean b)
```

The call `setEnabled(false)` disables a menu item. The item appears with a lighter text and any listener assigned to it is no longer informed when the item is clicked on. Hence, a disabled item does not trigger any reaction in the application. Calling `setEnabled(true)` will enable the item again. Its text becomes darker and listeners assigned to the item are again informed of events.

8.2.4 □ Constructing the GUI

We are now able to implement the GUI. The listings below show the code for the frame class `MenuFrame` and the driver class `MenuDriver`. A `MenuFrame` has a label centrally placed in its content pane. A menu bar is created and added. Then the two menus are created and added. Finally we generate the menu items and add them to the respective menus. Finally an action listener is created and assigned to all menu items. This listener is an instance of the class `MenuListener` which we define later in Section 8.3. The frame class also has three public methods for setting the text in the label, and enabling or disabling the menu item 'Test' in the first menu:

```
setText(String text)
enableTest()
disableTest()
```

File: `its/Menus/MenuFrame.java`

```
package its.Menus;                              1.
                                                2.
import its.SimpleFrame.SimpleFrame;             3.
import javax.swing.*;                           4.
import java.awt.BorderLayout;                   5.
                                                6.
public class MenuFrame extends SimpleFrame {    7.
                                                8.
```

```
9.    private JLabel display;
10.   private JMenuItem testItem;
11.
12.   public MenuFrame() {
13.     display = new JLabel("No menu selected.",JLabel.CENTER);
14.
15.     // Create a menu bar and add it to the frame
16.
17.     JMenuBar menubar = new JMenuBar();
18.     this.setJMenuBar(menubar);
19.
20.     // Create and add the menus
21.     JMenu firstMenu  = new JMenu("Menu 1");
22.     JMenu secondMenu = new JMenu("Menu 2");
23.     menubar.add(firstMenu);
24.     menubar.add(secondMenu);
25.
26.     // Create the menu items and add them to the menus
27.     JMenuItem firstItem   = new JMenuItem("Item 1");
28.              testItem    = new JMenuItem("Test");
29.     JMenuItem exitItem    = new JMenuItem("Exit");
30.     JMenuItem enableItem  = new JMenuItem("Enable Test");
31.     JMenuItem disableItem = new JMenuItem("Disable Test");
32.
33.     firstMenu.add(firstItem);
34.     firstMenu.add(testItem);
35.     firstMenu.addSeparator();
36.     firstMenu.add(exitItem);
37.
38.     secondMenu.add(enableItem);
39.     secondMenu.add(disableItem);
40.
41.     // Create a listener and add it to the menu items
42.     MenuListener menuList = new MenuListener(this);
43.     firstItem.addActionListener(menuList);
44.     testItem.addActionListener(menuList);
45.     exitItem.addActionListener(menuList);
46.     enableItem.addActionListener(menuList);
47.     disableItem.addActionListener(menuList);
48.
49.     // Add the label to the frame
50.     this.getContentPane().add(display,BorderLayout.CENTER);
51.   }
52.
53.   // Method to set the text in the label
54.   public void setText(String text){
```

```
      display.setText(text);                                        55.
    }                                                               56.
                                                                    57.
  // Method to enable the label                                     58.
  public void enableTest(){                                         59.
      testItem.setEnabled(true);                                    60.
  }                                                                 61.
                                                                    62.
  // Method to disable the label                                    63.
  public void disableTest(){                                        64.
      testItem.setEnabled(false);                                   65.
  }                                                                 66.
}                                                                   67.
```

File: `its/Menus/MenuDriver.java`

```
package its.Menus;                                                  1.
                                                                    2.
public class MenuDriver {                                           3.
  public static void main(String[] args) {                         4.
    MenuFrame mf = new MenuFrame();                                 5.
    mf.showIt();                                                    6.
  }                                                                 7.
}                                                                   8.
```

8.3 ■ The control part

The control part is realized by an action listener. We implement an `Action-Listener` in class `MenuListener`. As a reaction to events coming from the menu items the `MenuListener` has to update the information displayed in the `MenuFrame` and to enable or disable the 'Test' item. In order to have access to the frame the `MenuListener` receives a reference to a `MenuFrame` in the constructor.

As mentioned above, menu items behave much like buttons. If a menu item has a listener assigned to it and is clicked, the runtime system generates an object of type `ActionEvent`. This contains information on the type of event, e.g. which menu item was clicked. The runtime system calls method `actionPerformed` of the listener.

In our example, method `actionPerformed` exploits the action command to find out which button was clicked using nested if-then-else statements. Depending on the action command, a specific action is performed, namely the name of the selected menu item is displayed in the label. Below is the code listing for this class. Figure 8.2 shows the result of running the application.

Figure 8.2 The menu application. The first menu is rolled out and its second item, 'test', has been disabled

File: `its/Menus/MenuListener.java`

```
1. package its.Menus;
2.
3. import java.awt.event.ActionEvent;
4. import java.awt.event.ActionListener;
5.
6. public class MenuListener implements ActionListener {
7.
8.   private MenuFrame menuFrame;
9.
10.   public MenuListener(MenuFrame mf) {
11.     menuFrame = mf;
12.   }
13.
14.   public void actionPerformed(ActionEvent evt) {
15.     String actionCommand = evt.getActionCommand();
16.     if(actionCommand.equals("Item 1")){
17.       menuFrame.setText("Item 1 selected");
18.     }
19.     else if(actionCommand.equals("Test")){
20.       menuFrame.setText("Item Test selected");
21.     }
22.     else if(actionCommand.equals("Exit")){
23.       System.exit(0);
24.     }
25.     else if(actionCommand.equals("Enable Test")){
26.       menuFrame.enableTest();
27.       menuFrame.setText("Item \"Test\" in Menu 1 enabled.");
28.     }
29.     else if(actionCommand.equals("Disable Test")){
```

```
    menuFrame.disableTest();                                      30.
    menuFrame.setText("Item \"Test\" in Menu 1 disabled.");       31.
  }                                                               32.
  else{                                                           33.
    System.out.println("ERROR: unknown action command.");        34.
  }                                                               35.
  }                                                               36.
}                                                                 37.
```

Exercise

8.1 Construct a GUI consisting of a frame with a menu and an embedded panel. The menu has three items 'Red', 'Blue' and 'Yellow'. When a menu item is selected, the background colour of the panel is changed accordingly.

More on listeners

9

In this chapter we discuss how to use listeners in general. We also introduce some more listeners that react to events not considered so far. This chapter can be skipped in a first reading.

9.1 ■ Basics of listeners

Listeners are those components that link user actions to a running program. There are different listeners for different types of user actions. We have seen examples in Chapters 3, 4 and 6. These react to pressing a button or to using the mouse. There are many more listeners, some of which we shall briefly introduce here. Look in the `java.awt.event` library to see more.

A listener has to be assigned to a graphical component. The components have methods

```
addXXXXXXListener(XXXXXXListener listener)
```

for doing this, where XXXXXX is the type of the listener, e.g. `MouseMotion`. All listeners are *interfaces*. They require certain methods to be implemented by the programmer, e.g. `mouseMoved`. These methods are then automatically called by the operating system if the related event occurs, e.g. the mouse is moved. The code for the application's reaction to an event therefore has to be inside these methods.

Some listeners have only one method, such as `actionPerformed` in `Action-Listeners`, while others have more, like the five methods of a `MouseListener`. Every one of them reacts to a different event. If one only wants a reaction to some events, then the other methods are implemented with an empty body.

The methods of listener receive an event object as an argument. This event object contains more information about the event. Different listeners have different kinds of event objects (`ActionEvent` for `ActionListeners`, `MouseEvent` for `MouseListeners`). The event object is automatically generated by the runtime system when an event occurs and the appropriate method of the listener is called.

The information in the various types of events varies. A `MouseEvent` contains the coordinates at which the mouse pointer was when the event occurred. For an

`ActionEvent` this does not make sense. It is not of importance where a button was pressed. An `ActionEvent` on the other hand contains information on which button had been pressed. The different event types supply methods to access the information contained in the event, e.g. `getX()` and `getY()` allow one to get the co-ordinates of a `MouseEvent`, and `getActionCommand()` allows one to find the source of an action event.

9.2 ■ Implementing listeners

We have so far implemented listeners in classes of their own. We now see three more ways of implementing them. We return to our first GUI, the counter from Chapter 3. There, a class `CounterListener` is defined that implements an `ActionListener`. We illustrate the other methods for implementing listeners on this example.

9.2.1 □ Listeners as internal classes

In the counter example we defined the listener in a separate class `CounterListener`. The listener is assigned to two buttons and has to take actions when one of them is pressed. The reaction was to update the `CounterPanel`. The counter listener has to know *which* panel to update. Therefore we pass a reference to a `CounterPanel` in the constructor of the listener. Alternatively we can define the listener as an *internal class* inside `CounterPanel`. Then the methods of `CounterPanel` are known to the listener and can be called directly, i.e. the listener can use `decrement()` instead of `countPane.decrement()`. Therefore, no reference to a panel is passed to the listener. The constructor of the listener has an empty body. In fact, it can be omitted altogether; then the default constructor of `ActionListener` takes over. This is implemented in the package `its.CounterInternalGUI`, where the class `CounterInternalPanel` with an internally defined listener replaces both `CounterPanel` and `CounterListener`. We only print the listing of this class.

File: `its/CounterInternalGUI/CounterInternalPanel.java`

```
package its.CounterInternalGUI;                          1.
                                                         2.
import javax.swing.JPanel;                               3.
import javax.swing.JButton;                              4.
import javax.swing.JLabel;                               5.
import java.awt.BorderLayout;                            6.
import javax.swing.SwingConstants;                       7.
import java.awt.event.ActionListener;                    8.
import java.awt.event.ActionEvent;                       9.
                                                        10.
public class CounterInternalPanel extends JPanel {      11.
                                                        12.
    private CounterModel counter;                       13.
```

```
14.    private JLabel valueLabel;
15.
16.    public CounterInternalPanel() {
17.        counter = new CounterModel();
18.
19.        BorderLayout bordLay = new BorderLayout();
20.        this.setLayout(bordLay);
21.
22.        JButton upButton   = new JButton("Up");
23.        JButton downButton = new JButton("Down");
24.        valueLabel = new JLabel(""+counter.getValue(),SwingConstants.CENTER);
25.
26.        this.add(upButton,BorderLayout.WEST);
27.        this.add(downButton,BorderLayout.EAST);
28.        this.add(valueLabel,BorderLayout.CENTER);
29.
30.        // Definition of the listener, no reference
31.        // to "this" is passed on.
32.        InternalCounterListener countList =
33.            new InternalCounterListener();
34.        upButton.addActionListener(countList);
35.        downButton.addActionListener(countList);
36.    }
37.
38.    public void increment(){
39.        counter.increment();
40.        valueLabel.setText(""+counter.getValue());
41.    }
42.
43.    public void decrement(){
44.        counter.decrement();
45.        valueLabel.setText(""+counter.getValue());
46.    }
47.
48.    // Internal Listener Class
49.    class InternalCounterListener implements ActionListener{
50.
51.    //The constructor is empty
52.    public InternalCounterListener() {
53.    }
54.
55.    public void actionPerformed(ActionEvent evt){
56.        String actionCommand = evt.getActionCommand();
57.        if(actionCommand.equals("Up")){
58.            increment();
59.        }
60.        else if(actionCommand.equals("Down")){
```

```
      decrement();                                              61.
   }                                                            62.
   else{                                                        63.
      System.out.println("ERROR: Unexpected ActionCommand");    64.
   }                                                            65.
                                                                66.
  }// actionPerformed                                           67.
 }//internal class                                             68.
}                                                               69.
```

9.2.2 ☐ Listeners as part of the application class

In this section we will learn how to implement a listener as an interface inside another class. For users with no or very limited experience in using interfaces we give a very short survey about the *interface* mechanism in Java. In Java a class can extend only one other class and inherit its properties. For example, in the its-package class CounterFrame extends SimpleFrame and thus inherits the property of terminating the application when the frame is closed. Sometimes one would like a class to inherit the properties of more than one other class. The concept of interfaces allows this to a certain extent. A class can *extend* only one other class but it can *implement* more than one interface. An interface *requires* certain methods to be implemented. If a class NewClass is derived from OldClass and implements the interfaces IF1 and IF2 then the syntax for this is:

    class NewClass **extends** OldClass **implements** IF1, IF2

Inside the class NewClass we then have to implement the methods required by interfaces IF1 and IF2.

In our example we define class CounterInterfacePanel which we would like to inherit the properties of a JPanel and of an ActionListener. To this end we let CounterInterfacePanel *extend* JPanel and *implement* ActionListener.

    class CounterInterfacePanel **extends** JPanel **implements** ActionListener

The interface ActionListener requires method actionPerformed(ActionEvent evt) to be implemented inside CounterPanel (we get an error message from the compiler if we do not do this). After implementing actionPerformed in Line 50, the class CounterInterfacePanel also has the properties of an action listener, it 'has become' an action listener itself. Therefore, an instance of CounterInterfacePanel is assigned as an action listener to the buttons. Recall that the keyword this references the current instance.

```
   upButton.addActionListener(this);
   downButton.addActionListener(this);
```

We list the modified code for the counter panel. The class name is CounterInterfacePanel and it is located in the sub-package CounterInterfaceGUI.

File: `its/CounterInterfaceGUI/CounterInterfacePanel.Java`

```java
1.  package its.CounterInterfaceGUI;
2.
3.  import javax.swing.JPanel;
4.  import javax.swing.JButton;
5.  import javax.swing.JLabel;
6.  import java.awt.BorderLayout;
7.  import javax.swing.SwingConstants;
8.  import java.awt.event.ActionListener;
9.  import java.awt.event.ActionEvent;
10.
11.    public class CounterInterfacePanel extends JPanel
12.                                       implements ActionListener{
13.
14.    private CounterModel counter;
15.    private JLabel valueLabel;
16.
17.    public CounterInterfacePanel() {
18.        counter = new CounterModel();
19.
20.        BorderLayout bordLay = new BorderLayout();
21.        this.setLayout(bordLay);
22.
23.        JButton upButton   = new JButton("Up");
24.        JButton downButton = new JButton("Down");
25.        valueLabel = new JLabel(""+counter.getValue(),SwingConstants.CENTER);
26.
27.        this.add(upButton,BorderLayout.WEST);
28.        this.add(downButton,BorderLayout.EAST);
29.        this.add(valueLabel,BorderLayout.CENTER);
30.
31.        // A CounterInterfacePanel is now
32.        // also an ActionListener. Therefore, it
33.        // is assigned to the buttons using "this".
34.        upButton.addActionListener(this);
35.        downButton.addActionListener(this);
36.    }
37.
38.    public void increment(){
39.      counter.increment();
40.      valueLabel.setText(""+counter.getValue());
41.    }
42.
43.    public void decrement(){
44.      counter.decrement();
```

```
    valueLabel.setText(""+counter.getValue());          45.
  }                                                      46.
                                                         47.
  // Method actionPerformed is implemented               48.
  // inside the class CounterPanel.                       49.
  public void actionPerformed(ActionEvent evt){          50.
    String actionCommand = evt.getActionCommand();       51.
    if(actionCommand.equals("Up")){                      52.
      increment();                                       53.
    }                                                    54.
    else if(actionCommand.equals("Down")){               55.
      decrement();                                       56.
    }                                                    57.
    else{                                                58.
      System.out.println("ERROR: Unexpected ActionCommand");  59.
    }                                                    60.
  }//  actionPerformed                                   61.
                                                         62.
}                                                        63.
```

9.2.3 ☐ Anonymous listeners

Listeners can also be defined *anonymous* and *on-the-fly*. The syntax for assigning an anonymous listener to a component comp looks like this:

```
comp.addXXXXXXListener([Whole definition of XXXXXXListener goes here.]);
```

In our example, we have to implement one listener for each button. The anonymous implementation of the listener for the Up button then looks like this:

```
upButton.addActionListener(
    // Implementation of the listener begins
  new ActionListener(){
      // Implementation of required method begins
    public void actionPerformed (ActionEvent evt){
          increment();
    } // End of implementation of actionPerformed
  }// End of implementation of ActionListener
);//End of method addActionListener
```

The listener is *anonymous* because it does not receive a name. It is *on-the-fly* because it is placed where the listener is assigned to the button, namely inside the parentheses of method addActionListener. As the listener has no name, it cannot be referenced from anywhere. In particular, it cannot be reused for the Down button. Therefore we must define another listener for that button, which we again do as an anonymous listener.

As an anonymous listener is responsible for only a single button, it gets informed only when this specific button is pressed. There is no need to check which button it was. Therefore, we can immediately call methods `increment` and `decrement` for the `Up` respectively `Down` button. For other listeners, however, there still can be different events being triggered by the same component, e.g. for a mouse listener, one might have to check which mouse button has been used. The use of anonymous listeners is demonstrated in class `CounterAnonymousPanel`.

File: `its/CounterAnonymousGUI/CounterAnonymousPanel.java`

```
1. package its.CounterAnonymousGUI;
2.
3. import java.awt.BorderLayout;
4. import java.awt.event.ActionEvent;
5. import java.awt.event.ActionListener;
6. import javax.swing.*;
7.
8. public class CounterAnonymousPanel extends JPanel{
9.
10.    private CounterModel counter;
11.    private JLabel valueLabel;
12.
13.    public CounterAnonymousPanel() {
14.        counter = new CounterModel();
15.
16.        BorderLayout bordLay = new BorderLayout();
17.        this.setLayout(bordLay);
18.
19.        JButton upButton   = new JButton("Up");
20.        JButton downButton = new JButton("Down");
21.        valueLabel = new JLabel(""+counter.getValue(),SwingConstants.CENTER);
22.
23.        this.add(upButton,BorderLayout.WEST);
24.        this.add(downButton,BorderLayout.EAST);
25.        this.add(valueLabel,BorderLayout.CENTER);
26.
27.        // The listener for the up-button is defined
28.        // anonymous and on the fly.
29.        upButton.addActionListener(new ActionListener(){
30.          public void actionPerformed(ActionEvent evt){
31.                    increment();
32.          }// actionPerformed
33.        }//ActionListener
34.        );//addActionListener
35.
36.        // The listener for the down-button is defined
```

```
    // anonymous and on the fly.                          37.
    downButton.addActionListener(new ActionListener(){    38.
      public void actionPerformed(ActionEvent evt){       39.
            decrement();                                   40.
      }// actionPerformed                                  41.
     }//ActionListener                                     42.
    );//addActionListener                                  43.
  }                                                        44.
                                                           45.
  public void increment(){                                 46.
    counter.increment();                                   47.
    valueLabel.setText(""+counter.getValue());             48.
  }                                                        49.
                                                           50.
  public void decrement(){                                 51.
    counter.decrement();                                   52.
    valueLabel.setText(""+counter.getValue());             53.
  }                                                        54.
                                                           55.
                                                           56.
 }                                                         57.
```

9.2.4 □ Comparison of the four implementation techniques

We have seen four ways to implement a listener: in a separate class (Section 3.4), in an internal class (Section 9.2.1), as an interface (Section 9.2.2) or as an anonymous object (Section 9.2.3). The first method is especially suited to beginners with little experience of using interfaces. It also makes sense if the listener has to manipulate objects from many classes. Then references to all these classes are passed to the listener in the constructor, so the listener can access them.

The second method allows the listener to directly access methods and variables of the class it is defined in. This is suited for applications where the listener has to manipulate objects from only one class.

The third method completely avoids having to define a listener class of its own. This is considered a more elegant and efficient way by many authors. For beginners in graphics programming, however, it is often confusing, and a more structured approach with separate classes is preferred. It also limits the listener's range to the class that implements it.

The last method, anonymous listeners, assigns an individual listener to every component. This saves the trouble of checking which component triggered the listener. Also this method is not easy for beginners to understand.

Let us remark that philosophical wars are fought about what is the *best way* to implement listeners and to introduce them to beginners in graphics programming. The author's opinion on *teaching* listeners clearly is to use separate classes in the beginning. This is based on experience. Starting out with the method described in Section 9.2.2 or 9.2.3 only makes sense if students are experienced with using interfaces or anonymous definitions. If not, this approach causes confusion ('But, then where is my listener after all?').

In the three modifications of `CounterPanel` presented in this section, one can also avoid defining the methods `increment` and `decrement`. Instead one can transfer the respective code to the appropriate places in the listener.

9.2.5 □ Listeners and adapters

Listeners require the implementation of *all* their methods. Often one is interested in only one of them and the rest are implemented with empty bodies. To save some work, Java supplies *classes* that implement all the listener *interface* methods with empty bodies. The name for such a class is the name of the corresponding listener interface with 'Listener' replaced by 'Adapter', e.g. the class implementing a `MouseListener` is called a `MouseAdapter`.

Adapters are present for most listeners that require more than one method to be implemented. Then, instead of **implementing** all methods of the **listener interface** one only has to **override** the desired method of the corresponding **adapter class**.

9.3 ■ Other kinds of listener

There are other kinds of listeners that are of interest, for example `KeyListener`, `DocumentListener` and `WindowListener`. Key listeners react to key strokes. A document listener monitors changes in text documents; see Chapter 18. Window listeners react to events related to 'windows', i.e. 'frames' in Java. Such events are for example opening a window, closing it, turning it into an icon or activating it. We focus on closing the window here, i.e. on the event that occurs when the 'close' button of a frame is pressed.

In our basic frame class `SimpleFrame` we used the command

```
setDefaultCloseOperation(JFrame.EXIT_ON_CLOSE)
```

to immediately exit the application when the 'close' button is pressed. Often one would like to perform some clean-up or rescue work before termination, such as saving changed data to the disk. We define class `CleanUpFrame` which defines a method `cleanUp` to perform this work. In our example it just writes a message to the console and then exits the application. `CleanUpFrame` uses a window listener to activate this method.

As we use only one of the seven methods of interface `WindowListener` we actually use the corresponding adapter class `WindowAdapter` and thus avoid implementing six methods. We implement the class as an internal class `CleanUpAdapter`. It implements method `windowClosing(WindowEvent we)` which is automatically called by the runtime system when the 'close' button is pressed. Method `windowClosing` then calls the `cleanUp` method of the frame. In the constructor of `CleanUpFrame` an instance of `CleanUpAdapter` is created and assigned to the frame.

File: its/CleanUpFrame/CleanUpFrame.java

```
package its.CleanUpFrame;                                                1.
                                                                         2.
import javax.swing.JFrame;                                               3.
import java.awt.event.WindowAdapter;                                     4.
import java.awt.event.WindowEvent;                                       5.
                                                                         6.
public class CleanUpFrame extends JFrame                                 7.
{                                                                        8.
  public CleanUpFrame()                                                  9.
  {                                                                     10.
    this.setSize(200,200);                                             11.
    this.setLocation(200,200);                                         12.
    this.setTitle("CleanUpFrame");                                     13.
    CleanUpAdapter cleaner = new CleanUpAdapter();                     14.
    this.addWindowListener(cleaner);                                   15.
  }                                                                    16.
                                                                       17.
  public void showIt(){                                                18.
    this.setVisible(true);                                            19.
  }                                                                    20.
                                                                       21.
   public void hideIt(){                                               22.
    this.setVisible(false);                                          23.
  }                                                                    24.
                                                                       25.
  // Performs the clean up work before terminating the application.    26.
  private static void cleanUp(){                                       27.
    // Real code for the clean up goes here.                          28.
    System.out.println("Cleaning up and then terminating the program."); 29.
    System.exit(0);                                                   30.
  }                                                                    31.
  // Internal class                                                    32.
  private class CleanUpAdapter extends WindowAdapter{                  33.
                                                                       34.
  public void windowClosing(WindowEvent we)                            35.
        {                                                             36.
            // Call the cleanUp method of the frame.                  37.
            cleanUp();                                                38.
        }                                                             39.
}// internal class                                                    40.
}                                                                      41.
```

Exercises

9.1 Modify the text analysis GUI from Chapter 4 by implementing the listener as in internal class as described in Section 9.2.1. Decide into which class it should be implemented.

9.2 Modify the text analysis GUI from Chapter 4 by implementing the listener as a part of some other class as described in Section 9.2.1. Decide which class that should be.

Loading, saving and displaying text

10

In this chapter we begin to describe how graphical interfaces are used to display and manipulate text. We introduce the methods for reading and writing text files and for displaying text.

10.1 ■ Reading and writing text files

A *text* in Java is a sequence of *characters* in *Unicode* format. The Unicode character set contains more than 16,000 characters, including Japanese and Chinese ones. Every Unicode character is stored in 2 bytes (16 bit). Most text files contain data in *ASCII* format, which can express at most 256 characters and needs one byte (8 bit) to store one character. Depending on the format of the text file an appropriate way must be used to read or write it. If one reads an ASCII file as though it were a Unicode file then two consecutive ASCII characters are interpreted as one Unicode character. This looks funny but is not what we want. Nowadays, most text files are in ASCII format. Let us briefly look at how data transfer is handled in Java.

Input and output in Java are based on the concept of a *data stream*. Such a data stream is a sequence of characters (or other data objects). One distinguishes between an *input stream* from which one can extract (read) data and an *output stream* to which one can append (write) data. Streams are not limited to reading data from the hard disk. They can also be used to exchange data with the internet or with another application.

The data in a stream do not have to be human-readable text. There are streams in Java that consist of doubles or integers in binary representation. To extract data from a stream in the appropriate form (or to add it) one uses so-called *filters*. The stream is sent through a filter designed to handle the specific data format of this stream. The filter then extracts and interprets the data in the desired way. The names of filters for ASCII data streams end with *Reader* (input) or *Writer* (output).

The `java.io` library supplies the necessary classes and methods for file handling. The library is included by

```
import java.io.*;
```

We now present the most important classes for reading and writing ASCII text files and some of their methods.

10.1.1 ☐ The class `File`

The class `File` is the Java abstraction of a file or directory on the hard disk or some other storage medium; we shall use the term 'hard disk' in the following. Below we list a constructor and some methods we need:

```
File(String filename)

boolean exists()
boolean delete();
boolean renameTo(File newName)
boolean createNewFile()
boolean isDirectory()
String   getName()
String   getPath()
```

! `File(String filename)` creates a file object for a file with name `filename`. Note that neither an existing file with that name is opened nor is a file created on the hard disk.

`exists()` returns true if the file exists.

`delete()` deletes the file from the hard disk and returns `true` if successful or `false` otherwise, e.g. if the file did not exist.

`renameTo(File newName)` renames the file. The new name is that of the file object `newName`.

`createNewFile()` creates a file on the hard disk. The file name is that specified in the constructor, but only if the file does not already exist. If successful it returns `true` and `false` otherwise.

`isDirectory()` returns `true` if the file is a directory and `false` otherwise.

`getName()` returns just the file name, without the path but with extension.

`getPath()` returns the whole path including file name and extension.

Possible file names (the last one is directory) are, for example

```
testFile.txt
C:/Java/kurs/FileIO/scr/testFile.txt
C:\\Java\\kurs\\FileIO\\scr\\testFile.txt
~/Java/kurs/FileIO/testFile.txt
./FileIO/testFile.txt
C:/Java/
```

! Note that under MS Windows one can use both / or \ as a separator. Because of the special meaning of backslash in Java strings it has to be duplicated.

10.1.2 □ The classes `FileReader` and `FileWriter`

The classes `FileReader` and `FileWriter` supply methods for reading and writing ASCII files. These are *convenience classes* as they make it easy to access files. The programmer does not have to define a stream explicitly. We start by looking at a constructor and some methods of class `FileReader`:

```
FileReader(File aFile)

void close()
int  read()
int  read(char[] buffer,int start,int length)
```

`FileReader(File aFile)` opens the file `aFile` for reading. All further methods refer to this file.

`close()` stops the file reader and closes the file. It is important not to forget this command, otherwise the file might not be accessible by other applications.

`read()` reads a single character from the file and returns its integer value (ASCII code).

`read(buffer,start,length)` reads `length` and puts the characters into the char-array `buffer` starting at position `start` of the buffer. Returns the number of characters read or −1 if the file end is reached.

Most constructors and methods of `java.io` throw exceptions if errors occur, mostly `IOExceptions`. Thus they have to be embedded into `try-catch` blocks or the exceptions have to be thrown further.

Class `FileWriter` supplies methods for writing an ASCII file:

```
FileWriter(File aFile)

void close()
void write(char[] buffer)
void write(char[] buffer,int start,int length)
void write(String str, int start, int length)
```

`FileWriter(File aFile)` – this constructor opens the file `aFile` for writing. If the file is already present the old content is lost! All further methods refer to this file.

`close()` stops the file writer and closes the file. It is important not to forget this command, otherwise part of the data might not be written.

`write(char[] buffer)` writes the content of the buffer to the file by appending it to the previously written text.

`write(buffer,start,length)` writes the number of characters equivalent to the current value of `length` from `buffer` starting at position `start` of the buffer. The text is appended to the previously written text.

`write(str,start,length)` writes the number of characters equivalent to the current value of `length` of string `str` starting at position `start` of the string. The text is appended to the previously written text.

10.1.3 ☐ Dealing with text files

The program `FileReadWrite` is given below and demonstrates the methods described above. It reads some characters from the file `testtext1.txt` and stores them in a buffer (char-array) for potential further use. The buffer is initialized with dashes (-), so that the unused parts are visible when it is printed. The buffer is written to the standard output (screen). After this, a part of the buffer is written to another file `testtext2.txt`. If this file already exists, it is first erased. The constant `path` has to be changed if the directory structure is different from the one in the downloaded files. The path name has to end with a slash (/) or two backslashes. Below we list the content of file `testtext1.txt` on the left and that of `testtext2.txt` on the right:

```
Line  1               ne  1
Line  2               Line  2
Line  3               Line  3
Line  4               Line  4
Line  5               Line
Line  6
Line  7
Line  8
Line  9
The last line
```

When the buffer is printed, one can see that the line breaks appear as in the file because a `FileReader` reads the line break characters (\n).

File: `its/TextIO/FileReadWrite.java`

```java
1. package its.TextIO;
2.
3. import java.io.File;
4. import java.io.FileReader;
5. import java.io.FileWriter;
6.
7. public class FileReadWrite
8. {
9. // This variable has to be set according to your system
10. public static String path = "./its/TestData/";
11.
12.   public FileReadWrite(String ReadFileName,String WriteFileName)
13.   {
```

```
    //Buffer for the text                                                    14.
    char[] buffer = new char[128];                                           15.
    for (int i = 0; i < buffer.length; i++) {                                16.
      buffer[i] = '-';                                                       17.
    }                                                                        18.
                                                                             19.
    // Create two File-variables                                            20.
    File readfile  = new File(path+ReadFileName);                           21.
    File writefile = new File(path+WriteFileName);                          22.
                                                                             23.
//READING:                                                                   24.
    if (readfile.exists())                                                  25.
    {                                                                        26.
     try                                                                     27.
     {                                                                       28.
        // Create a reader.                                                 29.
        FileReader fr = new FileReader(readfile);                           30.
                                                                             31.
        // Read the file and store 100 characters in the                   32.
        // buffer starting at position 5 of the buffer.                    33.
        fr.read(buffer,5, 100);                                            34.
                                                                             35.
        // close file                                                      36.
        fr.close();                                                         37.
     }                                                                       38.
     catch (Exception ex)                                                   39.
     {                                                                       40.
      System.out.println("Problem opening file "+readfile.getName());      41.
     }                                                                       42.
    }//if                                                                    43.
    else                                                                     44.
    {                                                                        45.
      System.out.println("File not found "+readfile.getName());            46.
    }                                                                        47.
    System.out.println("Buffer>"+buffer+"<Buffer");                        48.
                                                                             49.
//WRITING:                                                                   50.
     try                                                                     51.
     {                                                                       52.
      if (writefile.exists())                                               53.
      {                                                                      54.
        writefile.delete();                                                 55.
      }                                                                      56.
      if (writefile.createNewFile())                                        57.
        {                                                                    58.
        // create a writer                                                 59.
        FileWriter fw = new FileWriter(writefile);                          60.
```

```
61.
62.        // writes 40 characters from the buffer
63.        // starting at position 7 of the buffer
64.
65.        fw.write(buffer,7,40);
66.
67.        // close file
68.        fw.close();
69.
70.    }//if
71.    else
72.    {
73.      System.out.println("File not created "+writefile.getName());
74.    }
75.    }
76.    catch (Exception ex)
77.    {
78.      System.out.println("Problem opening file "+writefile.getName());
79.    }
80. }
81.
82. public static void main(String[] args)
83.    {
84.    FileReadWrite RWF = new FileReadWrite("testtext1.txt","testtext2.txt");
85.    }
86. }
```

10.1.4 ☐ Reading text files line by line

Sometimes one would like to access a text file line by line. To do this another reader is used, a `BufferedReader`. We list the constructor and some methods:

```
BufferedReader(FilerReader fReader)

close()
String readLine()
```

`BufferedReader(FilerReader fReader)` constructs a buffered reader. A file reader is given as argument.

`close()` stops the buffered reader and closes the file.

`readLine()` returns a single line of text or null if the end of the stream has been reached. The line-end characters are not returned.

The following program `LineRead` reads a file line-wise. The while loop is terminated when the string read is `null`, i.e., when the file end is reached.

File: `its/TextIO/LineRead.java`

```
package its.TextIO;                                                       1.
                                                                         2.
import java.io.*;                                                         3.
                                                                         4.
public class LineRead                                                     5.
{                                                                         6.
  // This variable has to be set according to your system                7.
  public static String path = "./its/TestData/";                         8.
   public LineRead(String ReadFileName)                                   9.
   {                                                                     10.
     File readfile = new File(path+ReadFileName);                        11.
     String line;                                                        12.
     try                                                                 13.
     {                                                                   14.
       BufferedReader bfr = new BufferedReader(new FileReader(readfile)); 15.
       while((line = bfr.readLine()) != null)                            16.
       {                                                                 17.
         System.out.println("READ>"+line+"<");                          18.
       }                                                                 19.
     }                                                                   20.
     catch (Exception ex)                                               21.
     {                                                                   22.
       System.out.println("Problem opening file "+readfile.getName());  23.
     }                                                                   24.
   }                                                                     25.
                                                                        26.
   public static void main(String[] args)                               27.
   {                                                                    28.
    LineRead LR =  new LineRead("testtext1.txt");                       29.
   }                                                                    30.
}                                                                       31.
```

10.2 ■ Displaying text

We now show how to display text in a graphical component and not just on the console. We use a `JEditorPane` to do this. We could have used other components as well (`JTextArea` or `JTextPane`) but this one seems best suited for our purpose.

```
JEditorPane()

void    read(Reader myReader, Object description)
String getText()
```

JEditorPane() constructs an editor pane.

read(Reader myReader, Object description) reads the text supplied by myReader and displays it in the editor area. In the second argument description further information on the type of text can be given; we do not use this here, i.e. we set description = null.

getText() returns the text currently displayed in the editor area as one string, including the line-end characters.

The following listing TextDisplayFrame implements a text display. We derive a TextDisplayFrame from SimpleFrame and glue a JEditorPane into it as a central component. The constructor gets a file name as a string. It constructs a file readfile with this name. As in Section 10.1.3 a FileReader for file readfile is created. This reader is then passed to the read-method of JEditorPane. The pane then starts the reader and the text is displayed in the JEditorPane. Class TextDisplayDriver is just the start class.

File: its/TextDisplay/TextDisplayFrame.java

```
1. package its.TextDisplay;
2.
3. import its.SimpleFrame.SimpleFrame;
4. import java.io.File;
5. import java.io.FileReader;
6. import java.io.IOException;
7. import javax.swing.JEditorPane;
8. import java.awt.BorderLayout;
9.
10. public class TextDisplayFrame extends SimpleFrame
11. {
12.     private JEditorPane textDisplayPane;
13.
14.     public TextDisplayFrame(String filename)
15.     {
16.         textDisplayPane = new JEditorPane();
17.         this.getContentPane().add(textDisplayPane,BorderLayout.CENTER);
18.         this.setSize(200,160);
19.
20.         File readfile  = new File(filename);
21.
22.         try{
23.             FileReader fr = new FileReader(readfile);
24.             textDisplayPane.read(fr,null);
25.         }catch(IOException e){
26.             System.out.println("Problems opening or reading "
                              +readfile.getPath());
```

```
    }                                                                    27.
                                                                         28.
    }                                                                    29.
}                                                                        30.
```

File: `its/TextDisplay/TextDisplayDriver.java`

```java
package its.TextDisplay;                                                  1.
                                                                         2.
public class TextDisplayDriver                                           3.
  {                                                                      4.
  // Adjust paths if necessary!!                                         5.
  private static String path = "./its/TestData/";                        6.
  private static String fileName = "testtext1.txt";                      7.
                                                                         8.
  public static void main(String[] args)                                 9.
  {                                                                      10.
    TextDisplayFrame TAF = new TextDisplayFrame(path+fileName);          11.
    TAF.showIt("Text Display");                                          12.
  }                                                                      13.
}                                                                        14.
```

The result is shown in Figure 10.1. Obviously the frame is too small to display all the text. In the next section we shall see how to display long large texts using *scrolling*.

A `JEditorPane` supplies the basic functions of a text editor automatically. We can place the cursor, insert or delete text and also copy (using CNTR-C and CNTR-V). The reader is advised to try this. Other, more complex, functions such as searching are not provided.

!

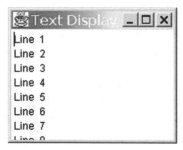

Figure 10.1 Display of `TextDisplayDriver`. Not all lines of the text are visible

Scrolling

11

In this chapter we see how to display long texts or large drawings that do not fit into the window. Only a part of them can be made visible. So-called scroll panes allow navigation in the text or the drawing and thus display different parts of the document.

11.1 ■ Scrolling text components

Scrolling allows us to roll a long text upwards, downwards or sideways in a graphical component or to change that part of a large drawing that is displayed. It is not important what kind of document is displayed, whether it is text or a drawing. Scrolling is realized as follows: imagine that the whole document is laid out somewhere. A scrollable graphical component has a small area where a part of the document is displayed. This area is called a *viewport*. The viewport can be around the document with the help of *sliders* or *scroll bars*, thus changing the part seen on the screen. See Figure 11.1. In Swing, scrolling is implemented by class JScrollPane. The scroll bars are on the right and at the bottom by default. We only use the following class JScrollPane:

```
JScrollPane(JComponent comp);
setHorizontalScrollBarPolicy(int policy)
setVerticalScrollBarPolicy(int policy)
```

JScrollPane(JComponent comp) this constructor generates a JScrollPane, the viewport of which displays part of comp. If the whole component fits into the viewport the scroll bars disappear. This behaviour can be changed using the next method.

setHorizontalScrollBarPolicy(int policy) determines when the scroll bars are visible. Class JScrollPane defines constant values for policy: HORIZONTAL_SCROLLBAR_ALWAYS, HORIZONTAL_SCROLLBAR_AS_NEEDED and HORIZONTAL_SCROLLBAR_NEVER and have obvious meanings.

setVerticalScrollBarPolicy(int policy) is the same as above, but for the vertical scroll bar.

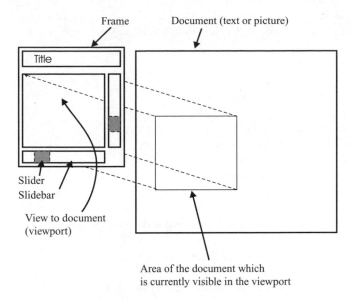

Figure 11.1 Structure of a scrollable component

Let us augment the application from Section 10.2 so that the text can be scrolled. Our text is still loaded into a JEditorPane. We then generate a scroll pane to display parts of it. The vertical scroll bar is visible at once. The horizontal one does not appear even though the text contains a very long line. The reason is that the JEditorPanel breaks long lines when reading them. One has to first make the panel wide (using the mouse) and then narrow to make the horizontal scroll bar appear. The functions of the scrollbars are automatically supplied. Moving the horizontal or vertical slider moves the viewport inside the document.

In the following we list the code for TextDisplayScrollFrame which displays scrollable text. The driver class TextDisplayScrollDriver is not listed. Figure 11.2 shows the result.

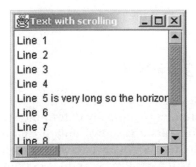

Figure 11.2 TextDisplayScrollFrame

File: `its/Scrolling/TextDisplayScrollFrame.java`

```
1.  package its.Scrolling;
2.
3.  import its.SimpleFrame.SimpleFrame;
4.  import java.io.File;
5.  import java.io.FileReader;
6.  import java.io.IOException;
7.  import java.awt.BorderLayout;
8.  import javax.swing.JEditorPane;
9.  import javax.swing.JScrollPane;
10.
11. public class TextDisplayScrollFrame extends SimpleFrame
12. {
13.   private JEditorPane TextDisplayPanel;
14.
15.   public TextDisplayScrollFrame(String filename)
16.   {
17.
18.    TextDisplayPanel = new JEditorPane();
19.
20.    JScrollPane scrollPane  = new JScrollPane(TextDisplayPanel);
21.    this.getContentPane().add(scrollPane,BorderLayout.CENTER);
22.
23.    File readfile  = new File(filename);
24.
25.    try{
26.     FileReader fr = new FileReader(readfile);
27.     TextDisplayPanel.read(fr,null);
28.    }catch(IOException e){
29.     System.out.println("Problems opening or reading "
                          +readfile.getName());
30.    }
31.  }
32. }
```

11.2 ■ Scrolling panels

If we use the default policy `HORIZONTAL_SCROLLBAR_AS_NEEDED` for the text component, the runtime system automatically determines the size of the area that is filled with text. The scroll bars are shown only if that area does not fit into the viewport. Using the default policy with panels will make the scroll bars appear when the area specified with a `setPreferredSize` command does not fit into the viewport.

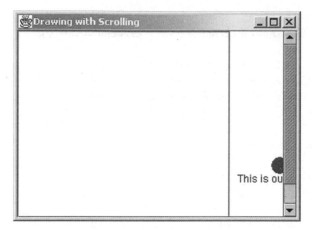

Figure 11.3 The drawing display application. The vertical scroll bar is visible because the height of the viewport is less than the preferred height of the panel to display. The horizontal scroll bar is not visible because the viewport is wider than the preferred width of the panel. The vertical line is the right edge of the preferred area. The drawing outside the preferred area is not considered by the runtime system when determining whether to show the scroll bar

As an example we construct a panel and add some drawing commands to its method `paintComponent`. The resulting class is called `DrawingDisplayScroll-Panel`. The size of the panel is set to 250×250 pixels. We draw a red rectangle to indicate the border of this area and a text to denote it. We then draw a circle and a text outside the area specified in the `setPreferredSize` command. We then create a scroll pane that displays the panel in its viewport. The scroll pane is embedded into a frame. We list class `DrawingDisplayScrollPanel` below but omit the listing of the frame class `DrawingDisplayScrollFrame` and the driver `DrawingDisplayScrollDriver`; both can be downloaded from the book's home page. Try resizing the frame in different ways to see when scroll bars appear or vanish.

Running this application and resizing the frame will show that the scroll bars become visible if the preferred size area of the panel does not fit into the viewport. The result can be seen in Figure 11.3. The runtime system does not recognize that there is some drawing outside this area. The programmer must take care of that by monitoring the current size of the drawing and adjusting the preferred size. In Chapter 21 we shall learn an elegant way to do this.

File: `its/Scrolling/DrawingDisplayScrollPanel.java`

```
package its.Scrolling;                    1.
                                          2.
import java.awt.Color;                    3.
import java.awt.Dimension;                4.
import java.awt.Graphics;                 5.
import javax.swing.JPanel;                6.
```

```
 7.
 8. public class DrawingDisplayScrollPanel extends JPanel {
 9.
10.    public DrawingDisplayScrollPanel() {
11.       this.setBackground(Color.white);
12.       this.setPreferredSize(new Dimension(250,250));
13.    }
14.
15.    public void paintComponent(Graphics g){
16.       super.paintComponent(g);
17.       Color oldColor = g.getColor();
18.       g.setColor(Color.red);
19.       g.drawRect(0,0,249,249);
20.       g.drawString("Border of preferred size.",10,240);
21.       g.setColor(Color.blue);
22.       g.fillOval(300,150,20,20);
23.       g.drawString("This is outside the preferred size",260,180);
24.       g.setColor(oldColor);
25.    }
26. }
```

Dialogues

12

In this chapter we introduce dialogues as a further means for user–program interaction. They are used when the application needs information from the user in order to proceed. First, we look at dialogues that are predefined in Swing and then turn to user-defined dialogues. We shall do this by extending the examples from previous chapters into a small editor. We will also learn how to transfer data between dialogues and the application.

In Chapter 10 we read a fixed file into our editor. In Section 11.1 we saw how to display the text so that it can be scrolled. The use of menus was presented in Chapter 8. Here, we combine these three things into an editor application. In addition to that, we add some dialogues for choosing a file, searching and showing a warning message. We begin by developing the skeleton of the application to which we then add more and more functions. No model is used for the actual data – the text – because our focus is on dialogues. Text models will be considered in Chapter 18.

12.1 ■ The basic editor application

Our editor should support the following operations. There should be menus where the user can select the actions 'Load', 'Save' and 'Search'. The first one allows the user to choose the text file to be loaded. The second one saves the currently loaded text file (under the same name). The third action allows the user to search for a word in the text. In order to implement these features, dialogues will be used. Before turning to dialogues we first set up the skeleton of the editor applications and fill in the relevant parts in later sections. The mechanism for editing a loaded text is automatically supplied by the Swing text component used.

In the following listing of class `EditorSkeletonFrame` we define a frame with a `JEditorPane` as a central component. The frame has a menu bar with two menus, 'File' and 'Tools'. The first menu has three items 'Load', 'Save' and 'Exit'. The second menu has only one item 'Search'. The implementation is a combination of the implementations from Chapter 10, Section 11.1 and Chapter 8.

The skeleton contains four methods that implement the reactions to selecting a menu item. For now, the only action is to print a message on the console.

The real actions are implemented later. We implement a listener in class EditortorListener which monitors the menu items. As a reaction to selecting a menu item, the appropriate method of the class EditorSkeletonFrame is called. Class EditorListener will not be changed later on, when we complete the editor.

File: its/Dialogs/EditorSkeletonFrame.java

```
1. package its.Dialogs;
2.
3.
4. import its.SimpleFrame.SimpleFrame;
5. import java.awt.*;
6. import javax.swing.*;
7. import java.io.*;
8.
9. public class EditorSkeletonFrame extends SimpleFrame {
10.
11.    private JEditorPane textDisplayPane;
12.
13.    public EditorSkeletonFrame()
14.    {
15.      textDisplayPane = new JEditorPane();
16.      JScrollPane scrollPane = new JScrollPane(textDisplayPane);
17.      this.getContentPane().add(scrollPane,BorderLayout.CENTER);
18.
19.  // Create menu bar, menus and menu items
20.      JMenuBar menubar = new JMenuBar();
21.      this.setJMenuBar(menubar);
22.      JMenu fileMenu = new JMenu("File");
23.      JMenu toolMenu = new JMenu("Tools");
24.      menubar.add(fileMenu);
25.      menubar.add(toolMenu);
26.      JMenuItem loadItem   = new JMenuItem("Load");
27.      JMenuItem saveItem   = new JMenuItem("Save");
28.      JMenuItem exitItem   = new JMenuItem("Exit");
29.      JMenuItem searchItem  = new JMenuItem("Search");
30.      fileMenu.add(loadItem);
31.      fileMenu.add(saveItem);
32.      fileMenu.addSeparator();
33.      fileMenu.add(exitItem);
34.      toolMenu.add(searchItem);
35.  // Create a listener and add it to the menu items
36.      EditorListener editorListener = new EditorListener(this);
37.      loadItem.addActionListener(editorListener);
38.      saveItem.addActionListener(editorListener);
39.      exitItem.addActionListener(editorListener);
```

```
      searchItem.addActionListener(editorListener);          40.
}                                                            41.
// The next four methods do not yet do anything             42.
// useful. The real code is supplied later.                 43.
public void openFile(){                                      44.
  //Code for loading a file has to go here.                  45.
  System.out.println("Menu item Load selected.");            46.
}                                                            47.
                                                             48.
public void saveFile(){                                      49.
  //Code for saving a file has to go here.                   50.
  System.out.println("Menu item Save selected.");            51.
}                                                            52.
                                                             53.
public void search(){                                        54.
  //Code for searching has to go here.                       55.
  System.out.println("Menu item Search selected.");          56.
}                                                            57.
                                                             58.
public void exitEditor(){                                    59.
  //Code for leaving the editor has to go here.              60.
  System.out.println("Menu item Exit selected.");            61.
}                                                            62.
}                                                            63.
```

File: its/Dialogs/EditorListener.java

```
package its.Dialogs;                                          1.
                                                             2.
import java.awt.event.ActionListener;                        3.
import java.awt.event.ActionEvent;                           4.
import javax.swing.JFrame;                                    5.
                                                             6.
public class EditorListener implements ActionListener {      7.
                                                             8.
  private EditorSkeletonFrame editor;                        9.
                                                            10.
  public EditorListener(EditorSkeletonFrame edi) {          11.
    editor = edi;                                           12.
}                                                           13.
                                                            14.
public void actionPerformed(ActionEvent evt) {              15.
  String actionCommand = evt.getActionCommand();            16.
  if(actionCommand.equals("Load")){                         17.
    editor.openFile();                                      18.
  }                                                         19.
```

```
20.    else if(actionCommand.equals("Save")){
21.       editor.saveFile();
22.    }
23.    else if(actionCommand.equals("Exit")){
24.       editor.exitEditor();
25.    }
26.    else if(actionCommand.equals("Search")){
27.       editor.search();
28.    }
29.    else {
30.      System.out.println("Error: Unexpected action command.");
31.    }
32.  }
33. }
```

12.2 ■ File selection dialogues

File selection dialogues allow the user to select a file from the computer's mass storage (hard disk). We will make this dialogue appear when the menu item 'Open' is clicked. The file selected by the user is returned to the class that started the dialogue.

12.2.1 ☐ The class `JFileChooser`

In Swing, file selection dialogues are predefined in the class JFileChooser. We present only a few of its methods; the class offers a lot more possibilities. The navigation in JFileChooser is (mostly) done as in the file selection dialogues of the operating system. One can change directories, to choose a file from a list, or by typing its name into a text field. There are buttons labelled 'Open' and 'Cancel'. We do not have to implement any listener for these buttons. All the functions one expects from a file selection dialogue are supplied by JFileChooser.

```
JFileChooser(String startDirectory);

int showOpenDialog(Component parent);
int showSaveDialog(Component parent);
File getSelectedFile();
```

JFileChooser(`String startDirectory`) generates a file selection dialogue which is not yet visible. When it becomes visible the files in startDirectory are listed, provided that this string specifies an existing directory.

showOpenDialog(`Component parent`) displays the file selection dialogue for **opening** files. Component parent is usually the component in which the showOpenDialog was called. This is important because a file selection dialogue is *modal*; see explanations below. On closing, a file selection dialogue returns an integer value which is one of the following integer constants: APPROVE_OPTION

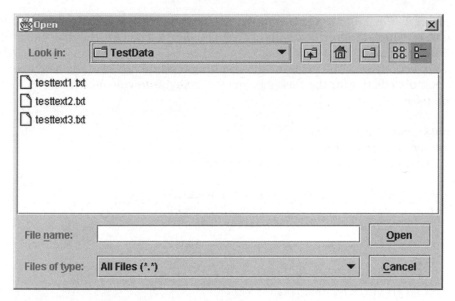

Figure 12.1 A file selection dialogue

indicates that the 'Open' (or 'Save', in case of a save dialogue) button of the dialogue has been clicked. CANCEL_OPTION indicates that the 'Cancel' button of the dialogue has been clicked.

showSaveDialog(Component parent) displays the file selection dialogue for **saving** files; the rest is as for showOpenDialog.

getSelectedFile() returns the selected file in a variable of type File if AP-PROVE_OPTION has been selected.

Methods that display a file selection dialogue receive a Component parent as an argument. Class Component from the AWT library is the mother class of all graphical components in Java. The reference to the parent is needed because a JFile-Chooser is modal. The parent component is blocked as long as it is visible itself. Only after the dialogue is closed can the parent component be used again. This is to avoid unwanted interactions such as modifying a file in the parent frame while it is being saved.

Figure 12.1 shows the result of creating a JFileChooser with the TestData directory of the ITS package, a start directory, and then making it visible by showOpenDialog.

12.2.2 □ Adding the file chooser to the editor

We declare a variable chooser of type JFileChooser and a variable selectedFile of type File in class EditorFrame by

```
private JFileChooser chooser;
private File selectedFile;
```

These variables are not yet instantiated using new; this will happen in method openFile which is described below. We then add the code for the dialogue at the position marked '//Code for opening a file has to go here.' in class EditorSkeletonFrame. The code for the resulting method openFile is listed below. The complete listing for the class EditorFrame can be downloaded from the book's home page.

```
1.  public void openFile(){
2.    if(chooser == null){
3.        chooser = new JFileChooser(startPath);
4.    }
5.    int returnVal = chooser.showOpenDialog(this);
6.    if(returnVal == JFileChooser.APPROVE_OPTION)
7.    {
8.      File selectedFile =  chooser.getSelectedFile();
9.      try{
10.      FileReader reader = new FileReader(selectedFile);
11.      textDisplayPane.read(reader,null);
12.      reader.close();
13.    }catch(IOException e){
14.    System.out.println("Problems opening or reading "
15.                                +selectedFile.getName());
16.    }
17.  }//if
18. }
```

The first lines create a file selection dialogue if this has not been done before. This is because we would like to avoid unnecessarily creating new instances of it. The condition in the if-statement in Line 2 is true only at its first execution. Then an instance of the file chooser is created and assigned to the variable chooser in Line 3. From that point on chooser is not null and hence the statement in Line 3 is not executed again.

We then make the file chooser visible in Line 5 as an 'Open'-dialogue using method showOpenDialog(this). The dialogue is modal and thus blocks its parent component as long as it is visible. In our case the parent component is the EditorFrame which is passed to the dialogue as this. The execution of the code of the EditorFrame is stopped at Line 5 until either the 'Open' or the 'Cancel' button of the dialogue is selected. Then the variable returnVal receives the value APPROVE_OPTION or CANCEL_OPTION respectively, the dialogue is made invisible and the execution of the code of EditorFrame is continued.

If APPROVE_OPTION is selected we find out which file has been selected using method getSelectedFile. Then a file reader for this file is created in Line 10. This reader is passed to the read method of JTextPanel which loads the file and displays the text. As explained in Section 10.1, readers have to be placed inside a try-catch block. This concludes the implementation of the file opening procedure of our editor.

The methods `saveFile` and `exitEditor` are implemented in a very simple way; exercises to extend the implementation are given at the end of the chapter. The `saveFile` method writes the current content of the editor area to a file with the same name as the one it loaded from. The `exitEditor` method exits the application.

```java
public void saveFile(){
  try{
    FileWriter fw = new FileWriter(selectedFile);
    fw.write(textDisplayPane.getText());
    fw.close();
    }catch(IOException e){
     System.out.println("Problems writing "+selectedFile.getName());
    }
    textDisplayPane.setText("");
}

public void exitEditor(){
 System.exit(0);
}
```

The implementation of the 'Search' feature is described in the next section.

12.3 ■ User-defined dialogues

We shall now augment the editor with a search function. To keep things simple, we search for a whole word only and report how often it occurs in the text. The user can specify whether the search should be case-sensitive or not.

We will create our own dialogue class `SearchDialog` by extending the Swing-class `JDialog`. A `JDialog` is much like a `JFrame` but it can be *modal*; see Section 12.2.1. A `JDialog` has a content pane into which further components are embedded. We glue a panel with 4 × 2 grid layout into the content pane of the dialogue. We then add components to the panel to get a layout as shown in Figure 12.2. The only new type of components here are the *radio buttons* which select whether the search is case sensitive. They are explained below. From class

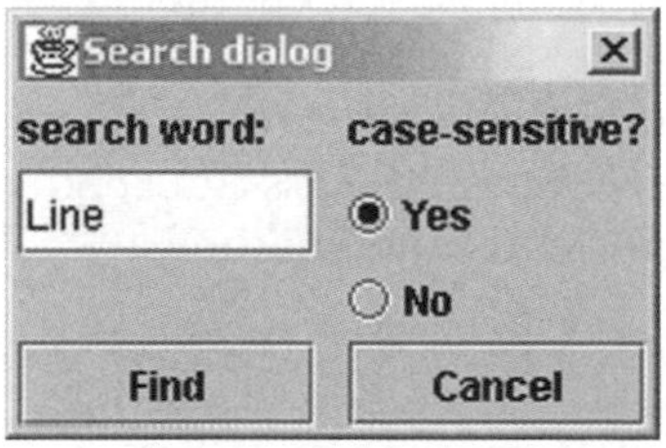

Figure 12.2 The search dialogue

`JDialog` we only need the constructor and some methods to add components. The semantics of the methods is the same as that for `JFrames`.

```
JDialog(Frame parent, String title, boolean modal)
```

```
getContentPane.add(Component comp)
setVisible(boolean b)
pack()
```

In order to have a proper display we call the default constructor of `JDialog` in the constructor of `SearchDialog` using the `super`-method.

12.4 ■ Radio buttons

The two buttons 'Find' and 'Cancel' are `JButtons`, as in `TextAnalysisGUI` in Chapter 4. The buttons 'Yes' and 'No' are *radio buttons*. Only one of them can be pressed at a time. These buttons are implemented using the class `JRadioButton`. A radio button is rectangular. It contains a circular area on the left and a label to the right of it. Radio buttons can be pressed and they can be *grouped*. They stay pressed until another radio button of the group is pressed. A black dot appears inside the circular area if the button is pressed. We need the following methods:

```
JRadioButton(String buttonName)
```

```
setSelected(boolean pressed)
setActionCommand(String command)
String getActionCommand()
```

`JRadioButton(String buttonName)` creates a button labelled `buttonName`.

`setSelected(boolean pressed)` determines whether the button is selected (`pressed = true`) or not (`pressed = false`). In the first case the black dot is visible inside the circular area of the button. This method is used initially to set which buttons are pressed before the first user action.

`setActionCommand(String command)` assigns the string `command` as the action command to the button. Radio buttons are **not** automatically assigned an action command. This is because their label is often not a text but a picture. We set the action command ourselves using method `setActionCommand`.

`getActionCommand()` returns the action command assigned to the button.

We still have to make sure that only one button is pressed at a time. This is done by *grouping* the buttons. We use the class `ButtonGroup` from the AWT library. Below we list the constructor and some methods:

```
JButtonGroup();
```

```
add(JRadioButton button)
String getSelection().getActionCommand()
```

`JButtonGroup()` constructs a button group not yet containing any button.

`add(JRadioButton button)` adds the radio button `button` to the group.

`getSelection().getActionCommand()` returns the action command of the button which is currently selected in the group. This statement combines methods from `ButtonGroup` and `ButtonModel`, a class we do not discuss here.

Once the buttons are in a group, only one at a time can be pressed. Pressing an unpressed one releases the one previously pressed. The listing of the whole dialogue can be found in Section 12.5.2.

12.5 ■ Exchange of information between dialogue and program

Now that the layout of the dialogue is completed we take care of the information exchange. We begin by describing the general principle and then apply it to our editor.

12.5.1 □ General scheme for information transfer

Depending on how much information has to be exchanged between a dialogue and the program that created it, different methods of information exchange can be used. Return values may be used to transfer a single variable from the dialogue back to the program. This is, for example, done by `JFileChooser`. Further information can then be accessed using `get`-methods of the dialogue such as `getSelectedFile` and `JFileChooser`. This approach is appropriate if the data format is fixed and not too much data have to be transferred.

A more flexible way of realizing information transfer is to define a special object for this purpose. The *data transfer object* has to be defined by the programmer to store all the information to be transferred between the program and the dialogue. It should also have `get` and `set` methods to access the data; see also Section B.3.

A data transfer object can be used to transfer data both ways, from the program to the dialogue and back. It might contain some initial information which is displayed by the dialogue. This is then altered by the user in the dialogue and the modified data are returned to the program. We describe the framework for this approach below and incorporate it into our editor after that. The basic steps for a data transfer using an object are:

1. Define a class for the *data transfer object*. Let us call it `DataTransferObject` here. A `DataTransferObject` contains the information that is to be exchanged between the dialogue and the application that created the dialogue. Define the `get` and `set` methods to access the data.

2. Define a dialogue class, say `MyDialog`, with the desired layout. The dialogue should also contain two buttons labelled, for example, 'OK' and 'Cancel'.

3. Define a method `showIt(DataTransferObject dto)` in class `MyDialog`. This method receives a data transfer object `dto` as an argument. It (possibly) extracts some data from `dto` which is to be displayed in the dialogue. It also makes the dialogue visible.

4. Define a listener for the dialogue (preferably as an internal class). This listener monitors the 'OK' and 'Cancel' buttons. When one of them is clicked the listener updates the data transfer object. Changes made by the user while the dialogue was visible, e.g. text inputs, are put into the data transfer object. In addition the data transfer object has to contain the information whether 'OK' or 'Cancel' was clicked. Finally the listener makes the dialogue invisible.

5. The information transfer then proceeds as follows:
    (a) The application creates an instance `myDialog` of `MyDialog` and an instance `dto` of `DataTransferObject`.
    (b) If desired, the application initializes some values of `dto` using the `set` methods.
    (c) The application makes the dialogue visible by calling `myDialog.showIt (dto)`. As a dialogue is modal, the application pauses until the dialogue is invisible again. During this time the user can change the information in the data transfer object through the dialogue.
    (d) Once the dialogue is invisible the application extracts the modified data from `dto` and uses it.

12.5.2 ☐ Exchanging data with the search dialogue

We define the class `DataTransferObject` to exchange data. An object of type `DataTransferObject` contains three fields: one string and two boolean variables. The string `searchWord` contains the text to search for. To indicate whether the search has to be case sensitive we use the boolean field `caseSensitive`. Finally the boolean field `search` indicates whether the dialogue was closed by clicking 'Find' (`true`) or 'Cancel' (`false`). The class also defines the `get`- and `set`-methods to read and write these fields. For convenience there is a `setAll` method to set all information.

The application `EditorFrame` can now check whether it has to search (`get-Search() == true`), which word to search for (`getSearchWord()`) and whether to obey cases (`getCaseSensitive() == true`).

Class `SearchDialog` has `SearchListener` as an internal class[1]. The listener keeps track of the two `JButtons` 'Find' and 'Cancel' (it does not monitor the radio buttons). On closing the dialogue, the current information of the dialogue is written into the `DataTransferObject`. Then the program can extract the information from it. In our example the search itself is done by just counting the number of occurrences of the word. The respective method `countWords` of `EditorFrame` is not listed here.

In order to avoid the generation of unnecessary objects from within the `EditorFrame` class, we generate the dialogue only once. After that, it is made visible or

---

[1] See Chapter 9 for information on listeners as internal classes.

invisible. We check whether the dialogue is already defined by checking whether the reference to it is `null` or not.

```
if (searchDialog == null)
  {
    searchDialog  = new SearchDialog(this);
    dataTransfer  = new DataTransferObject();
  }
```

The variables `searchDialog` and `dataTransfer` are previously declared, e.g.

```
private SearchDialog searchDialog;
private DataTransferObject dataTransfer;
```

but not instantiated using `new`. We now list the classes `SearchDialog` and `Data-TransferObject`.

File: `its/Dialogs/SearchDialog.java`

```
package its.Dialogs;                                              1.
                                                                 2.
import java.awt.*;                                               3.
import java.awt.event.*;                                         4.
import javax.swing.*;                                            5.
                                                                 6.
public class SearchDialog extends JDialog                        7.
{                                                                8.
  private JPanel mainPanel          = new JPanel();              9.
  private JTextField searchTextField = new JTextField();        10.
  private JRadioButton yesButton    = new JRadioButton("Yes");  11.
  private JRadioButton noButton     = new JRadioButton("No");   12.
  private JButton searchButton      = new JButton("Find");      13.
  private JButton cancelButton      = new JButton("Cancel");    14.
  private DataTransferObject dataTransfer;                      15.
  private ButtonGroup group = new ButtonGroup();               16.
                                                                17.
  public SearchDialog(Frame frame)                             18.
  {                                                            19.
    super(frame,"Search dialog",true);                        20.
                                                                21.
    JLabel questionS   = new JLabel("search word:");          22.
    JLabel questionCS  = new JLabel("case-sensitive?");       23.
    JLabel filler      = new JLabel();                        24.
                                                                25.
    this.getContentPane().setLayout(new BorderLayout());      26.
    this.setLocation(300,300);                                27.
    this.getContentPane().add(mainPanel,BorderLayout.CENTER); 28.
                                                                29.
```

```
30.      mainPanel.setLayout(new GridLayout(4,2,10,0));
31.      mainPanel.add(questionS);
32.      mainPanel.add(questionCS);
33.      mainPanel.add(searchTextField);
34.      mainPanel.add(yesButton);
35.      mainPanel.add(filler);
36.      mainPanel.add(noButton);
37.      mainPanel.add(searchButton);
38.      mainPanel.add(cancelButton);
39.
40.      group.add(yesButton);
41.      group.add(noButton);
42.      yesButton.setActionCommand("yesActionCommand");
43.      noButton.setActionCommand("noActionCommand");
44.      yesButton.setSelected(true);
45.      noButton.setSelected(false);
46.
47.      SearchListener SLis = new SearchListener();
48.      searchButton.addActionListener(SLis);
49.      cancelButton.addActionListener(SLis);
50.
51.      this.pack();
52.    }
53.
54.    public void showIt(DataTransferObject dto)
55.    {
56.      dataTransfer =dto;
57.      this.setVisible(true);
58.    }
59.
60. // Internal class
61.    class SearchListener implements ActionListener
62.    {
63.    // No constructor defined, default constructor is used
64.
65.    public void actionPerformed(ActionEvent evt)
66.      {
67.         String searchText = searchTextField.getText();
68.         boolean caseSensitive =
69.    (group.getSelection().getActionCommand().equals("yesActionCommand"));
70.         String command = evt.getActionCommand();
71.         if(command.equals("Cancel"))
72.         {
73.          dataTransfer.setAll(searchText,caseSensitive,false);
74.          //Note that setVisible is a method of class SearchDialog,
```

```
       //not of the internal class SearchListener!     75.
       setVisible(false);                              76.
       }                                               77.
       else if (command.equals("Find"))               78.
       {                                               79.
        dataTransfer.setAll(searchText,caseSensitive,true);  80.
        setVisible(false);                             81.
       }                                               82.
     }                                                 83.
   }// internal class                                 84.
}                                                      85.
```

File: its/Dialogs/DataTransferObject.java

```
package its.Dialogs;                                   1.
                                                       2.
public class DataTransferObject                        3.
{                                                      4.
  private String  searchWord;                          5.
  private boolean caseSensitive;                        6.
  private boolean search;                               7.
                                                       8.
  public DataTransferObject()                          9.
  {                                                    10.
   searchWord = "";                                    11.
   caseSensitive = true;                               12.
   search = true;                                      13.
  }                                                    14.
                                                       15.
  public void setAll(String w, boolean cs, boolean s)  16.
   {                                                   17.
     searchWord = w;                                   18.
     caseSensitive = cs;                               19.
     search = s;                                       20.
   }                                                   21.
                                                       22.
  public String getSearchWord()                        23.
  {                                                    24.
   return(searchWord);                                 25.
  }                                                    26.
                                                       27.
  public boolean getCaseSensitive()                    28.
  {                                                    29.
```

```
30.     return(caseSensitive);
31.   }
32.
33.   public boolean getSearch()
34.   {
35.     return(search);
36.   }
37. }
```

12.6 ■ Predefined option dialogues

For a number of simple but frequently used dialogues, Swing offers predefined components. Messages such as 'File Win.ini has been deleted' and questions such as 'Format hard disk? Yes/No' are examples. The Swing class JOptionPane supplies methods for making such simple dialogues appear. The following most frequently used ones are: showMessageDialog, showConfirmDialog and showOptionDialog.

We use such a dialogue – a message dialogue – to display the result of our search:

```
JOptionPane.showMessageDialog(Component parent,
  String title,
  String message,
  int type);
```

As for other kinds of dialogue, the parent component is blocked while the message is visible. The text title appears in the title bar of the dialogue. The text message is shown in the dialogue. Argument type determines which symbol (e.g. warning sign, exclamation mark) is shown next to the message. There are predefined constants in 'JOptionPane'. Figure 12.3 shows the result. This completes our editor. The editor also needs the classes SearchDialog and InfoTransferObject defined in Section 12.5. The whole program is found on the home page of the book.

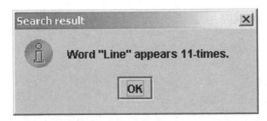

Figure 12.3 The dialogue used to display the search result

Exercises

12.1   Add a menu item 'Save as' to the first menu. When clicking it, a file selection dialogue should appear where one can select a file or input a new name. The text is then saved to this file.

12.2   Augment the 'Load' function as follows. If a file has already been loaded and is displayed, a dialogue box appears. The user is asked whether the displayed text should be saved before loading the new one. Depending on the user's choice the old text is simply erased (using `setText("")`) or saved and erased before loading the new one.

12.3   Augment the 'Exit' function as follows. If 'Exit' is selected while a text is displayed, a dialogue appears. The user is asked whether the text should be saved before exiting or not. Depending on the user's choice the appropriate action is performed. This procedure should also be executed when the close button to the frame is pressed.

12.4   Add another menu 'Help' to the editor. It should have two items 'Help' and 'About'. The first should display a help text in a dialogue window and the second some information on the program.

12.5   Add a status bar under the editor pane which displays some additional information, e.g. the number of lines or the file name.

More on graphics 13

In this chapter we discuss some techniques to improve drawings. This chapter can be skipped on a first reading.

13.1 ■ The class `Graphics2D`

In the previous examples for displaying drawings, we used the class `Graphics` from the AWT library to supply the drawings commands. This class offers only basic commands for drawing shapes. The line width, for example, is limited to one pixel. To draw wider lines one can draw more than one line in parallel. One has to consider the direction of the line in order to make this look nice. For thicker lines one would also like to allow different kinds of line ends, e.g. rounded, square. This and much more is provided by the class `Graphics2D` which is also found in the AWT library. This class together with its helper classes such as `Shape`, `AffineTransform` and `Stroke` provide very powerful methods to create and modify drawings. To use it in `paintComponent`, one casts the `Graphics` parameter to `Graphics2D`. As `Graphics2D` is derived from `Graphics`, all the 'old' drawing commands are available.

A complete description of these classes is beyond the scope of this book. We restrict ourselves to a brief description of strokes. This is, in the author's experience, the feature that is most missed in class `Graphics`. A *stroke* may be thought of as a drawing tool like a pen or a brush. The user can define such a tool with a given width and shape and then use it to draw lines on curves. Besides this, one can also set the line style. The use is quite simple: first define some strokes. Then choose the desired one and all following drawing commands use it until another stroke is selected.

Stokes in Java are realized by the interface `Stroke`. Java also supplies an implementation of `Stroke` in the class `BasicStroke`. This class allows us to define the line width, the line endings (rounded/square), and the way line segments are connected to form a nice looking polygon. The width is specified by parameter `width` in the constructors below, the style of the line end by parameter `cap` and the joining method by `join`. For example to have rounded line ends one uses `cap = BasicStroke.CAP_ROUND`. The class provides more features, such as dashed lines, which we do not discuss here.

`BasicStroke(float width)` constructs a solid `BasicStroke` with the specified line width and with default values for the cap and join styles.

`BasicStroke(float width, int cap, int join)` constructs a solid `Basic-Stroke` with the specified attributes.

The following code snippet shows how to use class `Graphics2D` and `BasicStroke` to draw lines 5 and 6 pixels wide and have rounded and square ends respectively:

```
// define strokes in the preamble
 BasicStroke stroke5 =
     new BasicStroke(5.0f,BasicStroke.CAP_ROUND,BasicStroke.JOIN_BEVEL);
 BasicStroke stroke6 =
     new BasicStroke(6.0f,BasicStroke.CAP_BUTT,BasicStroke.JOIN_BEVEL);


// using the strokes in paintComponent

 public void paintComponent(Graphics g){
    super.paintComponent(gr);
// cast to Graphics2D
    Graphics2D g2d = (Graphics2D) g;

// draw a line with width 5
    g2d.setStroke(stroke5);
    g2d.drawLine(10,10,30,40);

// draw a line with width 6
    g2d.setStroke(stroke6);
    g2d.drawLine(10,40,30,10);
 }
```

13.2 ■ Finding the screen parameters

When displaying a frame, one often wants to fill only a certain area of the screen. Those parts of the frame that are 'outside' the screen should be avoided because the frame is large and the screen resolution is low. The following lines show how to find the number pixels per column and row, and the screen resolution, i.e. the number of pixels per inch. We do not explain the class `Toolkit` used for this purpose. Just think of it as a class that allows access to information on the system.

```
    Toolkit tk        = Toolkit.getDefaultToolkit();
    Dimension screenDim = tk.getScreenSize();
    int screenHeight    = screenDim.height;
```

```
int screenWidth     = screenDim.width;
int pixPerInch      = tk.getScreenResolution();
```

13.3 ■ Scaling a drawing

Resizing the frame from Section 5.3 does not resize the drawing. Thus it might become partly invisible if the frame is made small or just fill a very small portion of the frame if the frame is large. To access a large drawing one can use scroll panes as described in Chapter 11. Sometimes this is not appropriate because one wants the whole drawing displayed regardless of the size of the window. Here we describe how to resize a drawing if the window is resized. This approach is suited for simple and more or less static drawings. In Chapter 21 a much more elaborate method is presented, which allows complex, highly dynamical and resizeable drawings to be displayed.

We derive a frame `ResizeFrame` from `SimpleFrame`. In its content pane we glue a `ResizePanel` which we derive from `JPanel`. A `ResizePanel` has a yellow background and a black rectangle in the middle. The black rectangle is one-third as wide and high as the panel. This ratio is preserved if the frame (and with it the panel) is resized.

In order to do this we have to know the **current** size of the panel. We use the methods

```
int getWidth();
int getHeight();
```

They return the current width and height of the panel in pixels. The left edge of the black rectangle is then one-third the width of the panel. We then place the black rectangle at the desired position by calling `drawRect` with the appropriate values. The following listings show the code including the start class `ResizeDriver`. Figure 13.1 shows the result.

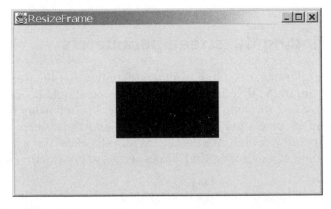

Figure 13.1 The resizeable frame

File: `its/ResizeDisplay/ResizeFrame.java`

```
package its.ResizeDisplay;                              1.
                                                        2.
import its.SimpleFrame.SimpleFrame;                     3.
                                                        4.
public class ResizeFrame extends SimpleFrame{           5.
                                                        6.
  public ResizeFrame(){                                 7.
    ResizePanel rp = new ResizePanel();                 8.
    this.setSize(500,300);                              9.
                                                        10.
    this.getContentPane().add(rp);                      11.
                                                        12.
  }                                                     13.
                                                        14.
}                                                       15.
```

File: `its/ResizeDisplay/ResizePanel.java`

```
package its.ResizeDisplay;                              1.
                                                        2.
import java.awt.Color;                                  3.
import java.awt.Graphics;                               4.
import javax.swing.JPanel;                              5.
                                                        6.
public class ResizePanel extends JPanel{                7.
                                                        8.
  public ResizePanel(){                                 9.
    this.setBackground(Color.yellow);                   10.
  }                                                     11.
                                                        12.
  public void paintComponent(Graphics g)               13.
  {                                                     14.
    super.paintComponent(g);                            15.
    // get the current dimensions of the panel          16.
    int currentWidth  = this.getWidth();               17.
    int currentHeight = this.getHeight();              18.
                                                        19.
    //  take a third of the current dimensions          20.
    int wThird  = currentWidth/3;                      21.
    int hThird  = currentHeight/3;                     22.
// set color to black                                   23.
```

```
24.      g.setColor(Color.black);
25. // and draw the rectangle
26.      g.fillRect(wThird, hThird, wThird, hThird);
27.    }
28.
29.
30. }
```

File: `its/ResizeDisplay/ResizeDriver.java`

```
1. package its.ResizeDisplay;
2.
3. public class ResizeDriver
4. {
5.   public static void main(String[] args){
6.     ResizeFrame rf = new ResizeFrame();
7.     rf.showIt("ResizeFrame");
8.   }
9. }
```

Exercise

13.1 Extend the resizeable frame as follows: add four buttons labelled 'up', 'down', 'left' and 'right'. When clicking one of them, the black rectangle has to move in that direction (by an amount you can specify). Make sure it is always fully contained in the panel!

An example project 14

In this chapter we present a small project based on the model–view–control approach. The aim is to implement a game that can be interactively played by the user. The design and implementation are described in some detail because this example is also to serve as a template for further projects. The aim is not to design a stylish layout, but a working graphical interface.

14.1 ■ Specification

Our example game is the *15-puzzle*. It consists of a 4 × 4 board with 15 movable blocks and one free space. One can move a block adjacent to the empty place in that direction. See Figure 14.1 for an example.

The user interface has to display the board and enable the user to move blocks. The implementation has to ensure that only legal moves are possible. These are moves that can be performed in the real puzzle.

14.2 ■ The model part

The first step in the model design is to find out what the essential components in the project are. Here it is quite natural that the 'hardware' of the game, the board, is one such component. Other components are more abstract, such as the current configuration of blocks on the board and the concept of a move. Every essential component should be implemented into a class of its own. In our example, it is more or less clear what the essential components are. In more complex projects there might be different ways to structure the problem, which would result in different definitions of the essential components. Which of the solutions is better cannot always be decided. In any case the use of large, all-purpose classes should be avoided.

The model part of the puzzle is implemented in the classes `BoardModel`, `Move-Model`, `ConfigurationModel` and `Constants`. They offer all the methods to make moves in an abstract way. In addition, class `BlockPuzzleTest` is a non-graphical

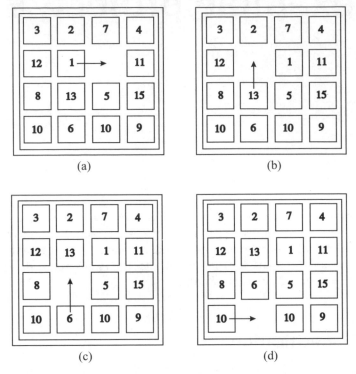

Figure 14.1 The 15-puzzle: (a) some configuration of the 15 blocks; (b), (c) and (d) are derived from (a) by moving one block at a time. The aim is to arrange the blocks in such a way that the numbers increase when read row-wise

driver to test the functionality of the non-graphical classes. One might argue whether a class for moves or constants is really necessary for this simple game. In fact, the use of these classes here helps to structure the project, speeds up the design, and makes the program easy to maintain.

The `BoardModel` is not restricted to a size of 4×4 but allows an arbitrary $n \times m$ board. The parameters determining the size are passed in the constructor. The blocks are numbered $0, 1, 2, \ldots, nm - 1$; where 0 stands for the empty place. The board is represented by the two-dimensional $n \times m$ array `board`. The array stores at `board[i][j]` the number of the block in row i column j. Two other arrays `rowOfBlock` and `colOfBlock` store for every block the number of the row and column that it is currently in. This way positions and numbers of the blocks can be easily linked. The board is initialized with the blocks consecutively numbered in a row-wise fashion with the empty place at the lower right corner.

The class supplies `get`-methods to access the current configuration and the board size. The dynamics of the game is provided by method `moveIt`. It receives an instance of `MoveModel`, checks whether the move is legal and – if so – moves the block. It returns a boolean value to indicate whether the move has been made or not.

File: `its/BlockPuzzle/BoardModel.java`

```java
package its.BlockPuzzle;                                         1.
                                                                2.
                                                                3.
public class BoardModel{                                        4.
  private int noOfRows, noOfCols;                               5.
  private int[][] board;      // The board as an array          6.
  private int[] rowOfBlock; // The number of the row of every block    7.
  private int[] colOfBlock; // The number of the column of every block 8.
                                                                9.
  public BoardModel(int nr, int nc){                           10.
      noOfRows = nr;                                           11.
      noOfCols = nc;                                           12.
      board = new int[noOfRows][noOfCols];                     13.
      rowOfBlock = new int[noOfRows * noOfCols];               14.
      colOfBlock = new int[noOfRows * noOfCols];               15.
      // initialize the board. The blocks are                 16.
      // numbered row-wise 1,2,...                             17.
      int kk = 1;                                              18.
                                                               19.
      for(int r=0; r < noOfRows; r++){                         20.
        for(int c=0; c < noOfCols; c++){                       21.
           if(kk < noOfRows * noOfCols){                       22.
             board[r][c] = kk;                                 23.
             rowOfBlock[kk] = r;                               24.
             colOfBlock[kk] = c;                               25.
             kk++;                                             26.
           }                                                   27.
        }//for c                                               28.
      }//for r                                                 29.
                                                               30.
      // ... and the missing block is at the lower right.      31.
      board [noOfRows-1][noOfCols-1] = 0;                      32.
      rowOfBlock[0] = noOfRows-1;                              33.
      colOfBlock[0] = noOfCols-1;                              34.
  }                                                            35.
                                                               36.
  public boolean moveIt(MoveModel mm){                         37.
      int dir   = mm.getDirection();                           38.
      int block = mm.getBlockNumber();                         39.
      int row   = rowOfBlock[block];                           40.
      int col   = colOfBlock[block];                           41.
      boolean ok = true;                                       42.
      // an UP move is possible if the missing block           43.
```

```
44.      // is above the position (r,c), i.e., at
45.      // (r-1,c). Esp. r has to be larger than 0.
46.      // The tests for the other directions are similar.
47.      if(dir == Constants.DIRECTION_UP){
48.       if((row > 0) && (board[row-1][col] == 0)){
49.          board[row-1][col] = board[row][col];
50.          rowOfBlock[block]--;
51.          board[row][col] = 0;
52.          rowOfBlock[0]++;
53.        }
54.       else{
55.          ok = false;
56.        }
57.      } else if(dir == Constants.DIRECTION_DOWN){
58.       if((row < noOfRows-1) && (board[row+1][col] == 0)){
59.          board[row+1][col] = board[row][col];
60.          rowOfBlock[block]++;
61.          board[row][col] = 0;
62.          rowOfBlock[0]--;
63.        }
64.       else{
65.         ok = false;
66.        }
67.      }else if(dir == Constants.DIRECTION_LEFT){
68.       if((col > 0) && (board[row][col-1] == 0)){
69.          board[row][col-1] = board[row][col];
70.          colOfBlock[block]--;
71.          board[row][col] = 0;
72.          colOfBlock[0]++;
73.        }
74.       else{
75.        ok = false;
76.        }
77.      }else if(dir == Constants.DIRECTION_RIGHT){
78.       if((col < noOfCols-1) && (board[row][col+1] == 0)){
79.          board[row][col+1] = board[row][col];
80.          colOfBlock[block]++;
81.          board[row][col] = 0;
82.          colOfBlock[0]--;
83.        }
84.       else{
85.         ok = false;
86.        }
87.      }       return(ok);
88.    }
89.
90.    public ConfigurationModel getCurrentConfiguration(){
```

```
    return(new ConfigurationModel(board));                    91.
  }                                                            92.
                                                               93.
  public int getNoOfCols(){                                    94.
    return(noOfCols);                                          95.
  }                                                            96.
                                                               97.
    public int getNoOfRows(){                                  98.
    return(noOfRows);                                          99.
  }                                                            100.
}                                                              101.
```

The class `MoveModel` provides the abstract description of a move. It specifies the number of the block to be moved and its direction. The direction is one of the constants defined in class `Constants`.

File: `its/BlockPuzzle/MoveModel.java`

```
package its.BlockPuzzle;                                       1.
                                                               2.
                                                               3.
public class MoveModel {                                       4.
                                                               5.
  private int direction;                                       6.
  private int blockNumber;                                     7.
                                                               8.
  public MoveModel(int dir, int bn) {                          9.
    direction = dir;                                           10.
    blockNumber = bn;                                          11.
  }                                                            12.
                                                               13.
   public int getBlockNumber(){                                14.
    return(blockNumber);                                       15.
  }                                                            16.
                                                               17.
  public int getDirection(){                                   18.
    return(direction);                                         19.
  }                                                            20.
}                                                              21.
```

Instances of class `ConfigurationModel` represent a snapshot of the board. This can be used to protocol the course of a game, or to store the current state of the game. Method `equals` checks whether two configurations are identical. This can be used for test purposes. The class provides a method `toString` which returns the configuration in a format that can also be printed on the console.

File: `its/BlockPuzzle/ConfigurationModel.java`

```java
1.  package its.BlockPuzzle;
2.
3.
4.  public class ConfigurationModel {
5.
6.   private int[][] board;
7.   int noOfRows, noOfCols;
8.
9.    public ConfigurationModel(int[][] b) {
10.    noOfRows = b.length;
11.    noOfCols = b[0].length;
12.    board = new int[noOfRows][noOfCols];
13.    for (int r=0;r < noOfRows ; r++ ) {
14.     for (int c=0;c < noOfCols ; c++ ) {
15.      board[r][c] = b[r][c];
16.      }//for
17.    }//for
18.    }
19.
20. public int getBlockNo(int r, int c){
21.   return(board[r][c]);
22. }
23.
24.    public String toString(){
25.      String confAsString = "";
26.      for(int r=0; r < noOfRows; r++){
27.          for(int c=0; c < noOfCols; c++){
28.              if(board[r][c] < 10)
29.              {
30.               confAsString += "  "+board[r][c];
31.              }
32.              else
33.              {
34.               confAsString += " "+board[r][c];
35.              }//ifelse
36.          }//for c
37.        confAsString += "\n";
38.        }//for r
39.     confAsString += "\n";
40.     return(confAsString);
41.    }
42.
43.    public boolean equals(ConfigurationModel conf){
44.      boolean result = true;
```

```
        for(int r=0; r < noOfRows; r++){                45.
          for(int c=0; c < noOfCols; c++){              46.
            if(this.board[r][c] != conf.board[r][c]){   47.
              result = false;                           48.
            }//if                                       49.
          }//for c                                      50.
        }//for r                                        51.
        return(result);                                 52.
      }                                                 53.
  }                                                     54.
```

Class constants define constants for the possible directions of the moves.

File: its/BlockPuzzle/Constants.java

```
package its.BlockPuzzle;                                1.
                                                        2.
                                                        3.
public class Constants {                                4.
                                                        5.
  public static final int DIRECTION_UP    = 1;          6.
  public static final int DIRECTION_DOWN  = 2;          7.
  public static final int DIRECTION_RIGHT = 3;          8.
  public static final int DIRECTION_LEFT  = 4;          9.
}                                                       10.
```

The test of the model is done by class BlockPuzzleTest. It constructs a 4 × 4 board, fetches the initial configuration of the board and prints it. Then two moves are generated and executed. The first one is legal but the second one is not. A thorough test should of course check more situations, such as attempting to move a block off the board or whether there are two blocks with the same number. The test is performed by comparing the true and expected configurations.

File: its/BlockPuzzle/BlockPuzzleTest.java

```
package its.BlockPuzzle;                                1.
                                                        2.
                                                        3.
public class BlockPuzzleTest{                           4.
                                                        5.
private static  boolean passed;                         6.
                                                        7.
public static void main(String[] args){                 8.
```

```
 9.      passed = true;
10.    //Generate a model and print it (also as string)
11.     BoardModel bm = new BoardModel(4,4);
12.     ConfigurationModel trueConf, expectedConf;
13.     trueConf = bm.getCurrentConfiguration();
14.     expectedConf = new ConfigurationModel(new int[][]
15.         {{1,2,3,4},{5,6,7,8},{9,10,11,12},{13,14,15,0}}));
16.     check(expectedConf,expectedConf);
17.
18.    //Make a move
19.     System.out.println("Move 15 right");
20.     MoveModel move1 = new MoveModel(Constants.DIRECTION_RIGHT,15);
21.     if(!bm.moveIt(move1)){
22.       System.out.println("Illegal Move!");
23.     }
24.     trueConf = bm.getCurrentConfiguration();
25.     expectedConf = new ConfigurationModel(new int[][]
26.         {{1,2,3,4},{5,6,7,8},{9,10,11,12},{13,14,0,15}}));
27.     check(expectedConf,expectedConf);
28.
29.    //Make another move
30.     System.out.println("Move 5 up");
31.     MoveModel move2 = new MoveModel(Constants.DIRECTION_UP,5);
32.     if(!bm.moveIt(move2)){
33.       System.out.println("Illegal Move!");
34.     }
35.     trueConf = bm.getCurrentConfiguration();
36.     expectedConf = new ConfigurationModel(new int[][]
37.         {{1,2,3,4},{5,6,7,8},{9,10,11,12},{13,14,0,15}}));
38.     check(expectedConf,expectedConf);
39.   // display the test result
40.     if (passed) {
41.       System.out.println("Test passed");
42.     }
43.     else {
44.        System.out.println("Test NOT passed");
45.     }
46. }
47.    private static void check(ConfigurationModel conf1,
48.                       ConfigurationModel conf2){
49.     if(conf1.equals(conf2)){
50.      System.out.println("Configuration ok:");
51.      System.out.println(conf1.toString());
52.     }
53.     else{
54.       System.out.println("Expected and true configurations"
55.                          + " do NOT match");
```

```
    System.out.println(conf2.toString());                    56.
    System.out.println(conf1.toString());                    57.
    passed = false;                                          58.
  }                                                          59.
 }                                                           60.
}                                                            61.
```

The listing below shows the test result as it is displayed on the console. It is correctly detected that the second move is illegal.

```
Configuration ok:
   1    2    3    4
   5    6    7    8
   9   10   11   12
  13   14   15    0

Move 15 right
Configuration ok:
   1    2    3    4
   5    6    7    8
   9   10   11   12
  13   14    0   15

Move 5 up
Illegal Move!
Configuration ok:
   1    2    3    4
   5    6    7    8
   9   10   11   12
  13   14    0   15

Test passed
```

14.3 ■ The view part

Once the model is implemented and tested, one can begin to design the display of the game. The layout we have chosen consists of two panels embedded side by side into a frame. The left one displays the current configuration of the board. The right one allows a direction to be selected for a move. The appearance is shown in Figure 14.2.

We begin by describing class `BlockPuzzlePanel` which displays the board. In the constructor, the panel receives a reference to the board model it has to display. By querying the board model it determines the number of rows and columns to display.

As usual, the painting is done by overriding method `paintComponent`. Here, the current configuration from the `BoardModel` is fetched. Then one queries the

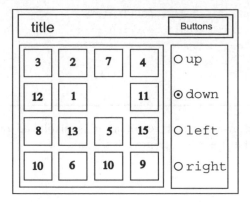

Figure 14.2 The layout of the GUI for the block puzzle

configuration on all positions (r, c), (r is the row number, c is the column number) to find the block number at this position. The blocks are drawn as rectangles with a number near the middle. The missing block is shown as a filled black rectangle. The code for drawing a block and the empty place is put into two private methods. Putting it into paintComponent is of course possible, but would make the structure hard to follow. The drawing is scalable (resizeable). We use the technique described in Section 13.3 for this purpose.

The panel does not know anything about the rules of the game, it can merely display the current state. Therefore, method makeMove(move) makes a move by calling the method moveIt(move) of the board model. The panel's display has to be updated if the configuration is changed. This update is made by calling the panel's repaint method. If the move has not been made a warning message is displayed. It uses a predefined message dialogue from class JOptionPane.

The class has a public method getBlockNoAtPixels(x,y) which will be used in the control part. It determines the number of the block that contains the pixel coordinates (x, y). In order to find out which row of blocks contains the given pixel y-coordinate we first divide the height of the panel by the number of rows. This is the height of a single row in pixels. Then we divide y by this height to get the row number. Note that all numbers involved are integers; then rounding is downwards and the correct row number is computed. The column number is computed analogously.

File: its/BlockPuzzle/BlockPuzzlePanel.java

```
1. package its.BlockPuzzle;
2.
3. import java.awt.Color;
4. import java.awt.Dimension;
5. import java.awt.Graphics;
6. import javax.swing.JPanel;
```

```
import javax.swing.JOptionPane;                                7.
                                                               8.
public class BlockPuzzlePanel extends JPanel{                  9.
                                                              10.
    private BoardModel boardMod;                              11.
    private ConfigurationModel currentConf;                   12.
    private int noOfRows, noOfCols;                           13.
    private int columnWidth,rowHeight;                        14.
                                                              15.
    public BlockPuzzlePanel( BoardModel bm){                  16.
        boardMod = bm;                                        17.
        noOfRows = bm.getNoOfRows();                          18.
        noOfCols = bm.getNoOfCols();                          19.
        this.setPreferredSize(new Dimension(300,300));        20.
        this.setBackground(Color.white);                      21.
    }                                                         22.
                                                              23.
    public void paintComponent(Graphics g){                  24.
        super.paintComponent(g);                              25.
        int w = getWidth();                                   26.
        int h = getHeight();                                  27.
        columnWidth = w/noOfCols;                             28.
        rowHeight = h/noOfRows;                               29.
        currentConf = boardMod.getCurrentConfiguration();     30.
        for(int r=0; r < noOfRows; r++){                      31.
         for(int c=0; c < noOfCols; c++){                     32.
            if(currentConf.getBlockNo(r,c) != 0){             33.
                drawBlock(r,c,currentConf.getBlockNo(r,c),g); 34.
            }                                                 35.
            else                                              36.
            {                                                 37.
                drawMissingBlock(r,c,g);                      38.
            }                                                 39.
         }//for c                                             40.
        }//for r                                              41.
    }                                                         42.
                                                              43.
    public void makeMove(MoveModel move){                     44.
    if(boardMod.moveIt(move)){                                45.
        this.repaint();                                       46.
    }                                                         47.
    else{                                                     48.
        JOptionPane.showMessageDialog(this,                   49.
        "Illegal Move","ITS BlockPuzzle",                     50.
         JOptionPane.WARNING_MESSAGE);                        51.
      }//ifelse                                               52.
```

```
53.       }
54.
55.      private void drawBlock(int r,  int c,  int n, Graphics g){
56.          g.drawRect(c*columnWidth+2,r*rowHeight+2,columnWidth-4,
57.                      rowHeight-4);
58.          g.drawString(""+n,c*columnWidth+(columnWidth/2),
59.                      r*rowHeight+rowHeight/2);
60.      }
61.
62.      private void drawMissingBlock(int r,  int c,   Graphics g){
63.          g.fillRect(c*columnWidth,r*rowHeight,columnWidth,rowHeight);
64.      }
65.
66.      public int getBlockNoAtPixels(int x,int y){
67.          int c =  x/(this.getWidth()/noOfCols);
68.          int r =  y/(this.getHeight()/noOfRows);
69.          return(currentConf.getBlockNo(r,c));
70.      }
71. }
```

Class `DirectionPanel` is quite simple. It receives a 4×1 grid layout, into which four radio buttons are placed. They are labelled with the four directions and receive action commands. The action commands will be used to determine which button is selected. The radio buttons are grouped as described in Section 12.4. The 'up'-button is selected. The class has only one method, `getDirection`. This returns the direction specified by the currently selected button. The return value is the corresponding direction-constant defined in class `Constants`.

File: its/BlockPuzzle/DirectionPanel.java

```
1. package its.BlockPuzzle;
2.
3. import java.awt.GridLayout;
4. import javax.swing.ButtonGroup;
5. import javax.swing.JPanel;
6. import javax.swing.JRadioButton;
7.
8.
9. public class DirectionPanel extends JPanel {
10.    private JRadioButton upBut, downBut, rBut, lBut;
11.    private ButtonGroup group;
12.
13.    public DirectionPanel(){
14.      this.setLayout(new GridLayout(4,1));
```

```
upBut    = new JRadioButton("up");           15.
downBut  = new JRadioButton("down");         16.
lBut     = new JRadioButton("left");         17.
rBut     = new JRadioButton("right");        18.
                                              19.
upBut.setActionCommand("u");                 20.
downBut.setActionCommand("d");               21.
lBut.setActionCommand("l");                  22.
rBut.setActionCommand("r");                  23.
                                              24.
group = new ButtonGroup();                   25.
group.add(upBut);                            26.
group.add(downBut);                          27.
group.add(lBut);                             28.
group.add(rBut);                             29.
upBut.setSelected(true);                     30.
                                              31.
this.add(upBut);                             32.
this.add(downBut);                           33.
this.add(lBut);                              34.
this.add(rBut);                              35.
  }                                           36.
                                              37.
public int getDirection(){                   38.
  String actionCommand = group.getSelection().getActionCommand();  39.
  int result = 0;                            40.
  if(actionCommand.equals("u")){             41.
    result = Constants.DIRECTION_UP;         42.
  } else if(actionCommand.equals("d")){      43.
    result = Constants.DIRECTION_DOWN;       44.
  } else if(actionCommand.equals("r")){      45.
    result = Constants.DIRECTION_RIGHT;      46.
  } else if(actionCommand.equals("l")){      47.
    result = Constants.DIRECTION_LEFT;       48.
  }                                           49.
  return( result );                          50.
  }                                           51.
}                                             52.
```

The class BlockPuzzleFrame is not derived from SimpleFrame but from JFrame to make this project independent of the its-package. In order to use it on its own, one has to replace the package name its.BlockPuzzle by BlockPuzzle. The frame implements a window listener, which terminates the application when the frame is closed; see Section 9.3.

File: `its/BlockPuzzle/BlockPuzzleFrame.java`

```
1. package its.BlockPuzzle;
2.
3.
4. import java.awt.event.WindowAdapter;
5. import java.awt.event.WindowEvent;
6. import java.awt.BorderLayout;
7. import javax.swing.JFrame;
8.
9.
10. public class BlockPuzzleFrame extends JFrame
11. {
12.     private DirectionPanel dirPanel;
13.     private BlockPuzzlePanel bpPanel;
14.
15.     // Constructor
16.     public BlockPuzzleFrame(int rows, int cols)  {
17.
18.         this.setLocation(200,200);
19.         this.setTitle("ITS Block Puzzle");
20.         BoardModel boardMod = new  BoardModel(rows,cols);
21.         bpPanel = new BlockPuzzlePanel(boardMod);
22.         dirPanel = new DirectionPanel();
23.         getContentPane().add(bpPanel,BorderLayout.CENTER);
24.         getContentPane().add(dirPanel,BorderLayout.EAST);
25.
26.         BlockPuzzleListener bpList = new BlockPuzzleListener(bpPanel,dirPanel);
27.         bpPanel.addMouseListener(bpList);
28.
29.         // Correct termination:
30.         // Otherwise only the frame disappears when clicking
31.         // on the "close" symbol but the process keeps running.
32.         addWindowListener(new WindowAdapter()
33.             { public void windowClosing(WindowEvent e)
34.             {
35.                 System.exit(0);
36.             }
37.         });
38.         pack();
39.     }
40.
41.
42.     public void showIt(){
43.         this.setVisible(true);
44.     }
```

```
                                                                        45.
                                                                        46.
                                                                        47.
public void hideIt(){                                                   48.
  this.setVisible(false);                                               49.
}                                                                       50.
                                                                        51.
                                                                        52.
}                                                                       53.
```

14.4 ■ The control part

The user–program interaction is specified as follows. The user selects a direction by clicking a radio button in the direction panel. This requires no listeners because the mechanism is supplied by `RadioButton` and `ButtonGroup`. Once a direction is selected a move can be made by clicking on a block in the `BlockPuzzlePanel`. This block is then moved in the specified direction if the move is legal, i.e. if the empty place is adjacent to the block in that direction.

A listener is used to detect when a click in the `BlockPuzzlePanel` occurs and to make the move. As we are reacting to a mouse click we extend a `MouseAdapter` in class `BlockPuzzleListener`. In order to be able to perform the desired task, the listener has to know the direction and the block of the desired move. The move is then made in the block puzzle panel. Therefore `BlockPuzzleListener` receives references to the `DirectionPanel` and the `BlockPuzzlePanel` in the constructor. The listener is assigned to the `BlockPuzzlePanel`.

If a mouse click occurs in the `BlockPuzzlePanel`, the listener's `mouseClicked` method is invoked. The listener extracts the *x*- and *y*-coordinates of the location of the click from the mouse event object. These are in pixels. The listener asks the panel which block is at that location. This is done by using the block panel's `get-BlockNoAtPixels(x,y)` method. The listener determines the direction by asking the direction panel using `getDirection()`.

Now that the block number and direction are known, the listener constructs an instance `MoveModel` for the desired move. The move is passed to the block puzzle panel using method `makeMove(move)`.

File: `its/BlockPuzzle/BlockPuzzleListener.java`

```
package its.BlockPuzzle;                                                 1.
import java.awt.event.MouseAdapter;                                      2.
import java.awt.event.MouseEvent;                                        3.
                                                                        4.
                                                                        5.
public  class BlockPuzzleListener extends MouseAdapter{                  6.
    private DirectionPanel dirPanel;                                     7.
```

```
8.        private BlockPuzzlePanel bpPanel;
9.
10.     BlockPuzzleListener (BlockPuzzlePanel bp, DirectionPanel m){
11.        dirPanel =  m;
12.        bpPanel = bp;
13.        }
14.
15.      public void mouseClicked(MouseEvent evt){
16.   //
17.          int x =  evt.getX();
18.          int y =  evt.getY();
19.          int blockNo = bpPanel.getBlockNoAtPixels(x,y);
20.     // Constructs the move
21.         MoveModel move =
22.             new MoveModel(dirPanel.getDirection(),blockNo);
23.     //  Request a move to made be in the BlockPuzzlePanel.
24.     //  Note that the BlockPuzzleListener does not know HOW to make
25.     //  a move.
26.         bpPanel.makeMove(move);
27.       }
28.
29. }
```

The driver class BlockPuzzle creates a BlockPuzzleFrame and makes it visible. A screen shot of the program is shown in Figure 14.3.

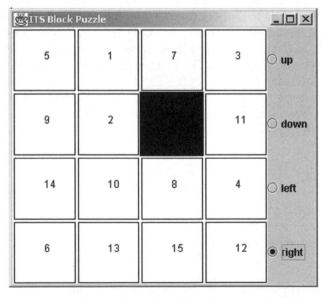

Figure 14.3 The block puzzle application after some moves have been made

File: `its/BlockPuzzle/BlockPuzzle.java`

```
package its.BlockPuzzle;                                          1.
                                                                 2.
                                                                 3.
class BlockPuzzle{                                               4.
                                                                 5.
 public static void main(String[] args){                        6.
    BlockPuzzleFrame g1f = new BlockPuzzleFrame(4,4);            7.
    g1f.showIt();                                                8.
  }                                                              9.
}                                                               10.
```

14.5 ■ Summary

The example in this chapter is to illustrate the design process of a graphical application. The non-graphical part is specified, implemented and tested separately from the graphical one. Both graphical and non-graphical classes supply the methods needed by the control part. For example `BoardModel` implements the move in `moveIt` and `BlockPuzzelPanel` supplies a pixel-to-block-number transformation in `getBlockNoAtPixels`.

The approach of separating data administration, graphics and user interaction is the key to a rapid save and easily maintainable implementation. An often-heard claim is that this slows down the program execution because, for example, the use of `get`- and `set`-methods is slower than direct access to public variables. This is almost always incorrect. One can achieve between 0 and 2 per cent speed-up for most applications by using a badly structured unsave and hard-to-maintain implementation. The time to debug such an implementation is, however, considerably larger.

In our block puzzle example we have been able to implement the model, view and control parts one after the other. Though a conceptional separation of these parts is always possible, a temporal separation is not. One will often have to develop the three parts separately, but parallel.

The block puzzle example is kept very short. It lacks a number of important tests, such as checking whether the numbers of rows and columns are positive in the constructor of `BoardModel`. Also the determination of the block clicked by method `getBlockNoAtPixels` is precise only to within a few pixels.

Exercises

14.1　Add a 'reset' button to the GUI. On pressing it the blocks are arranged in the initial configuration.

14.2 Add a text area to the GUI which displays the history of the game by displaying the moves made, one per line. It should be scrollable and cleared if the game is reset.

14.3 Add a menu to the GUI. There should be menu items 'Save' and 'Load'. On selecting them the current state of the game (the current configuration) is saved or a saved game is loaded and displayed, respectively. The files to save to or load from should be user selectable. Make sure that boards of different size can be handled.

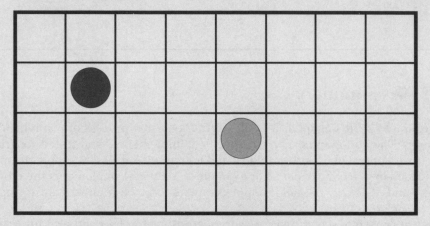

Figure 14.4 Sketch of the GUI for Exercise 14.6

Figure 14.5 Sketch of the GUI for Exercise 14.7

14.4   Add a menu item 'Select board size' to one of the menus. When selecting it, a dialogue appears, prompting the user for the numbers of rows and columns. On closing the dialogue, the board size is reset to the new values and the blocks are arranged in the original configuration.

14.5   Change the way the user selects a move as follows: the direction panel is removed. To make a move the user clicks on a block B. If the empty place is in the same row or column as B, then all blocks between the empty place and B are moved, including B. The empty place then is at the former position of B. Note that this requires changes in or re-implementation of many classes.

14.6   Implement the following GUI. There is a rectangular grid with $n \times m$ cells. Initially the cells are empty. A red chip is placed into one of the cells. Then the chip can be moved to another, different, cell. A yellow chip is put into the cell of the previous position of the red one. There are always at most two chips on the grid. The game can be restarted with an empty grid. See Figure 14.4.

14.7   Implement the following game (tic-tac-toe light). There is a rectangular grid with $n \times n$ cells, $n \geq 3$. Initially the cells are empty. Two players, called RED and BLACK, take turns to place chips of their colour into empty cells. RED begins. The game is over if one player has three chips next to one another in one row or all cells are occupied. The game can be restarted with an empty grid. See Figure 14.5.

More components and techniques

Pixel graphics 15

Pixel images are an essential ingredient in most graphical interfaces. They occur as small symbols on buttons or in messages or they are the main data object, for example in an application that displays photos. Such images are stored pixel by pixel. We shall not create such images ourselves. Instead we focus on displaying and manipulating existing ones.

We begin by discussing different types of pixel graphics and the Java classes for these kinds of image. We then show how images can be displayed and manipulated.

15.1 ■ Some graphics file types

Examples of pixel graphics are digital photos or scanned pictures. They are usually rectangular and are composed of *pixels*. A pixel is a small, coloured square. These squares are tiled to compose the picture. The possible colours vary with the type of picture. For scanned documents the pixels are usually white or black; then one bit is sufficient to store the information of a single pixel. Black-and-white photos are usually stored as grey-scales. Every pixel has a value representing its 'grey-ness', e.g. 0 white and 255 is black. For colour pictures every pixel describes a colour. There are different ways to represent a colour. The RGB-model uses three values which indicate the amount of red, green and blue in the colour. Often one byte is used for each of the values, thus one pixel requires 3 bytes or 24 bits. This allows us to define 16,777,216 different colours.

Storing pixel graphics requires a lot of memory. To store an image with 2048 × 1536 pixels and 24-bit colours (the format of a 3 mega-pixel digital photo) requires 9 megabytes. In order to save disk space, images are often stored in a *compressed* format. When a picture is compressed some image information might be lost. Roughly speaking, compression combines the information on adjacent or similar pixels. Decompressing such an image results in a coarser image than the original one. The higher the compression rate, the more image information is lost. With a reasonable, e.g. hardly visible, loss of image quality the aforementioned photo can be reduced to about 1.5 megabytes. Photos or drawings that are not too detailed and have a low contrast allow a higher compression rate than detailed and contrast-intense images in order to achieve the same visual quality. Some compressed image formats are loss-free, i.e. the original image can be precisely recovered.

The Java libraries support the following image formats. When loading such an image it is automatically decompressed and can be displayed.

■ **Graphics Interchange Format,** file extension GIF. This format stores images in 256-bit colours, one byte per pixel. The pictures are compressed without loss of information. It is often used for small icons or graphics on the Internet. Using this format might cause legal problems, because the CompuServe company holds patents for the compression method.

■ **Joint Photographic Experts Group,** file extensions JPG, JPEG. This format uses a compression method in which image information is lost. For photos a reduction to 20 per cent of the original image file size can be achieved while still maintaining a good quality. JPEG is probably the most widely used format to store larger photos or drawings.

■ **Portable Network Graphic,** file extension PNG. A newer image format with growing importance. It uses a loss-free compression and might replace the GIF format in the long run.

Most Internet browsers can render images in any of these three formats. In this book we shall mostly use PNG images; the examples work also when using JPEG or GIF. Using compressed image formats is especially advisable if the pictures have to be sent over a network: sending or loading times are drastically reduced.

Loading a large image into an application takes some time, even on a modern computer. To save the user from waiting for the image to be displayed, images are often loaded *asynchronously*. This means that a second process is started which runs in parallel to the main program and loads the image. This way the main program is not blocked and the user can go on working while the image is loaded. If, however, the image has to be processed right away by the application then it should be loaded *synchronously* and the main program has to wait until the image is available.

15.2 ■ Class `ImageIcon`

The Swing library provides class `ImageIcon` for pixel graphics. Although 'icon' is mostly used for small images this class is well suited to handle large images and supports the basic operations on images. For more elaborate manipulation, class `Image` from the AWT library can be used. Some constructors and methods of class `ImageIcon` are listed and described below:

```
ImageIcon()
ImageIcon(Image picture)
ImageIcon(String filename)
ImageIcon(URL webaddress)
```

```
int getImageHeight()
int getImageWidth()
```

`ImageIcon()` default constructor.

`ImageIcon(Image picture)` creates an `ImageIcon` out of an instance of the AWT class `Image`.

`ImageIcon(String filename)` creates an `ImageIcon` from an image file, the name of which is supplied in the argument `filename`.

`ImageIcon(URL webaddress)` creates an `ImageIcon` from a web address which is supplied in the argument `webaddress`. Class `URL` is from the `java.net` library.

`getImageHeight()` returns the image height in pixels.

`getImageWidth()` returns the image width in pixels.

15.3 ■ Displaying pixel graphics in Swing

Program `ImageFrame` demonstrates how a picture is loaded and displayed. We want to display the image `orange.png` in a frame. The image is a digitized photo of size 400×400 pixels. Instances of class `ImageIcon` are non-graphical components. They have to be displayed inside some graphical Swing component. We use a `JLabel` for this purpose. In Section 3.3.1 we introduced the constructor

```
public JLabel(ImageIcon picture)
```

which we shall use now. We create an `ImageIcon` by passing the file name of the image in the constructor. Note that you might have to adjust the path to match your directory structure. To keep the program short, we do not check whether the specified file really exists. The image is then displayed in the label. The size of the label is adjusted so that it matches the image size, provided the layout manager of the parent component allows that size. The label is centrally embedded into the frame. We use the `pack` method of the parent frame to guarantee this. The result is shown in Figure 15.1.

File: `its/Images/ImageFrame.java`

```
package its.Images;                                          1.
                                                             2.
import its.SimpleFrame.SimpleFrame;                          3.
import javax.swing.*;                                        4.
                                                             5.
                                                             6.
public class ImageFrame extends SimpleFrame               7.
{                                                            8.
                                                             9.
  private ImageIcon picture;                                10.
```

Figure 15.1 Application `ImageFrame`

```
11.   // Adjust the following path if necessary
12.   private final String picturePath  = "./its/TestData/";
13.   private final String imageFileName = "orange.png";
14.
15.   public ImageFrame()
16.   {
17.     picture = new ImageIcon(picturePath+imageFileName);
18.     JLabel pictureLabel = new JLabel(picture);
18.     this.getContentPane().add(pictureLabel);
20.     pack();
21.   }
22.
23.   public static void main(String[] args)
24.   {
25.     ImageFrame imfr = new ImageFrame();
26.     imfr.showIt("ImageFrame: loading image from a file");
27.   }
28. }
```

The picture to be displayed does not have to be on the local hard disk, it might just as well be on some place on the Internet. Internet locations are specified by their *uniform resource locator*, *URL* for short. In Java these are realized by class URL from the java.net library. One passes the address as a string in the constructor. More on accessing the net may be found in Chapter 22. The following application WebImageFrame fetches the picture of a pear pear.png from the specified net address and displays it. The file size is 190 kilobytes. Depending on the bandwidth of the network connection, it can take up to 10 seconds to load. The application works only if the computer has access to the Internet. Attempts to access net locations can fail for many reasons, which are beyond the control of the user. Therefore, the corresponding Java statements are embedded into try-catch blocks. This allows the program to continue in case network access fails.

File: its/Images/WebImageFrame.java

```
package its.Images;                                                         1.
                                                                            2.
import its.SimpleFrame.SimpleFrame;                                         3.
import java.net.URL;                                                        4.
import javax.swing.ImageIcon;                                               5.
import javax.swing.JLabel;                                                  6.
                                                                            7.
public class WebImageFrame extends SimpleFrame                              8.
{                                                                           9.
                                                                            10.
  public WebImageFrame()                                                    11.
  {                                                                         12.
    URL   picURL = null;                                                    13.
    JLabel pictureLabel = null;                                             14.
    try                                                                     15.
    {                                                                       16.
      picURL = new URL("http://www.imm.dtu.dk/swingbook/"+                  17.
                       "+HTMLTest/pear.png");                               18.
    }                                                                       19.
    catch (Exception ex)                                                    20.
    {System.out.println("Problems in creating URL"+picURL.getPath());}      21.
    if(picURL != null){                                                     22.
       ImageIcon picture = new ImageIcon(picURL);                           23.
       pictureLabel = new JLabel(picture);                                  24.
    }                                                                       25.
    else{                                                                   26.
       pictureLabel = new JLabel("Image not loaded");                       27.
    }                                                                       28.
    this.getContentPane().add(pictureLabel);                                29.
    pack();                                                                 30.
  }                                                                         31.
                                                                            32.
  public static void main(String[] args)                                   33.
```

```
34. {
35.   WebImageFrame wifr = new WebImageFrame();
36.   wifr.showIt("WebImageFrame: loading Image from the net");
37. }
38. }
```

15.4 ■ Manipulating images

You may want to resize, rotate or reflect your image, or display only part of it, rather than view it as it is stored on the hard disk. These operations are supported by classes from the AWT library. We shall now introduce some techniques to solve the aforementioned image manipulations. Class `Image` from the AWT library plays a central role for image manipulations.

15.4.1 □ Loading images asynchronously

As mentioned above, loading a picture might take some time, especially if the image has to be transferred over a network. To avoid blocking the main application while the image is fetched, the loading process can be run asynchronously. Class `Toolkit` from the AWT library supplies methods for this purpose. We shall use the `getImage`-method of the *default toolkit* to load images. One can specify the name of the image file or a web location (URL) where the image is stored. Method `getImage` returns an object of class `Image`:

```
Image picture = Toolkit.getDefaultToolkit.getImage(String filename);
Image picture = Toolkit.getDefaultToolkit.getImage(String url);
```

Once the picture is loaded into an object of class `Image`, it can be manipulated by methods of this class. As a first application we show how a number of images can be arranged. We derive class `ImagePanel` from `JPanel`. An image panel will automatically arrange pictures and display them. The background colour is set to be yellow to emphasize the contrast to the pictures.

The images are displayed in method `paintComponent` of the panel. We use the following method of class `Graphics`. The arguments are explained afterwards.

```
drawImage(Image picture, int left, int top, ImageObserver imObs)
```

The first argument (`picture`) contains the image to display. The two integer arguments `left` and `top` specify the pixel position of the upper left corner of the image inside the panel. The last argument is of type `ImageObserver`. This is an interface from the AWT library which is of great help when loading or displaying images. Fortunately, we do not have to implement this interface ourselves. Every graphical component, regardless whether it is AWT or Swing, implements this interface. We therefore can use `this` as image observer.

!

To determine the width or height of an image we use the following two methods of class `Image` which return, respectively, these two values in pixels. Note that these values refer to the size of the picture in the `Image` variable. The actual display might be enlarged or shrunk with techniques described later on.

```
int getWidth(ImageObserver imo)
int getHeight(ImageObserver imo)
```

An `ImagePanel` uses a vector `images` to store the images to be displayed. In method `paintComponent` this vector is traversed. For every image in the vector its width and height are determined for an adequate placement. This is done every time the panel is repainted. Thus the pictures are always arranged to fit the width of the panel, unless the panel is too small to fit a single picture in which case the picture is partly invisible. In `ImagePanel` we define three methods to add a picture:

```
addImage(Image picture)
addImage(String filename)
addImageAndTrack(String filename)
```

The first adds a picture that is already stored as an instance of class `Image`. The second one loads a picture from a file. The third one also loads a picture from a file but in a slightly different way that we shall explain later. In any case a re-drawing of the panel is initiated after a picture is added by calling `repaint`. The following listing contains the classes `ImagePanel` and `ImagePanelFrame`. The latter one creates an `ImagePanel` and adds some pictures to it. The result is shown in Figure 15.2.

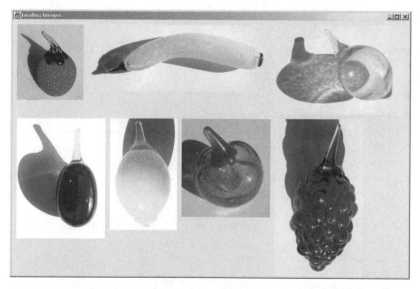

Figure 15.2 `ImagePanelFrame`. Resizing the frame might change the arrangement of the pictures

File: `its/Images/ImagePanel.java`

```
1.  package its.Images;
2.
3.  import java.awt.*;
4.  import javax.swing.JPanel;
5.  import java.util.Vector;
6.
7.  public class ImagePanel extends JPanel
8.  {
9.
10.    private Vector images;
11.    private int gap = 10;
12.    private MediaTracker mediTracker;
13.    private int imageID;
14.
15.    public ImagePanel()
16.    {
17.     this.setLayout(new BorderLayout());
18.     this.setBackground(Color.yellow);
19.     images = new Vector();
20.     mediTracker = new MediaTracker(this);
21.     imageID = 0;
22.     this.setPreferredSize(new Dimension(1000,1400));
23.    }
24.
25.    public void paintComponent(Graphics g)
26.    {
27.     super.paintComponent(g);
28.     int currentYPosition = gap;
29.     int currentXPosition = gap;
30.     int imageWidth, imageHeight;
31.     int maxHeight = -1;
32.     int panelWidth = this.getWidth();
33.     for (int i = 0; i < images.size(); i++) {
34.        Image currentImage = (Image)(images.get(i));
35.        imageWidth  = currentImage.getWidth(this);
36.        imageHeight = currentImage.getHeight(this);
37.        //  Check whether to start a new row.
38.        if((gap+imageWidth+currentXPosition) > panelWidth)
39.        {
40.          currentYPosition += maxHeight + gap;
41.          maxHeight = -1;
42.          currentXPosition = gap;
43.        }
44.        if (imageHeight > maxHeight)
```

```
        {                                                          45.
          maxHeight = imageHeight;                                 46.
        }                                                          47.
        g.drawImage(currentImage,currentXPosition,currentYPosition,this);  48.
        currentXPosition += gap + imageWidth;                      49.
    }// for i                                                      50.
  }                                                                51.
                                                                   52.
  public void addImage(String filename)                           53.
  {                                                                54.
    Image im = Toolkit.getDefaultToolkit().getImage(filename);     55.
    images.add(im);                                                56.
    repaint();                                                     57.
  }                                                                58.
                                                                   59.
  public void addImageAndTrack(String filename)                   60.
  {                                                                61.
    Image im = Toolkit.getDefaultToolkit().getImage(filename);     62.
    imageID++;                                                     63.
    mediTracker.addImage(im,imageID);                             64.
    try                                                            65.
      {                                                            66.
         //   Wait for the image to be completely loaded.          67.
         mediTracker.waitForID(imageID);                           68.
      }                                                            69.
      catch (InterruptedException ex){                             70.
        System.out.println("Error loading image "+filename+".");   71.
      }                                                            72.
    images.add(im);                                                73.
    repaint();                                                     74.
  }                                                                75.
                                                                   76.
  public void addImage(Image picture)                             77.
  {                                                                78.
    images.add(picture);                                           79.
    repaint();                                                     80.
  }                                                                81.
                                                                   82.
}                                                                  83.
```

File: `its/Images/ImagePanelFrame.java`

```
package its.Images;                                                1.
                                                                   2.
import its.SimpleFrame.SimpleFrame;                                3.
import java.awt.BorderLayout;                                      4.
```

```
 5.
 6. public class ImagePanelFrame extends SimpleFrame
 7. {
 8.    // Adjust the following path if necessary
 9.    private final String picturePath = "./its/TestData/";
10.
11.    public ImagePanelFrame()
12.    {
13.       this.setSize(900,600);
14.       ImagePanel ip = new ImagePanel();
15.       this.getContentPane().add(ip,BorderLayout.CENTER);
16.       ip.addImage(picturePath+"strawberry.png");
17.       ip.addImage(picturePath+"banana.png");
18.       ip.addImage(picturePath+"lime.png");
19.       ip.addImage(picturePath+"plum.png");
20.       ip.addImage(picturePath+"lemon.png");
21.       ip.addImage(picturePath+"apple.png");
22.       ip.addImage(picturePath+"grapes.png");
23.    }
24.    public static void main(String[] args)
25.    {
26.       ImagePanelFrame ipf = new ImagePanelFrame();
27.       ipf.showIt("Loading Images");
28.    }
29.
30.
31. }
```

Depending on the version of the SDK, the operation system and the hardware, one might observe slightly different behaviour. It might happen that only the yellow background of the panel is visible or only some of the images are displayed. The reason for this is the asynchronous loading. Let us look at three lines of code used in the `addImage` method of `ImagePanel`:

```
Image im = Toolkit.getDefaultToolkit().getImage(filename);
images.add(im);
repaint();
```

They suggest that the image stored in `filename` is first loaded, then added to the vector `images` and finally a re-drawing is initiated. As the image is in the vector it should be displayed. The real time line is, however, different. The first command initiates the loading process, which then runs in *parallel* to the main application. This means that the two other statements of the above code fragment might be executed *while* the image is being loaded. Thus the image added to the vector might be incomplete or even empty and `repaint` would display it only partly or not at all. If one resizes the frame later, when all images are loaded, the automatic repainting will make them appear. The time needed to load a picture depends on its size and the hardware used. Therefore the aforementioned problems might not occur on some systems. For more on the mechanism of asynchronous loading consult Chapter 20.

To solve this problem one uses the concept of a *media tracker*. This can be used to monitor the loading process, wait for the picture to be fully loaded and only then display it. Class `MediaTracker` can be found in the AWT library. A media tracker can monitor the loading process of many images. To distinguish the different images, every image receives an identification (ID) number. We use the following constructor and methods:

```
MediaTracker(Component comp)

addImage(Image picture, int id)
waitForID(int id)
waitForID(int id, int msec)
```

`MediaTracker(Component comp)` creates a media tracker which monitors images loaded for component `comp`.

`addImage(Image picture, int id)` adds `picture` to those images monitored by the media tracker. The picture gets identification number `id`.

`waitForID(int id)` waits for the loading process of the image with identification number `id` to finish. The application waits at this point until the picture is fully loaded. The statement has to be embedded into a `try-catch` block because it throws an `InterruptedException` if the loading process fails (e.g. due a network failure). The programmer can implement appropriate reactions for this case.

`waitForID(int id, int msec)` waits for the loading process of the image with identification number `id` to finish or for `msec` milliseconds to pass, whichever happens first. Also this statement has to be embedded into a `try-catch` block.

In method `addImageAndTrack` of class `ImagePanel` we implement this concept. The identification numbers are increased from one picture to the next to guarantee uniqueness. The `repaint` method is called only when the image is fully loaded. Class `ImagePanelTrackerFrame` is like `ImagePanelFrame` except that it uses `addImageAndTrack` instead of `addImage`. It can be downloaded from the book's home page.

15.4.2 ☐ Modifying images

Up to now, we displayed the images 'as they are', i.e. every pixel in the image file was shown on the screen. Pictures loaded into `Image` variables can also be rescaled or reflected or only a part of them can be displayed. To this end it suffices to use method `drawImage` from class `Graphics` with an appropriate set of arguments. Recall that only part of an image might be displayed if `drawImage` is used while the image is not yet fully loaded.

The various ways of calling `drawImage` are described below. They all expect an instance of `ImageObserver` as one of the arguments. As discussed in Section 15.4.1 we can use `this` here. In the following, we assume that we draw into a panel, the procedure remains the same for other components which can display images.

```
drawImage(Image picture, int left, int top, ImageObserver imo)
drawImage(Image picture, int left, int top, int width, int height,
          ImageObserver imo)
drawImage(Image picture, int tl, int tt, int tr, int tb, int sl,
          int st, int sr, int sb, ImageObserver imo)
```

`drawImage(Image picture, int left, int top, ImageObserver imo)` has already been described in Section 15.4.1. It displays image `picture` such that its upper left corner is at pixel coordinates `left` and `top` of the panel.

`drawImage(Image picture, int left, int top, int width, int height, Image-Observer imo)` draws image `picture`, such that its upper left corner is at pixel coordinates `left` and `top` in the panel. The displayed image is `width` pixels wide and `height` high. The image is shrunk or stretched to match these constraints. It is important to note that the image itself, i.e. the content of variable `picture`, is *not* changed. The resizing is only in the display.

`drawImage(Image picture, int tl, int tt, int tr, int tb, int sl, int st, int sr, int sb, ImageObserver imo)` draws a rectangular clip of the image `picture` into a rectangular target area of the panel. The integer values `tl`, `tt`, `tr` and `tb` specify, respectively, the pixel coordinates of the left, top, right and bottom edges of the target rectangle. The values `sl`, `st`, `sr` and `sb` specify, respectively, the pixel coordinates of the left, top, right and bottom edges of the source rectangle in `picture`. The width and height of the source rectangle do not have to match the corresponding values of the target rectangle; the clip will be resized to fit into the target area. See also Figure 15.3.

These commands can also be used to reflect an image. If one chooses a negative value for argument `width` in the second `drawImage` method then the image will be vertically reflected. The displayed image has a width that is the absolute value of argument `width` but left and right are interchanged. Using a negative value for `height` results in a horizontal reflection. This also affects the meaning of the parameters `left` or `top`. These always reference the position of the upper left corner of the *original picture*. After a vertical reflection this becomes the upper right corner of the displayed image.

Also the last `drawImage` method can be used to reflect the clipped part. Here, (sl, st) (the upper left corner of the source rectangle) is always mapped onto (tl, tt) (the upper left corner of the target rectangle). Similar for (sr, sb) and (tr, tb). In an unreflected display we have $sl < sr$, $st < sb$, $tl < tr$, $tt < tb$. To vertically reflect the clipped area one only has to swap left and right by choosing $tr < tl$, i.e. by choosing the 'right' edge of the target left of its 'left' edge. For a horizontal reflection $tt > tb$ is set.

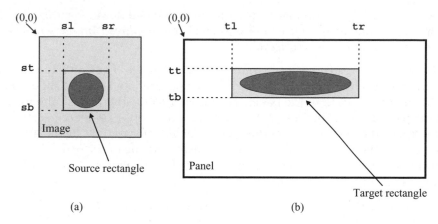

Figure 15.3 How to use method `drawImage` to display part of a picture. (a) A source rectangle is specified by its left, right, top and bottom coordinates. (b) A target rectangle is specified in the same way. The content of the source rectangle is stretched or shrunk to fit into the target rectangle and displayed there

Rotating an image is not supported by the `Graphics` class. As the pixels of images are normally organized in a row-wise fashion, rotations require substantial computational effort.

We illustrate the use of `drawImage` in application `ImageCutAndMirrorFrame`. The frame contains `CutAndMirrorPanel` as an internal class. In the constructor of the frame, the digitalized photo `orange.png` is loaded and passed to the panel. The photo is 400 × 400 pixels. The `paintComponent` method of the panel contains six `drawImage` commands which are described below. The `left` and `top` parameters are chosen such that there are always 10 pixels between any two images. The different `drawImage` commands are labelled A–G in the listing.

(A) draws the original image of size 400 × 400 at position (10, 10) of the panel.

(B) draws an image to the right of the original one at position (420, 10). The height is the original one (400) but the width is only 50, i.e. the image is horizontally shrunk to one-eighth.

(C) draws the image even further right in original height (400) but only 100 pixels wide and vertically reflected. The reflection is achieved by letting `width` be negative (−100). As mentioned above, this swaps left and right. Position (580, 10) therefore denotes the *right* upper corner of the *displayed image* which is the *left* upper corner of the original.

(D) draws an image below the original one at position (10, 420). The width is the original one (400) but the height is only 50, i.e. the image is vertically shrunk to one-eighth.

(E) draws the image even further down in original width (400) but only 100 pixels high and horizontally reflected. The reflection is achieved by letting `height` be negative (−100). Similar to (C) this swaps up and down. Position (10, 580) therefore denotes the *lower* left corner of the *displayed image* which is the *upper* left corner of the original.

(F) Draws an enlarged copy of a part of the original image. The first four numerical parameters 420, 420, 580, 580 specify the upper left and lower right corners of the target rectangle in the panel. This area is 160 × 160 pixels. The following four parameters 250, 130, 290, 170 determine a 40 × 20 source rectangle in the original image. Note that these coordinates refer to the original 400 × 400 picture in the Image variable, not to the displayed one in the panel. The source has to be horizontally stretched by a factor of four and vertically by a factor of eight to fit into the target area.

(G) To indicate the source for (F) area, a white rectangle is drawn in the panel.

The result is shown in Figure 15.4.

Figure 15.4 Application `ImageCutAndMirrorFrame`. Top left: original size picture. Lower right: enlarged images of the area in the white rectangle. Lower left and top right: the original image shrunk and reflected

File: its/Images/ImageCutAndMirrorFrame.java

```
package its.Images;                                                    1.
                                                                       2.
import its.SimpleFrame.SimpleFrame;                                    3.
import java.awt.*;                                                     4.
import javax.swing.JPanel;                                             5.
                                                                       6.
                                                                       7.
public class ImageCutAndMirrorFrame extends SimpleFrame {              8.
                                                                       9.
  // Adjust the following path if necessary                           10.
  private static final String picturePath ="./its/TestData/orange.png"; 11.
  private MediaTracker mediTracker;                                    12.
                                                                       13.
 public ImageCutAndMirrorFrame() {                                    14.
  this.setSize(600,610);                                              15.
  Image im =  Toolkit.getDefaultToolkit().getImage(picturePath);      16.
  CutAndMirrorPanel capp = new CutAndMirrorPanel(im);                 17.
  this.getContentPane().add(capp);                                    18.
  int imageID = 1;                                                    19.
  mediTracker = new MediaTracker(this);                               20.
  mediTracker.addImage(im,imageID);                                   21.
  try{                                                                22.
      mediTracker.waitForID(imageID);                                 23.
    }                                                                 24.
    catch (InterruptedException ex){                                  25.
      System.out.println("Error loading  "+picturePath+".");          26.
    }                                                                 27.
 }                                                                    28.
 public static void main(String[] args) {                            29.
   ImageCutAndMirrorFrame icamp = new ImageCutAndMirrorFrame();       30.
   icamp.showIt("ImageCutAndMirrorFrame");                            31.
 }                                                                    32.
                                                                       33.
                                                                       34.
// internal class                                                     35.
 private class CutAndMirrorPanel extends JPanel{                      36.
   private Image im;                                                  37.
                                                                       38.
   CutAndMirrorPanel(Image i){                                        39.
     im = i;                                                          40.
   }                                                                  41.
                                                                       42.
   public void paintComponent(Graphics g){                           43.
     super.paintComponent(g);                                        44.
```

```
45.        g.drawImage(im,10,10,this);                              //  (A)
46.        g.drawImage(im,420,10,50,400,this);                      //  (B)
47.        g.drawImage(im,580,10,-100,400,this);                    //  (C)
48.        g.drawImage(im,10,420,400,50,this);                      //  (D)
49.        g.drawImage(im,10,580,400,-100,this);                    //  (E)
50.        g.drawImage(im,420,420,580,580,250,130,290,150,this);    //  (F)
51.        g.setColor(Color.white);
52.        g.drawRect(260,140,40,20);                               //  (G)
53.    }
54.  }// internal class
55. }// class
```

The resizing done in the previous paragraphs affected only the displayed image, not the one contained in the `Image` variable. We now describe how an image can be physically resized. Such a resizing can, for example, be used to generate thumbnails for digitized photos. Think of an application that has to display an overview of a number of digitized photos. Such photos need several megabytes of memory each when stored as an instance of class `Image`. Using the appropriate `drawImage` method to display a miniaturized version does not solve the memory problem because only the display is resized while the picture in the `Image` variable maintains its full size. Then a few photos fill the main memory and the application is slowed down owing to swapping.

We now describe how smaller (or larger) copies of pictures can be generated. To overcome the aforementioned memory problem one can load the photos one at a time, generate small copies and keep just those. Only the copies are maintained in the memory. The programmer has to make sure that references to the original big image are destroyed (e.g. by use of local variables) so that the automatic garbage collection of Java releases the memory.

We use the following method of class `Image` to create a resized copy of an image:

```
Image getScaledInstance( int width, int height, int hints)
```

Arguments `width` and `height` specify the width and height of the resulting new image. The third argument `hints` determines which technique is used to enlarge or shrink the image. For an enlargement additional pixels have to be generated, for a miniaturization several pixels have to be combined. The quality of the resulting picture depends on the way this is done. A better quality usually requires a longer conversion time. We list the constants for `hints` which are defined in class `Image` together with the qualities achieved by the corresponding conversion techniques.

SCALE_DEFAULT	Good trade-off between speed and quality
SCALE_FAST	Fast conversion and moderate quality
SCALE_SMOOTH	Reasonably good quality
SCALE_REPLICATE	Good quality
SCALE_AREA_AVERAGING	Good quality

Figure 15.5 Application `ImageScaleFrame`. Top: original size image and a copy that is linearly scaled by 0.5. Bottom: upper part of the copy scaled by 2.0. The scroll pane can be used to show the hidden parts

Scaling is done asynchronously. To ensure that the resulting image is only displayed after it is completed one can again use a media tracker. The following application `ImageScaleFrame` demonstrates scaling a picture. The main program loads a photo into the `Image` object `original`. Then two copies `small` and `large` are generated. They are copies of the original scaled by a factor of 0.5 and 2.0, respectively. We defined method `scaleImage(image, factor)` which determines the size of the resulting picture from the dimensions of `image` and the scale factor `factor`. Horizontal and vertical scaling factors are equal; it is left as an exercise to extend the method to different factors. `ImagePanel` is used to display the three images. It is embedded into a scroll pane to be able to access all of the pictures. See Figure 15.5.

File: `its/Images/ImageScaleFrame.java`

```
package its.Images;                             1.
                                                2.
import its.SimpleFrame.SimpleFrame;             3.
import java.awt.*;                              4.
import javax.swing.*;                           5.
                                                6.
                                                7.
public class ImageScaleFrame extends SimpleFrame {   8.
```

```
9.
10.    // Adjust the following path if necessary
11.    private static final String picturePath ="./its/TestData/orange.png";
12.    private MediaTracker mediTracker;
13.    private int imageID = 0;
14.
15.    public ImageScaleFrame() {
16.      this.setSize(800,600);
17.      ImagePanel ip  = new ImagePanel();
18.      JScrollPane sp = new JScrollPane(ip);
19.      sp.setHorizontalScrollBarPolicy
             (JScrollPane.HORIZONTAL_SCROLLBAR_ALWAYS);
20.      sp.setVerticalScrollBarPolicy(JScrollPane.VERTICAL_SCROLLBAR_ALWAYS);
21.      this.getContentPane().add(sp);
22.      mediTracker = new MediaTracker(this);
23.
24.      Image original = loadImageAndTrack(picturePath);
25.      ip.addImage(original);
26.      Image klein     =  scaleImage(original,0.5);
27.      ip.addImage(klein);
28.      Image gross     =  scaleImage(original,2.0);
29.      ip.addImage(gross);
30.      repaint();
31.    }
32.
33.   private Image scaleImage(Image im, double factor){
34.       imageID++;
35.       int newWidth  = (int)(im.getWidth(this)*factor);
36.       int newHeight = (int)(im.getWidth(this)*factor);
37.
38.       Image scaledIm =
               im.getScaledInstance(newWidth,newHeight,Image.SCALE_FAST)
39.
40.       mediTracker.addImage(scaledIm,imageID);
41.       try {
42.         mediTracker.waitForID(imageID);
43.       }
44.       catch (Exception ex) {
45.         ex.printStackTrace();
46.       }
47.     return(scaledIm);
48.   }
49.
50.   private Image loadImageAndTrack(String filename)
51.     {
52.      Image im = Toolkit.getDefaultToolkit().getImage(filename);
53.      imageID++;
```

```
      mediTracker.addImage(im,imageID);                          54.
      try                                                        55.
        {                                                        56.
          mediTracker.waitForID(imageID);                        57.
        }                                                        58.
        catch (InterruptedException ex){                         59.
          System.out.println("Error loading "+filename+".");     60.
        }                                                        61.
      return(im);                                                62.
  }                                                              63.
                                                                 64.
  public static void main(String[] args) {                      65.
    ImageScaleFrame isf = new ImageScaleFrame();                 66.
    isf.showIt("ImageScaleFrame: Scaled images");                67.
  }                                                              68.
  }                                                              69.
```

More Swing components

16

In this chapter we introduce more graphical components from the Swing library. Some of them, such as lists and tables, are used to display data in a structured way. Others, such as split panes or tabbed panes, are used to embed other components so that one can easily switch between them.

16.1 ■ Borders

One can draw a line – a *border* – around most Swing components in order to separate them from one another. Swing offers class `Border` and the utility class `BorderFactory` for this purpose. There are various different types of borders. We show only how to get an 'etched border'; for others see the documentation. Let `comp` be a Swing component. To get a border, use the appropriate methods of the class `BorderFactory` namely:

```
Border bdr = BorderFactory.createEtchedBorder();
comp.setBorder(bdr);
```

To create a border with a text, one first creates a border `bdr` and then adds the text:

```
Border bdr     = BorderFactory.createEtchedBorder();
Border textbdr = BorderFactory.createTitledBorder(Border bdr,
                                                  Stringtext);
```

! Here is an example consisting of four panels with borders, two have a text. The result is shown in Figure 16.1. Note that the border is **inside** the panel, so leave a margin if you draw in the panel.

File: its/Borders/BorderPanel.java

```
1.  package its.Borders;
2.
3.  import java.awt.*;
4.  import javax.swing.JPanel;
```

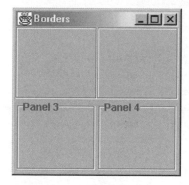

Figure 16.1 A frame with four embedded bordered panels

```java
import javax.swing.border.*;                                                5.
import javax.swing.BorderFactory;                                           6.
                                                                            7.
public class BorderPanel extends JPanel                                     8.
{                                                                           9.
  public BorderPanel()                                                     10.
  {                                                                        11.
    this.setBackground(Color.lightGray);                                   12.
    Border bdr       = BorderFactory.createEtchedBorder();                 13.
    this.setBorder(bdr );                                                  14.
  }                                                                        15.
public BorderPanel(String text)                                            16.
  {                                                                        17.
    this.setBackground(Color.lightGray);                                   18.
    Border bdr       = BorderFactory.createEtchedBorder();                 19.
    Border titlebdr = BorderFactory.createTitledBorder(bdr ,text);         20.
    this.setBorder(titlebdr );                                             21.
  }                                                                        22.
                                                                           23.
}                                                                          24.
```

File: `its/Borders/BorderFrame.java`

```java
package its.Borders;                                                        1.
                                                                            2.
import java.awt.*;                                                          3.
import its.SimpleFrame.SimpleFrame;                                         4.
                                                                            5.
                                                                            6.
                                                                            7.
public class BorderFrame extends SimpleFrame                                8.
{                                                                           9.
```

```
10.
11.  public BorderFrame()
12.  {
13.    this.getContentPane().setLayout(new GridLayout(2,2));
14.    BorderPanel borderPanel1 = new BorderPanel();
15.    BorderPanel borderPanel2 = new BorderPanel();
16.    BorderPanel borderPanel3 = new BorderPanel("Panel 3");
17.    BorderPanel borderPanel4 = new BorderPanel("Panel 4");
18.    this.getContentPane().add(borderPanel1);
19.    this.getContentPane().add(borderPanel2);
20.    this.getContentPane().add(borderPanel3);
21.    this.getContentPane().add(borderPanel4);
22.  }
23.
24.  public static void main(String[] args){
25.    BorderFrame borderFrame = new BorderFrame();
26.    borderFrame.showIt("Borders");
27.
28.  }
29. }
```

16.2 ■ Lists

Lists serve two purposes. They can be used to display text information in rows and they enable the user to select rows and use the selected information in the program. The graphical concept of a list should not be confused with the data structure with the same name. Java contains an implementation of the latter in the class LinkedList. The graphical component for lists is the Swing class JList. The list entries are shown as rows.

Instances of JList allow arbitrary Objects as list entries. The data are internally stored in a ListModel, a class we describe in Section 16.2.3. An explicit use of list models is advisable if the data displayed in a list change as the program is running. If the data in the list are fixed, it is not really necessary to use the model explicitly. An example for this can be found in Section 16.2.1. JLists also allow the user to select one or more entries. One can display an image or augment a text with an icon but the programmer has to specify how the display should be drawn by implementing a ListCellRenderer. We shall use Strings only as list entries, which can be displayed without implementing a user-defined renderer.

We describe the constructor and some methods of JList in the following:

```
JList()
JList(String[] entries)

void setListData(String[] entries)
void setSelectionMode(int selectionMode)
```

```
void getSelectionMode()
void setVisibleRowCount(int rowNo)
int   getSelectedIndex()
int[] getSelectedIndices()
Object   getSelectedValue()
Object[] getSelectedValues()
```

JList() creates an empty list.

JList(String[] entries) creates a list which contains the strings of array entries. The first string is the first, i.e. top-most, list entry.

setListData(String[] entries) sets the list entries to the strings in array entries. The first string is the first, i.e. top-most, list entry.

setSelectionMode(int) sets the way in which the user is allowed to select list entries. One can choose between the following: SINGLE_SELECTION – only one list entry can be selected, if a new one is selected the old selection is dropped; SINGLE_INTERVAL_SELECTION – one group of adjacent entries can be selected; MULTIPLE_INTERVAL_SELECTION – arbitrary combinations of entries can be selected. The three constants are defined in class ListSelectionModel.

getSelectionMode() determines which selection mode is currently used. The returned integer value is one of those described for method setSelectionMode above.

setVisibleRowCount(int rowNo) sets the number of rows visible of the list. This adjusts the height of the graphical component such that rowNo shows how many rows are displayed.

getSelectedIndex() returns the index of the (first) selected entry or −1 if no entry is selected.

getSelectedIndices() returns the indices of the selected entries in an integer array.

getSelectedValue() returns the (first) selected entry (not the index but the entry itself) or null if nothing is selected.

getSelectedValues() returns the selected entries (not the indices but the entries themselves), or null if nothing is selected.

16.2.1 ☐ Filling a list with data

To get text entries into a list one can pass an array of strings in the constructor. The following program ListDemo creates a list with the names of the German provinces. The visible length of the list is set to 8. To make all entries accessible we place the list into the viewport of a scroll pane. The scroll pane is then embedded into the frame. We do not set the selection mode, so the list has the default selection mode which is MULTIPLE_INTERVAL_SELECTION. The main-method is placed in the frame class so no driver class is needed.

File: `its/Lists/ListDemoFrame.java`

```
1. package its.Lists;
2.
3. import its.SimpleFrame.SimpleFrame;
4. import java.awt.BorderLayout;
5. import javax.swing.JList;
6. import javax.swing.JScrollPane;
7.
8. public class ListDemoFrame extends SimpleFrame {
9.   private String[] entries = {"Schleswig-Holstein", "Niedersachsen",
10.    "Hamburg", "Bremen", "Mecklenburg-Vorpommern", "Brandenburg",
11.    "Berlin", "Nordrhein-Westfalen","Hessen","Sachsen-Anhalt",
12.    "Rheinland-Pfalz","Thüringen","Sachsen","Saarland", "Bayern",
13.    "Baden-Württemberg"};
14.
15.   public ListDemoFrame() {
16.     JList provinces = new JList(entries);
17.     JScrollPane scrollPane = new  JScrollPane(provinces);
18.     this.getContentPane().add(scrollPane,BorderLayout.CENTER);
19.     this.pack();
20.   }
21.
22.   public static void main(String[] args) {
23.     ListDemoFrame ldf = new ListDemoFrame();
24.     ldf.showIt("List demo");
25.   }
26. }
```

16.2.2 ☐ Specification of a GUI with dynamic lists

We now consider lists where entries are added or removed and the user can select entries and trigger an action as a response to that. We want to design a GUI with two lists side by side. Initially only the left one contains some items. The user is allowed to select single entries in the left list. Whenever an item is selected in the left list which is not in the right list, it is copied to the right list. If the item selected in the left list is already in the right list, it is deleted from the latter. The left list is not changed during this process; only the right list changes. We use two components to implement the desired functions: list models to handle the data and listeners, which react to selecting list entries. We introduce these components in the following sections.

16.2.3 ☐ List models

When lists are dynamic, i.e. when list entries are added or deleted in the course of the program, the explicit use of a model for the list entries is recommended. The user can implement the interface `ListModel` for this purpose. However, there is a predefined implementation of list models in class `DefaultListModel` which is sufficient for many purposes. In a list with n entries, the list entries are numbered $0, 1, \ldots, n-1$, where 0 denotes the first (topmost) entry. When a list element is added or removed then the numbering is updated. In the following we describe class `DefaultListModel` which is located in the `javax.swing` library.

```
DefaultListModel()

int size()
boolean contains(Object entry)
Object get(int position)
void insertElementAt(Object entry, int position)
void addElement(Object entry)
void removeElementAt(int position)
boolean removeElement(Object entry)
void removeAllElements()
```

`DefaultListModel()` is the constructor which creates a list model without any entries.

`size()` returns the number of entries currently in the list model.

`contains(Object entry)` returns `true` if object `entry` is in the list model, and `false` otherwise.

`get(int position)` returns the list entry at position `position`. Throws an exception if `position` is negative or greater than or equal to the current number of list entries. As the return type is `Object`, an explicit cast to the correct type might be needed.

`insertElementAt(Object entry, int position)` adds entry `entry` at position `position` to the list model. Throws an exception if `position` is an invalid index.

`addElement(Object entry)` adds an `entry` at the end of the list.

`removeElementAt(int position)` removes the entry at position `position`. Throws an exception if `position` is an invalid index. The remaining list entries are renumbered to maintain a consecutive indexing.

`removeElement(Object entry)` removes the entry `entry`. If successful `true` is returned, otherwise `false` is returned.

`removeAllElements()` removes all entries from the list model.

Once the list model is defined, one passes it to a `JList` in the constructor or by using the `set`-method:

```
JList(ListModel lModel)
setModel(ListModel lModel)
```

! Changes in the list model (additions or deletions of entries) are *automatically* displayed by the corresponding list. No call to `repaint` is necessary.

16.2.4 □ List listeners and list events

As specified above, our application has to react to a list entry being selected. The appropriate listener for this purpose is a `ListSelectionListener`. It is assigned to a `JList`, say `myjlist`, by

```
myjlist.addListSelectionListener(listener)
```

Interface `ListSelectionListener` requires the implementation of only one method:

```
public void valueChanged(ListSelectionEvent evt)
```

! This method is automatically called by the runtime system every time the selection is changed. It is not executed if the selection is unchanged, for example if the user clicks in an item that is already selected. The body of this method has to contain the code that should be executed in response to the selection.

Method `valueChanged` receives an object of type `ListSelectionEvent` as an argument. This is automatically generated by the runtime system and contains further information on the selection event that has occurred. We shall use the following methods of `ListSelectionEvent`:

```
int getFirstIndex()
int getLastIndex()
boolean getIsAdjusting()
```

`getFirstIndex()` returns the position of the first (top-most) entry, the selection mode of which might have changed (from selected to non-selected or vice versa). 'Might' refers to the fact that the section state might be the same as before. For example if entries 5 to 8 were selected and the user now selects 5 to 10 then the first selected index remains unchanged. Which entries are selected can be found by using method `getSelectedIndices` of class `JList`.

`getLastIndex()` returns the position of the last (bottom-most) entry, the selection mode of which might have changed. See also `getFirstIndex()`.

! `getIsAdjusting` – changing the selection in a list triggers a series of actions, each of which generates a list selection event. For example previously selected entries become unselected before new ones become selected. Usually, one would prefer this series of events to be completed before the application reacts to the change. For such a rapid series of events all but the last one return `true` as a result of `getIsAdjusting`. Only the last one returns `false` as a result of `getIsAdjusting`. This can be used to wait for the end of the series of adjustments before taking further action.

! At the moment, `ListSelectionEvent` supports only the selection modes `SINGLE_SELECTION` and `SINGLE_INTERVAL_SELECTION`.

16.2.5 ☐ **Implementation of the list GUI**

The following program `ListTransferFrame` demonstrates the use of dynamic lists. The view part consists of two lists. Both are embedded into scroll panes which are then glued into a panel. The panel is glued centrally into a frame. The panel has a 1 × 2 grid layout so that the lists are side by side. We do not derive classes for these lists, because we do not add any additional functionality to them.

The list on the left contains the names of the German provinces. As mentioned in the specification this list does not change. Therefore, do we not explicitly define a model for it. The selection mode is set such that only a single entry can be selected. As the right list is dynamic, we define our own list model. Entries are inserted into or deleted from the model. The display of the right list is automatically updated as a response to this.

For the control part we use class `TransferListener` which implements the interface `ListSelectionListener`. It is implemented as an internal class of the frame so that it has direct access to fields of the frame. When the listener's `valueChanged`-method is informed, we first make sure that we are not in the middle of a sequence of events that change the selection. If that is not the case, we find out which entry is selected in the left list. This is stored in the string variable `sel`. We then check whether `sel` is already an entry in the right list and – if so – delete it there. Otherwise `sel` is added as an entry to the right list.

The program is listed below. When using it, note the following. If an entry `A` is selected on the left it is copied to the right list (assuming it was not already there). If this entry `A` is clicked again the corresponding entry `A` is not removed from the right list. One first has to select a different entry `B` on the left and select `A` again to remove it from the right list. The reason is, as explained above, that the selection has to change in order for `valueChanged` to be activated. Figure 16.2 shows the result.

Figure 16.2 The result of `ListTransferFrame`

File: `its/Lists/ListTransferFrame.java`

```java
1. package its.Lists;
2.
3. import its.SimpleFrame.SimpleFrame;
4. import java.awt.GridLayout;
5. import java.awt.BorderLayout;
6. import javax.swing.*;
7. import javax.swing.event.*;
8.
9. public class ListTransferFrame extends SimpleFrame
10. {
11.    private JList leftList, rightList;
12.    private DefaultListModel rightListModel;
13.    JButton transferButton;
14.    String[] entries = {"Schleswig-Holstein","Niedersachsen","Hamburg",
15.                        "Bremen","Mecklenburg-Vorpommern","Brandenburg",
16.                        "Berlin","Nordrhein-Westfalen","Hessen",
17.                        "Sachsen-Anhalt","Rheinland-Pfalz","Thüringen",
18.                        "Sachsen","Saarland","Bayern","Baden-Württemberg"};
19.
20.    public ListTransferFrame()
21.    {
22.     this.setSize(400,300);
23.     leftList  = new JList(entries);
24.
25.     rightListModel = new DefaultListModel();
26.     rightList = new JList(rightListModel);
27.     leftList.setSelectionMode(ListSelectionModel.SINGLE_SELECTION);
28.
29.     TransferListener selLis = new TransferListener();
30.     leftList.addListSelectionListener(selLis);
31.
32.     JPanel listPanel = new JPanel();
33.     listPanel.setLayout(new GridLayout(1,2));
34.     JScrollPane leftScrollPane  = new JScrollPane(leftList);
35.     JScrollPane rightScrollPane = new JScrollPane(rightList);
36.     listPanel.add(leftScrollPane);
37.     listPanel.add(rightScrollPane);
38.     this.getContentPane().add(listPanel,BorderLayout.CENTER);
39.    }
40.
41.    public static void main(String[] args)
42.    {
43.     ListTransferFrame LLF = new ListTransferFrame();
44.     LLF.showIt("List Transfer Frame");
45.    }
```

```
//Listener as internal class
  class TransferListener implements ListSelectionListener{

    public TransferListener(){}

    public void valueChanged(ListSelectionEvent evt){
     if(!evt.getValueIsAdjusting())
     {
     String sel = (String)leftList.getSelectedValue();
     if(rightListModel.contains(sel))
      {
         rightListModel.removeElement(sel);
      }
     else
      {
         rightListModel.addElement(sel);
      }//ifelse
     }//if
    }//valueChanged

  }//internal class
 }
```

46.
47.
48.
49.
50.
51.
52.
53.
54.
55.
56.
57.
58.
59.
60.
61.
62.
63.
64.
65.
66.
67.
68.

16.3 ■ Tables

Tables are used to display data with a two-dimensional structure. Examples are price lists, distance tables on maps, address books, etc. In Swing class JTable is used to visualize tables. As for lists, a model is internally used to handle the data. If the data are complex or change while the program is running, it advisable to explicitly define such a table model.

A *table* consists of cells arranged in a rectangular grid. It is possible to add headings to every column. JTables are *column*-oriented. This means that there is support for the manipulation of columns (for example swapping two columns or rendering the column content) but only limited support for row manipulation. When designing a table one should therefore try to arrange the data in such a way that a column contains data of the same type (strings, integers, images, etc.).

In the following we show how tables can be used to display static data, how table models work and how they can be used to dynamically or interactively change data in a table.

16.3.1 □ A simple static table

If a table displays data that do not change, then the explicit use of a table model is not necessary. Instead the data can be passed directly to the table in the constructor. The data are organized in a two-dimensional array content[][].

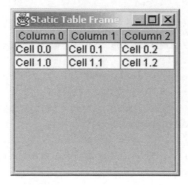

Figure 16.3 A static table

It is interpreted as an array consisting of the rows, i.e. `content[i][]` is the one-dimensional array containing the entries of the ith row of the table. In a second, one-dimensional array `columnNames` the headers of the columns are passed. The rows and the array with the column names all have to have the same length! The constructor then looks like this:

```
JTable(Object[][] content,Object[] columnNames)
```

Note that the arrays are of type `Object`. If 'non-standard' types are used, one has to ensure that the program knows how to render them by supplying a user-defined renderer. This is done by implementing the interface `TableCellRenderer`. By default, `JTable` uses a `DefaultTableCellRenderer` which can display the 'standard' types such as strings, images and boolean values. For most purposes this is sufficient. In order to make the column names visible the table should be embedded into a scroll pane. The heads remain visible even if the table is vertically scrolled. By default, the widths of the columns are all the same and they are automatically adjusted such that all columns fit into the visible area. This is done even though a scroll pane is used to display the table. If the visible area is small then the columns become too narrow to properly display the content of some or all the cells. In those cells some dots (. . .) are shown instead. To switch the automatic width adjustment off one uses the command:

```
setAutoResizeMode(JTable.AUTO_RESIZE_OFF)
```

The following listing `StaticTableFrame` is an example for creating and displaying a table. The resulting display is shown in Figure 16.3.

File: `its/Tables/StaticTableFrame.java`

```
1. package its.Tables;
2.
3. import its.SimpleFrame.SimpleFrame;
4. import javax.swing.JScrollPane;
5. import javax.swing.JTable;
```

```
public class StaticTableFrame extends SimpleFrame
{

  private String[][] entries  = {{"Cell 0.0","Cell 0.1","Cell 0.2"},
                                 {"Cell 1.0","Cell 1.1","Cell 1.2"}};
  private String[] columnNames = {"Column 0","Column 1","Column 2"};


  public StaticTableFrame()
  {
    JTable table = new JTable(entries,columnNames);
    JScrollPane scrollpane = new JScrollPane(table);
    this.getContentPane().add(scrollpane);
  }

  public static void main(String[] args)
  {
    StaticTableFrame STF = new StaticTableFrame();
    STF.showIt("Static Table Frame");
  }
}
```

6.
7.
8.
9.
10.
11.
12.
13.
14.
15.
16.
17.
18.
19.
20.
21.
22.
23.
24.
25.
26.
27.

16.3.2 ☐ Table models

The method of explicitly passing the table data in the constructor is not suitable when using tables with complex content or very large tables. So-called *table models* provide an elegant method in this situation. Changing the table content at runtime is also easy when using table models. Table models implicitly describe the content to be rendered into a cell. The whole table does not have to exist in the form of a two-dimensional array. The table model has to be able to provide the content of every cell on demand. The following application is an example of this.

We construct a multiplication table. The cell in row r and column c displays the product $r \cdot c$ of the row and column number. As rows and columns are indexed beginning with zero, the first row and column consist entirely of zeros. The model then just specifies the following rule: 'The content of cell (r, c) is $r \cdot c$'. The model does not have to construct a two-dimensional array with these values[1].

We derive our own table model from the class `AbstractTableModel` which is defined in the library `javax.swing.table`. Class `AbstractTableModel` requires the implementation of the following `abstract` methods:

```
int getRowCount()
int getColumnCount()
Object getValueAt(int r, int c)
```

---

[1] The current implementation of the Java runtime system seems to explicitly construct the table as a two-dimensional array.

`getRowCount()` has to be implemented to return the number of rows in the table.

`getColCount()` has to be implemented to return the number of columns in the table.

`getValueAt(r,c)` has to be implemented to return the content of the table cell in column c of row r.

Besides these three abstract methods `AbstractTableModel` contains some non-abstract methods one would often like to override:

```
String getColumnName(int c)
Class getColumnClass(int c)
boolean isCellEditable(int r, int c)
void setValueAt(Object val, int r, int c)
```

`getColumnName(c)` returns the name of column c as a string. By default, an `AbstractTableModel` assigns the names $A, B, C, \ldots, Z, AA, AB, AC, \ldots$ to the columns. Overriding `getColumnName` by your own implementation allows you to specify other names.

`getColumnClass(c)` returns the class of the objects in column c. By default, an `AbstractTableModel` returns class `Object`. One should override `getColumnClass(c)` to return the correct class of the objects in column c. This way one ensures that the correct renderer is used to display the entries. As mentioned above, tables are column-oriented and in every column the objects should be of the same class. To determine the appropriate class for column c one can look at the entry in the first row: `getValueAt(0,c).getClass()`.

`isCellEditable(r, c)` the return value is `true` if the cell is editable and `false` otherwise. The default implementation returns `false`, i.e. the user cannot change the content of the cell. The programmer can override this method to make some cells editable by the user.

`setValueAt(Object val, r, c)` can be used to set the value of the cell in row r and column c to `val`. The default implementation has an empty body, i.e. it does not change the value of the cell. The programmer can override this method to change the values of editable cells.

In the following listing we provide an implementation of `MultiplicationTableModel`. The numbers of rows and columns are given as an argument in the constructor. Method `getValueAt(r,c)` is implemented to return the product of r and c. Method `getColumnName(c)` is overridden to return the string `Col` followed by the number c as a string. In Figure 16.4 the results are shown when using automatic resizing of the column width and without using it.

We also list the class `MultiplicationTableFrame`. Such a frame generates a `MultiplicationTableModel` and a `JTable` using this model. The table is embedded into a scroll pane which in turn is embedded into the frame.

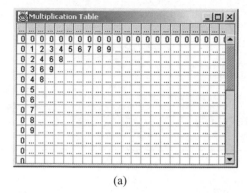
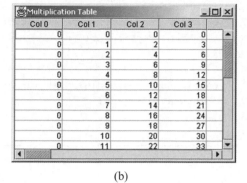

(a)   (b)

Figure 16.4 `MultiplicationTableFrame`. (a) The column widths are reduced to fit the width of the display. As there is a minimum column width (15 pixels on most platforms) this is not always possible. (b) The automatic resizing is switched off and all columns have their default width (75 pixels on most platforms)

File: `its/Tables/MultiplicationTableModel.java`

```
package its.Tables;                                                    1.
                                                                       2.
import javax.swing.table.AbstractTableModel;                           3.
                                                                       4.
public class MultiplicationTableModel extends AbstractTableModel{      5.
                                                                       6.
  private int noOfRows, noOfCols;                                      7.
  public MultiplicationTableModel(int r, int c) {                      8.
    noOfRows = r;                                                      9.
    noOfCols = c;                                                     10.
  }                                                                   11.
                                                                      12.
// Implementing the tree abstract methods:                            13.
  public int getColumnCount() {                                       14.
    return(noOfRows);                                                 15.
  }                                                                   16.
                                                                      17.
  public Object getValueAt(int r,int c) {                             18.
   return(new Integer(r*c));                                          19.
  }                                                                   20.
                                                                      21.
  public int getRowCount() {                                          22.
    return(noOfRows);                                                 23.
  }                                                                   24.
                                                                      25.
```

```
26.  // Overriding some methods:
27.    public Class getColumnClass(int c){
28.      return( getValueAt(0,c).getClass() );
29.    }
30.
31.    public String getColumnName(int c){
32.      return("Col "+c);
33.    }
34. }
```

File: `its/Tables/MultiplicationTableFrame.java`

```
1. package its.Tables;
2.
3. import its.SimpleFrame.SimpleFrame;
4. import javax.swing.JScrollPane;
5. import javax.swing.JTable;
6.
7. public class MultiplicationTableFrame extends SimpleFrame {
8.
9.    public MultiplicationTableFrame(int r, int c) {
10.      MultiplicationTableModel multModel = new MultiplicationTableModel(r,c);
11.      JTable multTable = new JTable(multModel);
12.      multTable.setAutoResizeMode(JTable.AUTO_RESIZE_OFF);
13.      JScrollPane scrollPane = new JScrollPane(multTable);
14.      this.setSize(350,250);
15.      this.getContentPane().add(scrollPane);
16.    }
17.
18.    public static void main(String[] args) {
19.      MultiplicationTableFrame mtf30 =
20.          new MultiplicationTableFrame(30,30);
21.      mtf30.showIt("Multiplication Table");
22.    }
23. }
```

16.3.3 ☐ Editable tables

In this section we show how different objects are used in different columns and how the content of table cells can be interactively changed by the user.

The table is an order form where the user can order some products. In our example three products are available: circles, triangles and rectangles. The table has five columns which contain the product's name, a picture of the product, the price per piece, the quantity ordered and the price for the ordered quantity. Initially, no products are ordered, i.e. the quantities are 0. The user can edit the quantities. As a result the price for the ordered quantity in the last column is updated. Our order form has an additional fourth row where the total price for all ordered products is displayed and updated with every change of the order.

The table is implemented by our table model `OrderTableModel`. This model is then passed to a `JTable` which displays it. We organize the data as follows: the first three rows contain the product information. The first column (column number 0) contains the product names as `Strings`. The next column contains the pictures `ImageIcons`. The following column contains the price per piece as `double`. The fourth column (number 3) contains the number of pieces ordered as `int`. This column is editable: the user can change the quantities. In the last column the total price for every item is listed as `double`. The values of these cells are computed as (price per piece) times (quantity ordered). The last cell of the fourth row contains the total amount of the order.

The values are computed in method `getValueAt` which determines the values by a large case distinction (switch statement). In particular, the first three rows containing the three products are treated differently from the last row containing the total amount. One has to make sure that a re-computation is performed when the user changes the quantity ordered. This is achieved by using method `fireTableDataChanged()` of class `AbstractTableModel`. It not only initiates a re-computation but also an update of the display of the associated `JTable`. In Java the so-called *fire method* of a class informs the listeners which are associated to that class. We have not explicitly defined a listener in our application. However, using a table with table model automatically implements listeners for the basic functions. These are responsible for the re-computation of the cell values and the update of the display.

We now list the classes `OrderTableModel` and `OrderTableFrame` and show a screen shot of the application in Figure 16.5.

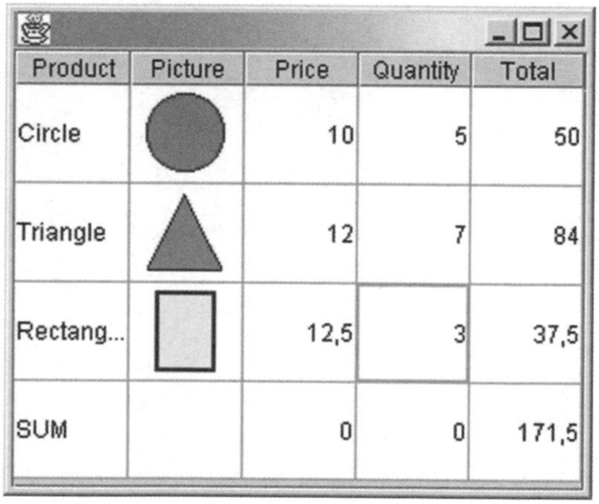

Figure 16.5 `OrderTableFrame` after some orders have been placed

File: `its/Tables/OrderTableModel.java`

```java
1.  package its.Tables;
2.
3.  import javax.swing.ImageIcon;
4.  import javax.swing.table.AbstractTableModel;
5.
6.  public class OrderTableModel extends AbstractTableModel
7.  {
8.    private String[] columnNames = {"Product","Picture","Price",
9.                                      "Quantity","Total"};
10.   private String[] products    = {"Circle","Triangle","Rectangle"};
11.   private String[] imageName    = {"circ.png","tria.png","rect.png"};
12.   private int[] quantities      = {0,0,0};
13.   private double[] prices        = {10.00, 12.00, 12.50};
14.   private static final String Path = "./its/TestData/";
15.   public boolean[] bv= {true,false,true};
16.
17.   public OrderTableModel()
18.   {
19.   }
20.   public int getColumnCount()
21.   {
22.     return(columnNames.length);
23.   }
24.
25.   public int getRowCount()
26.   {
27.     return(products.length+1);
28.   }
29.
30.    public String getColumnName(int c) {
31.        return(columnNames[c]);
32.     }
33.
34.    public Class getColumnClass(int c) {
35.       return getValueAt(0, c).getClass();
36.     }
37.
38.    public Object getValueAt(int r, int c)
39.    {
40.     Object result = new Object();
41.      if( r < products.length) {
42.       switch(c){
43.        case 0: result = products[r]; break;
44.        case 1: result = new ImageIcon(Path+imageName[r]);  break;
```

```
      case 2: result = new Double(prices[r]); break;          45.
      case 3: result = new Integer(quantities[r]);   break;   46.
      case 4: int quantity = ((Integer)getValueAt(r,3)).intValue();  47.
              double price = ((Double)getValueAt(r,2)).doubleValue();  48.
              result = new Double(quantity * price); break;   49.
    }//switch                                                  50.
  }                                                            51.
  else{                                                        52.
   switch(c){                                                  53.
    case 0: result = new String("SUM"); break;                54.
    case 1: result = new Object();     break;                 55.
    case 2: result = new Double(0.0); break;                  56.
    case 3: result = new Integer(0);   break;                 57.
    case 4: double sum = 0.0;                                 58.
            double ee;                                         59.
            for (int i = 0; i < products.length; i++) {       60.
              sum += ((Double)getValueAt(i,4)).doubleValue(); 61.
            }                                                  62.
            result = new Double(sum);  break;                 63.
   }                                                           64.
  }                                                            65.
  return(result);                                              66.
 }                                                             67.
                                                               68.
//cells in column 3 can be edited                             69.
   public boolean isCellEditable(int r, int c) {              70.
       return(c == 3);                                        71.
   }                                                           72.
                                                               73.
   public void setValueAt(Object obj, int r, int c)           74.
   {                                                           75.
     if(c == 3){                                               76.
       quantities[r] = ((Integer)obj).intValue();             77.
     }                                                          78.
       this.fireTableDataChanged();                           79.
   }                                                           80.
                                                               81.
}                                                              82.
```

File: its/Tables/OrderTableFrame.java

```
package its.Tables;                                            1.
                                                               2.
import its.SimpleFrame.SimpleFrame;                            3.
import javax.swing.JScrollPane;                                4.
```

```
 5. import javax.swing.JTable;
 6.
 7. public class OrderTableFrame extends SimpleFrame
 8. {
 9.
10.    public OrderTableFrame()
11.    {
12.       this.setSize(300,250);
13.       OrderTableModel otmodel = new OrderTableModel();
14.       JTable JTab = new JTable(otmodel);
15.       JTab.setRowHeight(50);
16.
17.       JScrollPane SP = new JScrollPane(JTab);
18.       this.getContentPane().add(SP);
19.
20.    }
21.
22.    public static void main(String[] args)
23.    {
24.       OrderTableFrame otframe = new OrderTableFrame();
25.       otframe.showIt();
26.    }
27. }
```

16.4 ■ Trees

Hierarchical structures can often be represented by *trees*. Examples of hierarchical structures are family trees, the organization structure of a company, the directory structure on a computer hard disk, or the embedding structure of Swing components as explained in Section 4.5. The notion of a tree comes from the area of combinatorics and graph theory, a field of mathematics that considers discrete structures. A hierarchy is reflected in a tree as follows: there is a most important component, the root. The tree then *branches* into (less important) subcomponents that, in turn, branch into sub-subcomponents. The bottom-most components of the hierarchy form the *leaves* of the tree, they do not branch any further. The parts of the tree that correspond to the components are called *nodes* and the connecting links are called *edges*. Figure 16.6 shows an example of this concept. The sub-nodes of a node are called its *children*. The children are numbered 0, 1, 2, ... In graphical representations the numbering is usually from left to right or from top to bottom. Trees are often drawn to grow downwards. The root is on top and the leaves (lowest in hierarchy) are at the bottom. In graphical interfaces trees are often drawn to grow from left to right. Swing offers predefined components to represent and display trees. For the abstract representation of the tree structure we use the non-graphical classes DefaultTreeModel and DefaultMutableTreeNode. The classes are located in javax.swing.tree. The graphical component is

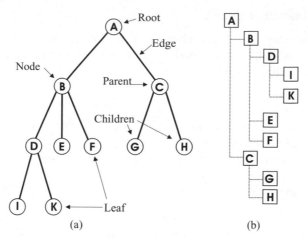

Figure 16.6 Two graphical representations of the same tree: (a) mathematical and (b) used in graphical interfaces

defined in class `JTree` which displays the abstract information of the tree model. The individual nodes of the tree are defined as `DefaultMutableTreeNode`. These are then inserted into the tree model together with the structural information, i.e. the information that tells you which node is a child of which other node. We describe these three classes in the following sections and then show two examples of applications using trees.

16.4.1 □ The class `DefaultMutableTreeNode`

Class `DefaultMutableTreeNode` is a convenience implementation of the interface `TreeNode`. For our applications, the following methods are sufficient:

```
DefaultMutableTreeNode(Object label)
add(DefaultMutableTreeNode node)
```

`DefaultMutableTreeNode(Object label)` defines a mutable tree node. The node receives object `label` as label. When a node is displayed one sees a symbol and the label to the right of the symbol. The label is often a string. The term 'mutable' refers to the fact that clicking on such a node in the display makes the subtree under this node appear or disappear. This function is automatically supplied by `DefaultMutableTreeNode`.

`add(DefaultMutableTreeNode node)` adds node `node` as the right-most child to `this` node. We shall not use this method in our examples but it can be helpful in some situations.

When nodes are displayed, they receive a default symbol. For `DefaultMutableTreeNode` this is the 'folder' symbol of Java if the node is not a leaf. If the node is a leaf the 'file' symbol of Java is displayed.

16.4.2 ☐ Class `TreeModel`

Instances of this class define the abstract structure of the tree. This is done by specifying the root and, for every node, specifying its children and their order. We shall use the following methods.

```
DefaultTreeModel(TreeNode root)

int getChildCount(TreeNode parent)
boolean isLeaf(TreeNode node)
insertNodeInto(MutableTreeNode newChild, MutableTreeNode parent, int k)
Object getChild(TreeNode parent, int k)
removeNodeFromParent(TreeNode child)
```

`DefaultTreeModel(TreeNode root)` creates a tree model with root node `root`. We may use a `DefaultMutableTreeNode` instead of `TreeNode`. There is no parameterless constructor; you must always specify a root node!

`int getChildCount(TreeNode parent)` returns the number of children of parent. If parent has n children they are numbered $0, 1, \ldots, n-1$.

`boolean isLeaf(TreeNode node)` returns `true` if node is a leaf, i.e. has no children, and `false` otherwise.

`insertNodeInto(MutableTreeNode newChild, MutableTreeNode parent, int k)` makes `newChild` the kth child of parent. If parent has n children then k has to be one of $0, 1, 2, \ldots, n$ otherwise a runtime error will occur. If k is strictly less than n then the former children k through $n-1$ become children $k+1$ through n and `newChild` is squeezed in between children $k-1$ and $k+1$.

`Object getChild(TreeNode parent, int k)` returns the kth child of parent as an `Object` and null if the parent does not have a kth child.

`removeNodeFromParent(TreeNode child)` removes child from its parent. Note that the whole subtree with root child is also removed.

16.4.3 ☐ Class `JTree`

The graphical component for displaying trees in Swing is defined in the class `JTree`. We only need the following methods:

```
JTree(TreeModel treeModel)

setTreeModel(TreeModel treeModel)
putClientProperty("JTree.lineStyle","Angled");
```

`JTree(TreeModel treeModel)` receives a `TreeModel` (or a `DefaultTreeModel`) as parameter.

`setTreeModel(TreeModel treeModel)` is used to set the tree model.

`putClientProperty("JTree.lineStyle","Angled")` is used to display the angled lines corresponding to tree's edges. Alternatives to 'Angled' are 'Horizontal', where horizontal lines between the nodes indicate the structure, and 'None' where only indentation is used.

16.4.4 □ Sample applications

In the first sample application we define a tree manually. The structure is like the one in Figure 16.6. The labels are to reflect a simple taxonomy of plants. Class `BiologyTree` is derived from `JTree`. It contains an instance `biologyTreeModel` of class `DefaultTreeModel`. The tree model is constructed by defining the root node and adding other nodes as children of existing ones.

The classes `TreeFrame` and `TreeDemoDriver` are also listed.

File: `its/Trees/BiologyTree.java`

```
package its.Trees;                                                      1.
                                                                        2.
import javax.swing.JTree;                                               3.
import javax.swing.tree.DefaultMutableTreeNode;                         4.
import javax.swing.tree.DefaultTreeModel;                               5.
                                                                        6.
public class BiologyTree extends JTree {                                7.
                                                                        8.
  private DefaultTreeModel biologyTreeModel;                            9.
                                                                       10.
  public BiologyTree(){                                                11.
    makeModel();                                                       12.
    this.setModel(biologyTreeModel);                                   13.
    this.putClientProperty("JTree.lineStyle","Angled");                14.
  }                                                                    15.
                                                                       16.
  private void makeModel(){                                            17.
    DefaultMutableTreeNode root = new DefaultMutableTreeNode("Trees"); 18.
    DefaultMutableTreeNode leaved                                      19.
        = new DefaultMutableTreeNode("Leaved Trees");
    DefaultMutableTreeNode conifer                                     20.
        = new DefaultMutableTreeNode("Conifers");
    DefaultMutableTreeNode beech   = new DefaultMutableTreeNode("Beech"); 21.
    DefaultMutableTreeNode oak     = new DefaultMutableTreeNode("Oak");  22.
    DefaultMutableTreeNode birch   = new DefaultMutableTreeNode("Birch"); 23.
    DefaultMutableTreeNode pine    = new DefaultMutableTreeNode("Pine"); 24.
    DefaultMutableTreeNode fir     = new DefaultMutableTreeNode("Fir");  25.
    DefaultMutableTreeNode beechR                                      26.
        = new DefaultMutableTreeNode("Red Leaved");
```

```
27.      DefaultMutableTreeNode beechG
             = new DefaultMutableTreeNode("Green Leaved");
28.
29.      biologyTreeModel = new  DefaultTreeModel(root);
30.      biologyTreeModel.insertNodeInto(leaved ,root    ,0);
31.      biologyTreeModel.insertNodeInto(conifer,root    ,1);
32.      biologyTreeModel.insertNodeInto(beech   ,leaved ,0);
33.      biologyTreeModel.insertNodeInto(oak     ,leaved ,1);
34.      biologyTreeModel.insertNodeInto(birch   ,leaved ,1);
35.      biologyTreeModel.insertNodeInto(pine    ,conifer,0);
36.      biologyTreeModel.insertNodeInto(fir     ,conifer,1);
37.      biologyTreeModel.insertNodeInto(beechR ,beech   ,0);
38.      biologyTreeModel.insertNodeInto(beechG ,beech   ,1);
39.    }
40. }
```

File: `its/Trees/TreeFrame.java`

```java
1. package its.Trees;
2.
3. import its.SimpleFrame.SimpleFrame;
4. import java.awt.*;
5.
6. public class TreeFrame extends SimpleFrame {
7.
8.    public TreeFrame() {
9.       this.setSize(300,500);
10.      BiologyTree bioTree = new BiologyTree();
11.      this.getContentPane().add(bioTree,BorderLayout.CENTER);
12.   }
13.
14.   public static void main(String[] args) {
15.       TreeFrame treeFrame = new TreeFrame();
16.       treeFrame.showIt("Tree Frame");
17.   }
18. }
```

In the second application we generate a directory tree. The tree is constructed recursively by method `recursion`. We only list the class `Directory-Tree`. The tree displays the directory structure of the `its`-package. The frame class `DirectoryFrame` and the driver class `DirectoryDriver` can be downloaded from the book's home page. The results of both applications are shown in Figure 16.7.

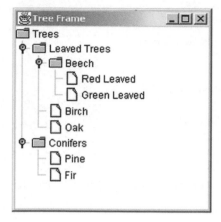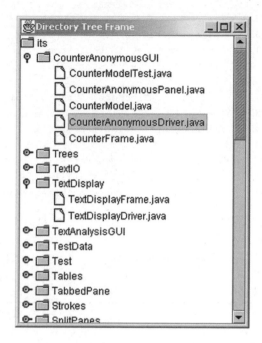

Figure 16.7 The two tree applications

File: its/Trees/DirectoryTree.java

```
package its.Trees;                                                      1.
                                                                        2.
import javax.swing.JTree;                                               3.
import javax.swing.tree.DefaultMutableTreeNode;                         4.
import javax.swing.tree.DefaultTreeModel;                               5.
import java.io.File;                                                    6.
                                                                        7.
public class DirectoryTree extends JTree {                              8.
                                                                        9.
   private DefaultTreeModel directoryTreeModel;                         10.
   //The following path might have to be changed.                       11.
   private  String startDir = "./its";                                  12.
   private File startFile;                                              13.
                                                                        14.
  public DirectoryTree() {                                              15.
    startFile = new File(startDir);                                     16.
    recursion(startFile);                                               17.
    this.setModel(directoryTreeModel);                                  18.
  }                                                                     19.
                                                                        20.
  public DefaultMutableTreeNode recursion(File currentFile)            21.
```

```
22.     {
23.        DefaultMutableTreeNode curNode =
24.             new DefaultMutableTreeNode(currentFile.getName());
25.        if(currentFile == startFile)
26.        {
27.          directoryTreeModel = new DefaultTreeModel(curNode);
28.        }
29.        if(currentFile.isDirectory())
30.         {
31.          File[] files = currentFile.listFiles();
32.           for (int i = 0; i < files.length; i++) {
33.               directoryTreeModel.insertNodeInto(recursion(files[i]),curNode,0);
34.
35.           }//for i
36.         }
37.         return(curNode);
38.       }
39. }
```

16.5 ■ Combo boxes

Combo boxes are graphical components that combine text fields and lists. Like lists, they offer a selection of items to choose from and, like text fields, the user can type a text. Combo boxes are used if there is a predefined set of options that cover most cases but not all. For example, if one wants to enter a date into an electronic appointment book, the current year and the following two will do most of the time. Only rarely are there dates further in the future. It is then convenient to have a list with the current year and the following two to choose from. If the date is at least three years ahead, then one can enter the year number.

16.5.1 ☐ Class `JComboBox`

A combo box looks like a text field with a small button attached at its right side. The button shows an arrow pointing downwards. If the arrow is clicked, a list rolls down out of the text field. Items can be selected from the list or text can be typed into the text field. After selecting an item or hitting the return key the list is rolled up again. Note that text written by the user is not permanently added to the list. We describe some features of class `JComboBox` which implements combo boxes in Swing and then present an application using this graphic component.

```
JComboBox()
JComboBox(String[] listEntries)
JComboBox(Vector[] listEntries)

additem(String listEntry)
```

```
insertItemAt(String listEntry, int pos)
int getSelectedIndex()
Object getSelectedItem()
int getItemCount()
setEditable(boolean b)
setMaximumRowCount(int rowCount)
```

`JComboBox()` generates a combo box with an empty list.

`JComboBox(String[] listEntries)` generates a combo box with a list containing the items of array `listEntries`. The first entry is the first string.

`JComboBox(Vector[] listEntries)` generates a combo box with a list containing the items of vector `listEntries`. The first list entry is the object at position 0 of the vector. If necessary, one has to implement a renderer to draw the objects.

`additem(String listEntry)` adds item `listEntry` at the end of the list.

`insertItemAt(String listEntry, int pos)` inserts `listEntry` at position `pos` into the list. The elements previously at `pos` and further down the list are moved one position down the list.

`getSelectedIndex()` returns the position of the selected list entry. If no item is selected or the user typed in new text then the return value is -1.

`getSelectedItem()` returns either the selected list item or the text entered by the user. As the return type is `Object` one might have to cast it to the desired type.

`getItemCount()` returns the number of items currently in the list.

`setEditable(boolean b)` – if `b` is `false` then the user cannot enter a text into the combo box but is only allowed to select an item from the list. If `b` is `true` the user may also enter a text. The appearance of the combo box depends on this property. Non-editable combo boxes have a grey background, editable ones are white.

`setMaximumRowCount(int rowCount)` sets the length of the visible part of the list to the current value of `rowCount`. If the list contains more items than `rowCount`, a scroll bar automatically appears on the right.

As for lists, there is a data model available for combo boxes: interface `ComboBox-Model` or a class `DefaultComboBoxModel` which implements enough features for most applications. We do not describe the models here; their use is similar to the list models in Section 16.2.3.

16.5.2 □ A calendar with combo boxes

The main part of our application is a panel `CalendarPanel` where the user can select a date. The panel provides only one public method `getDate` which returns the selected date as a string. The date is selected using three combo boxes. One box

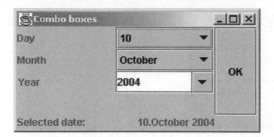

Figure 16.8 The calendar application

contains the day numbers. It cannot be edited but its content changes depending on the setting of month and year. The next combo box contains the month names. It is not editable; we do not allow the user to invent new months. The third combo box contains a list of years from 2004 to 2007. It is editable so the user can select another year by entering its number.

The month box is filled by passing an array with the months' names to the box in the constructor. The day and year boxes are filled in method `initBoxes` by adding the items in for-loops. Also in this method the visible length of boxes are set. For the day box the value is 10 so that a scroll bar will appear in the list.

A listener class `CalendarListener` is defined as an internal class. A `CalendarListener` is associated with the combo boxes for year and month. If an entry is selected in one of these boxes (or a new year is entered by the user) then the listener's `actionPerformed` method is engaged. It has to adjust the days displayed in the day combo box depending on the currently selected year and month. It does so by first determining the year and month. From this the length of the month is computed as one of 28, 29, 30 or 31. The actual adjustment of the day combo box is done by method `setDayListTo`. It compares the current length of the list of the day combo box with the desired one. If the list is too short the appropriate entries are added; if it is too long the last entries are removed.

The method to adjust the length of February is only correct from 1901 to 2099. If the user enters a number outside this range, then the listener sets the year to 2000. The code for `CalendarPanel` is listed below. The test program consists of a frame (`ComboBoxFrame`) and a panel (`DisplayDatePanel`). A `CalendarPanel` is centrally embedded into the frame and a `DisplayDatePanel` is embedded to the south. The frame also has a button labelled 'OK' on the right (east). If clicked, the date currently selected in the `CalendarPanel` is displayed in the `Display-DatePanel`. We do not list the latter classes; they can be downloaded from the book's home page. A screen shot is shown in Figure 16.8.

File: `its/ComboBox/CalendarPanel.java`

```
1. package its.ComboBox;
2.
3. import java.awt.GridLayout;
4. import java.awt.event.ActionEvent;
```

```java
import java.awt.event.ActionListener;                                    5.
import javax.swing.JComboBox;                                            6.
import javax.swing.JLabel;                                               7.
import javax.swing.JPanel;                                               8.
                                                                         9.
public class CalendarPanel extends JPanel {                             10.
private String[] months = {"January","February","March","April",       11.
                           "May","June","July","August",                12.
                           "September","October","November","December"};13.
private JComboBox yearBox   = new JComboBox();                          14.
private JComboBox monthBox = new JComboBox(months);                     15.
private JComboBox dayBox    = new JComboBox();                          16.
private JLabel yearLabel    = new JLabel("Year ");                      17.
private JLabel monthLabel   = new JLabel("Month ");                     18.
private JLabel dayLabel     = new JLabel("Day ");                       19.
private JLabel dummy        = new JLabel("");                           20.
private int startyear;                                                  21.
private int endyear;                                                    22.
                                                                        23.
public CalendarPanel() {                                                24.
  this.setLayout(new GridLayout(4,2));                                  25.
  startyear = 2004;                                                     26.
  endyear   = 2007;                                                     27.
  initBoxes();                                                          28.
  this.add(dayLabel);                                                   29.
  this.add(dayBox);                                                     30.
  this.add(monthLabel);                                                 31.
  this.add(monthBox);                                                   32.
  this.add(yearLabel);                                                  33.
  this.add(ycarBox);                                                    34.
  this.add(dummy);                                                      35.
                                                                        36.
  yearBox.setEditable(true);                                           37.
  CalenderListener cList = new CalenderListener();                      38.
  yearBox.setActionCommand("YearChanged");                             39.
  yearBox.addActionListener(cList);                                    40.
  monthBox.setActionCommand("MonthChanged");                           41.
  monthBox.addActionListener(cList);                                   42.
}                                                                       43.
                                                                        44.
 private void initBoxes()                                              45.
 {                                                                      46.
   for (int y=startyear;y <= endyear;y++ )                             47.
   {                                                                    48.
     yearBox.addItem(Integer.toString(y));                             49.
   }//for                                                              50.
   for (int d=1;d<=31 ;d++ )                                           51.
```

```
52.    {
53.       dayBox.addItem(Integer.toString(d));
54.    }//for
55.    monthBox.setMaximumRowCount(12);
56.    dayBox.setMaximumRowCount(10);
57.    yearBox.setMaximumRowCount(4);
58.  }
59.
60.  private void  setDayListTo(int desiredLength){
61.    int currentLength = dayBox.getItemCount();
62.    if(currentLength < desiredLength){
63.      for (int i = currentLength+1; i <= desiredLength; i++) {
64.        dayBox.addItem(Integer.toString(i));
65.      }//for i
66.      }
67.    else if (currentLength > desiredLength)
68.    {
69.      for (int i = currentLength-1; i >= desiredLength; i--) {
70.        dayBox.removeItemAt(i);
71.      }//for i
72.    }
73.  }
74.
75. public String getDate(){
76.  return((String)dayBox.getSelectedItem()+"."+
77.         (String)monthBox.getSelectedItem()+" "+
78.         (String)yearBox.getSelectedItem());
79. }
80.
81. class CalenderListener implements ActionListener
82. {
83.    public void actionPerformed(ActionEvent evt){
84.    String actionCommand = evt.getActionCommand();
85.    int year = Integer.parseInt(((String)yearBox.getSelectedItem()).trim());
86.    int month = monthBox.getSelectedIndex();
87.    if((year > 2099) || (year < 1901)){
88.      year = 2000;
89.      yearBox.setSelectedItem("2000");
90.    }
91.    if(actionCommand.equals("YearChanged"))
92.    {
93.       if((year % 4 == 0) && (month == 1)){
94.        setDayListTo(29);
95.       }
96.    }
97.    else if(actionCommand.equals("MonthChanged"))
```

```
{                                                                        98.
  if((month == 0) || (month == 2) || (month == 4) || (month == 6) ||     99.
     (month == 7) || (month == 9) || (month == 11)){                    100.
          setDayListTo(31);                                             101.
     }                                                                  102.
  else if(month == 1){                                                  103.
     if(year % 4 == 0){                                                 104.
       setDayListTo(29);                                                105.
     }                                                                  106.
     else                                                               107.
     {                                                                  108.
       setDayListTo(28);                                                109.
     }//ifelse                                                          110.
   }//ifelse                                                            111.
  else{                                                                 112.
    setDayListTo(30);                                                   113.
    }//ifelse                                                           114.
  }//ifelse                                                             115.
 }//actionPerformed                                                     116.
}//internal class                                                       117.
}                                                                       118.
```

16.6 ■ Split panes

Split panes can be seen as a pair of panels inside a rectangular area. The pro-grammer can embed graphical components into each of the areas. The two com-ponents are separated by a vertical or horizontal bar, called a *divider*. The divider bar can be moved by using the mouse, thus adjusting the visible area of the two components. If the divider is moved to the left or right margin of the split pane (in case of a vertical separation) then only the right (or left), component is visible.

Split panes are used, for example, if information is displayed in different for-mats. Think of stock market data which can be displayed as a chart in one com-ponent while another contains textual information such as high/low quotes and trading volume. The split pane then allows the user to focus on one or the other by moving the divider.

Class `JSplitPane` implements these functions in Swing. We introduce some methods of this class and show a small example application `SplitPaneFrame`.

```
JSplitPane(int division)

setLeftComponent(Component comp)
setRightComponent(Component comp)
setTopComponent(Component comp)
setBottomComponent(Component comp)
```

```
setDividerSize(int width)
setDividerLocation(int pos)
setDividerLocation(double fraction)
setOneTouchExpandable(boolean b)
```

JSplitPane(int division) is the constructor. Parameter division specifies whether the division is horizontal or vertical. There are predefined constants HORIZONTAL_SPLIT and VERTICAL_SPLIT in class JSplitPane. Observe that choosing HORIZONTAL_SPLIT determines that the two components are placed horizontally next to each other; the divider bar is the vertical. Similarly VERTICAL_SPLIT results in placing one component on top of the other and a horizontal divider bar.

setXXXComponent(Component comp) embeds component comp into one of the two areas. For XXX = Left, comp becomes the left component if HORIZONTAL_SPLIT is used. If XXX = Left is used with VERTICAL_SPLIT then comp becomes the top component. The other choices for XXX then have the obvious meanings.

setDividerSize(int width) determines the width of the divider bar in pixels.

setDividerLocation(int pos) determines the position of the divider bar. Parameter pos is the distance of the divider bar from the left margin of the split pane when HORIZONTAL_SPLIT is used, and from the upper margin when VERTICAL_SPLIT is used.

setDividerLocation(double fraction) determines the position of the divider bar. Parameter fraction is the fraction of the JSplitPane's size horizontal or vertical size, depending on the way it is split. Therefore fraction has to be in the interval [0, 1], otherwise an IllegalArgumentException is thrown. The fraction refers to the *current* width of the split-pane. If this method is called before the component is visible then the width is zero and the divider will be at the left (or top) margin.

setOneTouchExpandable(boolean b) – if parameter b is true then two small arrows appear on the divider bar. They point towards the two areas. When clicking on one arrow the divider bar jumps in that direction. If the divider bar is not at a margin of the split pane, it jumps to that margin to which the arrow points. If it is at the margin it jumps back to the previous position. If parameter b is false the arrows are not shown and the described functions are not available.

In our demonstration SplitPaneFrame we use nested split panes. At first a split pane splitPane1 with a vertical divider (HORIZONTAL_SPLIT) is centrally embedded into a frame. The width of the divider is set to 20 pixels and it receives an arrow to enable jumping. Into its right area another split pane splitPane2 is embedded. This has a horizontal divider. This arrangement results in three areas. Into the left area of splitPane1 we embed a JList which lists the file names of some directory. Into each of the two areas of splitPane2 we embed a JLabel which displays an ImageIcon. All three aforementioned components are embedded using scroll panes so that their whole content can be accessed by scrolling.

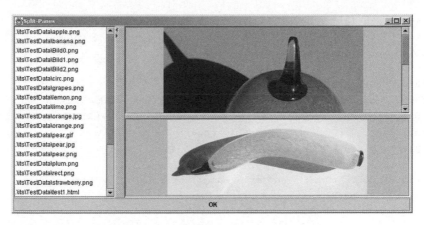

Figure 16.9 Demonstration of split panes in application SplitPaneFrame

The control part of the application allows the user to select an image from the list on the left and display it in the lower right area. To this end he or she has to select a file name in the list and press the button that is embedded into the frame's 'South' position. The control part is here implemented as an anonymous listener. The program checks whether the selected file has an extension which indicates an image file. Only files with extensions .jpg or .png are loaded; other selections are ignored. One of the images, the one of the orange, is available as an uncompressed PNG-format and a strongly compressed JPG-format. Loading the latter into the lower right component and comparing it with the constantly displayed PNG-image at the upper right makes the loss of quality visible. We list the program below and a screen shot is shown in Figure 16.9.

File: its/SplitPanes/SplitPaneFrame.java

```
package its.SplitPanes;                                    1.
                                                           2.
import its.SimpleFrame.SimpleFrame;                        3.
import java.awt.*;                                         4.
import java.awt.event.ActionEvent;                         5.
import java.awt.event.ActionListener;                      6.
import java.io.File;                                       7.
import javax.swing.*;                                      8.
                                                           9.
public class SplitPaneFrame extends SimpleFrame           10.
{                                                         11.
  private JButton okButton;                               12.
  private JList list;                                     13.
  private JLabel picLabel1, picLabel2;                    14.
  private ImageIcon picture1, picture2;                   15.
                                                          16.
```

```
17.    private static String picturePath = "./its/TestData/";
18.
19.    public SplitPaneFrame()
20.    {
21.      this.setSize(800,400);
22.      JSplitPane splitPane1 = new JSplitPane(JSplitPane.HORIZONTAL_SPLIT);
23.      JSplitPane splitPane2 = new JSplitPane(JSplitPane.VERTICAL_SPLIT);
24.      splitPane1.setOneTouchExpandable(true);
25.      splitPane1.setDividerSize(20);
26.
27.      this.getContentPane().add(splitPane1,BorderLayout.CENTER);
28.      splitPane1.setRightComponent(splitPane2);
29.
30.      picture1 = new ImageIcon(picturePath+"/Orange.png");
31.      picture2 = new ImageIcon(picturePath+"/Banana.png");
32.
33.      picLabel1 = new JLabel(picture1);
34.      JScrollPane sp2a = new JScrollPane(picLabel1);
35.      splitPane2.setTopComponent(sp2a);
36.      picLabel2 = new JLabel(picture2);
37.      JScrollPane sp2b = new JScrollPane(picLabel2);
38.      splitPane2.setBottomComponent(sp2b);
39.      splitPane2.setDividerLocation(150);
40.      splitPane1.setDividerLocation(100);
41.
42.      File startFile = new File(picturePath);
43.      list = new JList(startFile.listFiles());
44.      JScrollPane sp = new JScrollPane(list);
45.      splitPane1.setLeftComponent(sp);
46.
47.      okButton = new JButton("OK");
48.      okButton.setBackground(Color.cyan);
49.      this.getContentPane().add(okButton,BorderLayout.SOUTH);
50.      okButton.addActionListener(new ActionListener()
51.      {
52.        public void actionPerformed(ActionEvent e)
53.        {
54.           String filename = ((File)(list.getSelectedValue())).getPath();
55.          if((filename.endsWith(".png")) || (filename.endsWith(".jpg")) ||
56.             (filename.endsWith(".PNG")) || (filename.endsWith(".JPG")))
57.          {
58.            picLabel2.setIcon(new ImageIcon(filename));
59.          }
60.        }
61.      });
62.    }
63.
```

```
public static void main(String[] args)                          64.
{                                                               65.
  SplitPaneFrame spf = new SplitPaneFrame();                    66.
  spf.showIt("Split-Panes",200,200);                            67.
}                                                               68.
}                                                               69.
```

16.7 ■ Tabbed panes

Split panes are used to display two documents and to vary the view of them. A different Swing component should be considered if an application generates a large number of documents. In this section we introduce *tabbed panes*. They can administer a large number of documents, only one of which is visible at a time. The user can rapidly switch between them. One can imagine a tabbed pane as a stack of papers each of which contains some textual or pictorial information. In addition every page has a *tab*. Only the topmost page is visible. Another page can become the topmost one by grabbing its tab, pulling it out and putting it on top of the stack. See Figure 16.10 for an example.

In Swing, this mechanism is implemented in class JTabbedPane. A tabbed pane is initially empty, i.e. it contains no pages. Then components are added and each of them becomes a new page. When adding a component, the text for the tab should be provided. The tabs are arranged from left to right (or from top to bottom) in the order in which the components are added. Selecting a component as the topmost one does not change the order of the tabs. This order is reflected in the so-called indices. Every page has an index (index). A tabbed pane with n pages has indices $0, 1, \ldots, n - 1$. The index of the component with the left most (topmost) tab is 0. The indices can, for example, be used to remove a component or to insert a new one at a certain position.

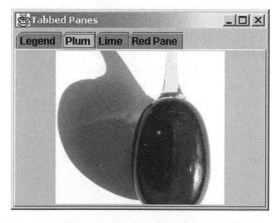

Figure 16.10 The third page of the example application for tabbed panes

```
TabbedPane();
TabbedPane(int tabPosition);

add(Component comp);
add(String tabText, Component comp);
add(Component comp, int index);
setTitleAt(int pos, String tabTitle);
setSelectedComponent(Component comp);
setSelectedIndex(int pos)
```

`TabbedPane()` – constructor. The tabs are placed on the upper edge.

`TabbedPane(int tabPosition)` – constructor in which one can specify the position of the tabs. The four values for parameter `tabPosition` are predefined in class `JTabbedPane`: `TOP`, `BOTTOM`, `LEFT`, `RIGHT`.

`add(Component comp)` adds `comp` as last page. 'Last' means that the tab is the right-most (or bottom-most) one. The tab does not have any text.

`add(String tabText, Component comp)` adds `comp` as last page. 'Last' means that the tab is the right-most (or bottom-most) one. The tab is labelled by `tabTitle`.

`add(Component comp, int index)` adds `comp` such that the corresponding tab is at position `index`. The tab does not have any text.

`setTitleAt(int pos, String tabTitle)` assigns a new text `tabTitle` to the tab at position `pos`.

`setSelectedComponent(Component comp)` selects the page containing component `comp`, i.e. this page is made visible.

`setSelectedIndex(int pos)` selects the page whose tab is at position `pos`, i.e. this page is made visible.

The listing `TabbedPaneFrame` below shows how to use a tabbed pane. As we do not add any new functions we use a `JTabbedPane` and do not extend it into a new class. The tabbed pane is glued into a frame. Then four components are added to to the tabbed pane. At first we add two `JLabel`s, each displaying an image. Then we add red `ColorPanel`. This is defined in the package `its.SimpleFrameWithPanels`. Finally we add a `JTextArea` which contains some text describing what the four components are. The `JTextArea` is added at position 0 so that its tab is the left-most. We then set the selected index to 1 which makes the image of the plum visible. The result is shown in Figure 16.10.

File: `its/TabbedPane/TabbedPaneFrame.java`

```
1. package its.TabbedPane;
2.
3. import its.SimpleFrame.SimpleFrame;
4. import its.SimpleFrameWithPanels.ColorPanel;
```

```
import java.awt.Color;                                              5.
import javax.swing.*;                                               6.
                                                                    7.
public class TabbedPaneFrame extends SimpleFrame                    8.
{                                                                   9.
                                                                    10.
  private static String picturePath = "./its/TestData/";           11.
                                                                    12.
  public TabbedPaneFrame()                                          13.
  {                                                                 14.
   // Create a tabbed pane and glue into the frame                  15.
    JTabbedPane tabbedPane = new JTabbedPane();                     16.
    this.getContentPane().add(tabbedPane);                          17.
                                                                    18.
   // Generate two labels each of which contains an image           19.
   // and add them to the tabbed pane                               20.
    ImageIcon plum = new ImageIcon(picturePath+"plum.png");        21.
    JLabel plumLabel = new JLabel(plum);                            22.
    ImageIcon lime = new ImageIcon(picturePath+"lime.png");        23.
    JLabel limeLabel = new JLabel(lime);                            24.
                                                                    25.
    tabbedPane.add("Plum",plumLabel);                               26.
    tabbedPane.add("Lime",limeLabel);                               27.
                                                                    28.
   // Generate a red panel from its.SimpleFrameWithPanels.ColorPanel 29.
   // and add it.                                                   30.
    ColorPanel redPane = new ColorPanel(Color.red);               31.
    tabbedPane.add("Red Pane", redPane);                           32.
                                                                    33.
   // Generate a text area and add it as the first (0-th)           34.
   // component.                                                    35.
    JTextArea legend = new  JTextArea();                            36.
    legend.setText("Legend in a JTextArea\n"+                       37.
                   "JLabel showing a plum\n"+                       38.
                   "JLabel showing a lime\n"+                       39.
                   "A red Panel");                                  30.
    tabbedPane.add(legend,0);                                       41.
    tabbedPane.setTitleAt(0,"Legend");                              42.
    tabbedPane.setSelectedIndex(1);                                 43.
  }                                                                 44.
                                                                    45.
  public static void main(String[] args) {                          46.
    TabbedPaneFrame tpf = new TabbedPaneFrame();                    47.
    tpf.setSize(300,200);                                           48.
    tpf.showIt("Tabbed Panes",200,200);                             49.
  }                                                                 50.
}                                                                   51.
```

Class JTabbedPane offers a large number of ways to change the appearance. One can, for example, use icons as labels for the tabs or change the background colour of the pages. If a tabbed pane contains a large number of pages and the tabs do not fit into a single line then they are arranged in rows. This can have the effect that the space for displaying the selected page is very small. Since version 1.4 of the SDK it is possible to use *scrollable tabs*. The tabs are then arranged in a single row which can be scrolled left or right.

Exercises

16.1 Implement a GUI with the same layout as ListTransferFrame and the following functions. When an entry in the left list is selected it is *moved* to the right one, i.e. removed from the left and added to the right list. When an entry in the right list is selected it is *moved* to the left one.

16.2 Implement a GUI with a similar layout as ListTransferFrame and the following functions. Add two buttons labelled 'Move to right' and 'Move to left' to the GUI and allow arbitrary selections in both lists. Selecting entries in one of the lists does not trigger any action. Pressing one of the buttons causes the appropriate selection to be moved to the other list.

Grid-bag layout

17

We present the most powerful but also the most complicated layout manager of Java, the grid-bag layout. This layout manager allows us to design complex arrangements of components without using stacks of nested intermediate components.

The grid layout described in Chapter 2 allows a component to be embedded in one cell of the grid and all cells have the same size. The *grid-bag layout* discussed here allows different widths or heights for different columns and rows. In addition, a component can be embedded to cover more than one cell. These cells then form a *bag*, i.e. a rectangular sub-grid.

When using grid-bag layout, the components are not placed according to the order of the add commands. The placement is done by passing to the layout manager information on the position of every component and on the size of the bag it has to be embedded into.

The grid-bag layout is a bit tricky to use. Many beginners give up using this very powerful tool after a few tries because 'it does not do what it is told to do'. We first discuss and analyse these problems and then show how to solve them. Only then do we turn to describing the Java classes involved in realizing a grid bag layout.

The example layout is specified in Figure 17.1. The layout consists of six panels that are embedded into a parent component, e.g. the content pane of frame. As a first step we determine the size of the grid, i.e. the number of rows and columns. Here a 4×4 grid seems appropriate. The grid is indicated by dashed lines in Figure 17.1. The columns and rows are numbered from left to right and from top to bottom, both starting with zero. The grid structure, i.e. the number of rows and columns, is **not** explicitly specified by the programmer. Instead the programmer specifies the size and location of the embedded components. The layout manager then computes the necessary grid structure. This computation is, however, not always done in the way we expect, as we shall shortly see.

The *size* of a component is specified as the number of columns and rows it spans. In Figure 17.1 panel A spans two columns and three rows and panel D spans one column and two rows. The *location* of a component is specified by the left-most column and top-most row it covers. In Figure 17.1 panel A is located at $(0, 0)$ and B is at $(2, 0)$. Table 17.1 summarizes the parameters for the six panels. In the next section we describe how these values are passed to the layout manager.

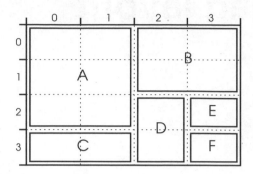

Figure 17.1 Sketch of the desired layout. The tick marks at the upper and left margins indicate the dimensions of the panels. For example, panels A and C should be half as wide as the parent component and panel A should be three-quarters the height of the parent component. The underlying 4 × 4 grid is shown as dashed lines. With respect to this grid, panel C has a width of 2 (columns) and a height of 1 (row). Its position is column 0 and row 3

Table 17.1 The size and location parameters for the six panels in the layout of Figure 17.1

Panel	Width	Height	Left	Top
A	2	3	0	0
B	2	2	2	0
C	2	1	0	3
D	1	2	2	2
E	1	1	3	2
F	1	1	3	3

Using these values would give the result shown in Figure 17.2. The corresponding program GridBagFrameBad is not listed here but can be downloaded from the book's home page. The figure shows two deficiencies: the panels A and C are only one-third the width of the frame (not a half) and panel B is only one-third the height of the frame, not a half. This is because when the layout manager computes the grid size from the values in Table 17.1 it deletes unnecessary column and row boundaries. These are boundaries that do not coincide with the boundary of some component. In our example the boundary between columns 0 and 1 in Figure 17.1 is unnecessary. At no place does it coincide with a component boundary. On the other hand the boundary between columns 2 and 3 is necessary; it coincides with the right boundary of panel D and the left boundaries of panels E and F. Inspecting the other row and column boundaries shows that the one between row 0 and row 1 is unnecessary and is thus deleted by the layout manager. All other bounds are necessary. The layout used by the layout manager is then a 3 × 3 grid. All columns are equally wide and all rows are equally high. This explains why the result shown in Figure 17.2 differs from the specification in Figure 17.1.

The way to adjust the width and height of components is thus not to introduce additional columns and rows but to assign *weights* to the columns and rows. We

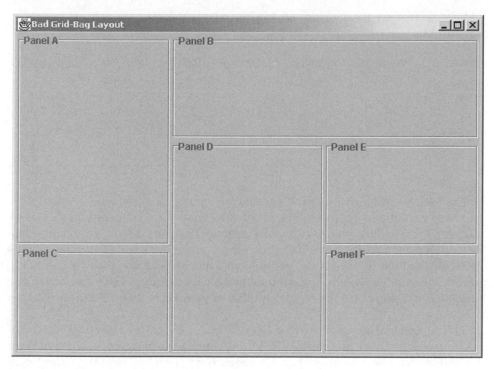

Figure 17.2 The result of application `GridBagFrameBad`

sketch the desired layout in Figure 17.3. Only the necessary columns and rows are introduced. Recall that the columns and rows are not explicitly defined by the user. They are computed by the layout manager from dimensions and locations of the embedded components. The figure also shows the weights given to the columns and rows. The first column gets weight 2.0, the second and third ones both have

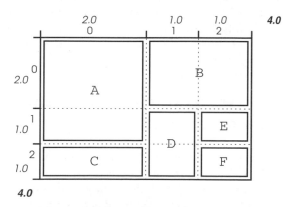

Figure 17.3 A sketch of the desired layout that reflects the column–row structure implicitly used by the layout manager. The resulting 3 × 3 grid is shown by dashed lines. The weights are shown at the top and left. The sums of the column and row weights are shown in **bold**

Table 17.2 The size, location and weight parameters for the six panels in the layout of Figure 17.3

Panel	Width	Height	Left	Top	Weightx	Weighty
A	1	2	0	0	2.0	1.0
B	2	1	1	0	1.0	2.0
C	1	1	0	2	1.0	1.0
D	1	2	1	1	1.0	1.0
E	1	1	2	1	1.0	1.0
F	1	1	2	2	1.0	1.0

weight 1.0. We still have the problem that we cannot directly set the weights for the rows or columns because rows and columns are internal concepts of the layout manager. We can, however, assign two weights to the embedded components. The horizontal weight (called weight$x$) affects the component's width and the vertical one (called weight$y$) affects the component's height. The weight of a column is then the maximum weight of a component in that column. Thus, by setting the horizontal weight of panel A to 2.0 and that of panel C to 1.0, column 0 receives weight 2.0.

The weight of the topmost row (row 0) is set by using a vertical weight of 2.0 for panel B. Using the vertical weight of panel A for this purpose would have side-effects on row 1 because panel A spans rows 0 and 1. All other horizontal and vertical weights are set to 1.0. Then row 1, row 2, column 1 and column 2 all receive weight 1. The parameters are listed in Table 17.2. These settings will result in the desired layout.

The column widths (or row heights) are then computed as follows. Let $w_0, \ldots, w_n$ be the $n+1$ column weights. Let $W = w_0 + \cdots + w_n$ be the sum of the weights. Then the width of column i is a fraction of w_i/W of the width of the parent component. In our case $w_0 = 2.0$, $w_1 = 1.0$, $w_2 = 1.0$ and $W = 4.0$. Hence column 0 gets $2.0/4.0 = 1/2$ of the width of the parent component while columns 1 and 2 each get $1.0/4.0 = 1/4$. This shows that the absolute values of the weights are irrelevant; only their ratio is important. We might have used the set $w_0 = 0.2, w_1 = 0.1, w_2 = 0.1$ or $w_0 = 6.0, w_1 = 3.0, w_2 = 3.0$ without changing the result.

17.1 ■ The classes `GridBagLayout` and `GridBagConstraints`

Two classes are needed to use a grid-bag layout, both of which are defined in the library `java.awt`. Class `GridBagLayout` defines the actual layout manager. The other class, `GridBagConstraints`, is a helper class to specify the size, dimension and weight parameters for every component. Basically, an instance of `GridBag-Constraints` represents one row of Table 17.2. Every component to be embedded into a grid-bag layout has its own `GridBagConstraints` object.

A `GridBagConstraints` object has a number of fields to store the layout parameters of a component. The class does not have any `set` or `get` methods to access these parameters. Instead the fields are `public` and can be directly accessed from the outside – quite a non-object-oriented approach. In the following we list some of the fields and their interpretation.

int	gridwidth	the number of columns spanned
int	gridheight	the number of rows spanned
int	gridx	the left-most column
int	gridy	the top-most row
double	weightx	the horizontal weight
double	weighty	the vertical weight
int	fill	determines whether the component is resized to fit the bag.

The layout parameter `fill` determines whether an embedded component should be resized such that it fills the bag. The possible values NONE, BOTH, HORIZONTAL and VERTICAL are defined as constants in `GridBagConstraints`. We always use `fill = BOTH` here, which resizes the component to precisely fit its bag. The reader is encouraged to try other settings for the various components. Class `GridBagConstraints` has more fields which we do not discuss here; the user is referred to the Java documentation.

The following code snippet shows how to set the constraints for panel A of our application. First an instance of `GridBagConstraints` is generated, then the fields are set to the desired values. The values are those of the corresponding line in Table 17.2.

```
GridBagConstraints constraintsA = new  GridBagConstraints();

constraintsA.gridwidth  = 1;   // The width of panel A.
constraintsA.gridheight = 2;   // The height of panel A.
constraintsA.gridx      = 0;   // Left column of panel A.
constraintsA.gridy      = 0;   // Top row of panel A.
constraintsA.weightx    = 2.0; // The horizontal weight of panel A.
constraintsA.weighty    = 1.0; // The vertical weight of panel A.
constraintsA.fill       = GridBagConstraints.BOTH; // resize panel A
                                                   // to fit its bag.
```

We still have to link the constraints to the panel. This is done by using method:

```
setConstraints(Component embeddedComp,GridBagConstraints constraints);
```

of class `GridBagLayout`. In our case the panel is called `panelA` and the constraints `constraintsA`:

```
setConstraints(panelA,constraintsA);
```

Summarizing, the following steps are necessary to use a grid-bag layout for embedding components `comp0`, `...,compK`, `...compN` into parent component `parent`:

- Sketch the desired layout on paper and determine how many rows and columns are necessary. Also determine the weights you want to use.

- Create an instance `gbl` of `GridBagLayout` and assign it to `parent` by `parent.setLayout(gbl)`.

- For every component `compK` to be embedded do the following:
  - (a) Create an instance `constraintsK` of `GridBagConstraints` and set the parameters.
  - (b) Link the constraints `constraintsK` to `compK` using `gbl.setConstraints-(compK,constraintsK)`.
  - (c) Embed `compK` into `parent` by `parent.add(compK)` (or `parent.getContentPane().add(compK)` in case `parent` is a frame).

Creating and setting the constraints for every component would result in many lines of nearly identical code. In the example application `GridBagFrame` we defined a private method `easyConstraints` that does all this work. It receives the constraint values, the component and the layout as arguments. It then creates an instance of `GridBagConstraints`, sets the values, and links constraints and components. The field `fill` is always set to `BOTH`. The GUI created by this program is shown in Figure 17.4.

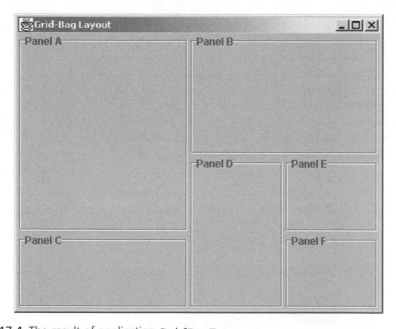

Figure 17.4 The result of application `GridBagFrame`

File: `its/GridBag/GridBagFrame.java`

```
package its.GridBag;                                              1.
                                                                 2.
import its.Borders.BorderPanel;                                  3.
import its.SimpleFrame.SimpleFrame;                              4.
import java.awt.GridBagConstraints;                              5.
import java.awt.GridBagLayout;                                   6.
import javax.swing.JComponent;                                   7.
                                                                 8.
public class GridBagFrame extends SimpleFrame                    9.
{                                                                10.
  private GridBagLayout gbl = new GridBagLayout();               11.
  public GridBagFrame()                                          12.
  {                                                              13.
    this.getContentPane().setLayout(gbl);                        14.
    BorderPanel panelA = new BorderPanel("Panel A");             15.
    BorderPanel panelB = new BorderPanel("Panel B");             16.
    BorderPanel panelC = new BorderPanel("Panel C");             17.
    BorderPanel panelD = new BorderPanel("Panel D");             18.
    BorderPanel panelE = new BorderPanel("Panel E");             19.
    BorderPanel panelF = new BorderPanel("Panel F");             20.
                                                                 21.
    this.getContentPane().add(panelA);                           22.
    this.getContentPane().add(panelB);                           23.
    this.getContentPane().add(panelC);                           24.
    this.getContentPane().add(panelD);                           25.
    this.getContentPane().add(panelE);                           26.
    this.getContentPane().add(panelF);                           27.
                                                                 28.
    easyConstraints(gbl,panelA,1,2,0,0,2.0,1.0);                 29.
    easyConstraints(gbl,panelB,2,1,1,0,1.0,2.0);                 30.
    easyConstraints(gbl,panelC,1,1,0,2,1.0,1.0);                 31.
    easyConstraints(gbl,panelD,1,2,1,1,1.0,1.0);                 32.
    easyConstraints(gbl,panelE,1,1,2,1,1.0,1.0);                 33.
    easyConstraints(gbl,panelF,1,1,2,2,1.0,1.0);                 34.
  }                                                              35.
                                                                 36.
  private void easyConstraints(GridBagLayout GLB,JComponent Comp, 37.
              int w, int h, int x, int y,double wx, double wy){  38.
    GridBagConstraints constraints = new  GridBagConstraints();  39.
    constraints.fill = GridBagConstraints.BOTH;                  40.
    constraints.gridwidth =  w;                                  41.
    constraints.gridheight = h;                                  42.
    constraints.gridx = x;                                       43.
    constraints.gridy = y;                                       44.
```

```
45.        constraints.weightx = wx;
46.        constraints.weighty = wy;
47.        gbl.setConstraints(Comp,constraints);
48.      }
49.
50.    public static void main(String[] args){
51.      GridBagFrame gridbagFrame = new GridBagFrame();
52.      gridbagFrame.showIt("Grid-Bag Layout");
53.
54.    }
55. }
```

Exercises

17.1   Change the constraint parameters for some of the panels in application Grid-BagFrame. Look at the result and explain why it looks the way it does.

17.2   Change method easyConstraints so that the fill value can also be set. Try different settings and explain the result.

17.3   Design a grid-bag layout for the GUI in Figure 17.5.

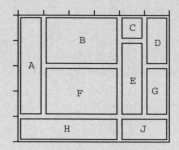

Figure 17.5 Sketch of the GUI to be designed in Exercise 17.3

Advanced topics

Styling text

18

When text is displayed, there is often a need to use different font styles, sizes or colours to emphasize parts of the text. We now show how this can be done by using a so-called document model for the text. The model allows style attributes to be assigned to parts of the text that are automatically moved when text is inserted or deleted.

Swing provides non-graphical classes that model text documents. They allow manipulations of the text such as insertion and deletions and the assignment of different styles to different parts of the text. When such a text model is displayed in a text component, the styles become visible. By using a text model the style and formatting are done abstractly and are independent of the display used. Listeners can be attributed to documents to trigger actions in response to changes in the text.

The `javax.swing.text` sub-library contains the interface `Document` and some classes implementing this interface. We will use class `DefaultStyledDocument` which supplies many methods to modify the layout of normal (ASCII) text. There is another predefined class, `HTMLDocument`, which provides a method for styling HTML formatted text. If these classes do not provide the layout features for the text under consideration, then one has to define one's own document class by implementing interface `Document` or by extending an existing class. We proceed by introducing a number of helper classes for formatting text documents and then show how they are used.

18.1 ■ Positions

Most operations on documents rely on the concept of a *position marker*. These are defined in class `Position`[1]. A *text* is a sequence of letters or symbols. We prefer the word 'symbols' because spaces and punctuation signs are also considered. A *position* designates a place between two consecutive symbols. The *offset* of a position is the number of symbols between it and the beginning of the text. The position before the first symbol (symbol number zero) has offset 0, the one after

---

[1] The name `Position` is misleading. An instance of `Position` does not specify a position in the document that is fixed, but one that moves if text is deleted or inserted.

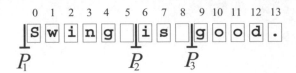

Figure 18.1 A text of 14 symbols. The numbering of the symbols begins with 0 and is shown above the text. Three positions markers, P_1, P_2 and P_3, are shown. P_1 has offset 0 as there is no symbol between it and the start of the text, P_2 has offset 6 because it is immediately before the 6th symbol and P_3 has offset 9

the first symbol has offset 1, etc. In the next section we use position markers to specify the beginning and end of text parts that receive specific formatting. Figure 18.1 illustrates the concept of position markers.

Let us now see what happens to position markers when the text is changed. We begin by inserting a single symbol, an m say, between the symbols 5 and 6 of the text in Figure 18.1. Then all symbols of the original text beginning with the one numbered 6 are moved one place to the right and the new symbol is inserted at place 6. Position marker P_3 is moved with the text; its offset is increased from 9 to 10. The new letter is inserted precisely at the position occupied by marker P_2. The convention is that the insertion happens *before* the marker. Hence the offset of P_2 is increased to 7. The result is shown in Figure 18.2.

Let us now see what happens to position markers when text is deleted. Let us first assume that the deleted text does not contain a position marker. In the original text of Figure 18.1 let us delete the symbols 2 to 5 (ing_). All position markers to the right of the deleted text will move left, i.e. their offsets are decreased. The result is shown in Figure 18.3.

Let us now delete the symbols 4 to 10 (g_is_go) in Figure 18.1, including both spaces. This range includes position markers P_2 and P_3. Though the symbols are deleted, the two markers are not. They are now at the position formerly occupied by the deleted text. Figure 18.4 shows the result.

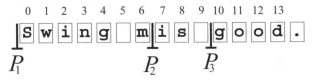

Figure 18.2 Inserting letter m at position 6 moves P_2 and P_3 to the right

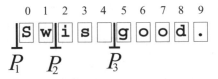

Figure 18.3 The result of deleting symbols ing_ in Figure 18.1. P_2 and P_3 move left to offsets 2 and 5

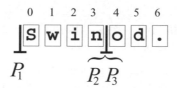

Figure 18.4 As a result of deleting symbols g_is_go the two position markers P_2 and P_3 now occupy the same place. Both have offset 4

Position markers are implemented in interface `Position` in the `javax.swing.text` library. There is only one method

```
int getOffset()
```

which returns the current offset of the position marker.

18.2 ■ Text attributes

In a text document, one can assign *text attributes* to parts of the text. These specify the text style (bold, italics), size, colour and more.

In Swing, text attributes are provided by interface `AttributeSet`. A predefined implementation of this interface is class `SimpleAttributeSet`, which we shall use in the following. Both are found in the library `javax.swing.text`. In an attribute set one can, for example, specify that the text should be bold or italic and have size (height) 14 points (pixels). Then this attribute set can be assigned to different text parts and all these parts are displayed in the specified way. We only need the constructor from this class:

```
SimpleAttributeSet();
```

To set the attribute values of an attribute set `attrSet` one uses methods from another class, namely `StyleConstants`. We list and explain some of them:

```
setForeground(SimpleAttributeSet attrSet, Color c)
setBackground(SimpleAttributeSet attrSet, Color c)
setFontSize(SimpleAttributeSet attrSet, int size)
setBold(SimpleAttributeSet attrSet, boolean b)
setItalic(SimpleAttributeSet attrSet, boolean b)
setUnderline(SimpleAttributeSet attrSet, boolean b)
setSuperscript(SimpleAttributeSet attrSet, boolean b)
setSubscript(SimpleAttributeSet attrSet, boolean b)
```

`setForeground(SimpleAttributeSet attrSet, Color c)` sets the text colour in `attrSet` to `c`. The default is the text colour of the graphical component which displays the text, usually black.

`setBackground(SimpleAttributeSet attrSet, Color c)` sets background colour in `attrSet` to `c`. The default is the background colour of the graphical component that displays the text, usually white.

`setFontSize(SimpleAttributeSet attrSet, int size)` sets font size in `attrSet` to `size` points (pixels). The default is the default size of the graphical component that displays the text, often 12 or 14 points.

`setBold(SimpleAttributeSet attrSet, boolean b)` determines whether the text formatted according to `attrSet` should be **bold** (b = `true`) or not (b = `false`). The default value is b = `false`.

`setItalic(SimpleAttributeSet attrSet, boolean b)` determines whether the text formatted according to `attrSet` should be in *italics* (b = `true`) or not (b = `false`). The default value is b = `false`.

`setUnderline(SimpleAttributeSet attrSet, boolean b)` determines whether the text formatted according to `attrSet` should be <u>underlined</u> (b = `true`) or not (b = `false`). The default value is b = `false`.

`setSuperscript(SimpleAttributeSet attrSet, boolean b)` determines whether the text formatted according to `attrSet` should appear as superscript (b = `true`) or not (b = `false`). The default value is b = `false`.

`setSubscript(SimpleAttributeSet attrSet, boolean b)` determines whether the text formatted according to `attrSet` should appear as subscript (b = `true`) or not (b = `false`). The default value is b = `false`.

Once an attribute set is defined, it can be assigned to parts of the text. The assignment is done using the following method from class `Document`:

```
setCharacterAttributes(int offset, int length,
                    AttributeSet attrSet, boolean replace)
```

This formats the text part consisting of as many symbols as the current value of `length` and beginning with the symbol at place `offset` as specified by the attribute values in `attrSet`. The parameter `replace` determines whether the attributes previously assigned to that text part should be removed first.

In the following example we define an attribute set `ugly` for formatting a text part in yellow, italic font on red background. Then the text in the document `doc` from symbols 203 to 234 (32 symbols) is formatted in this way. Another attribute set `greenText` just defines the font colour to be green. This is then used to format symbols 200 to 214. By setting the parameter `replace` to `false` the attributes of `ugly` other than the colour are maintained where the ranges overlap (symbols 203 to 214). In this range we have green, italic text on a red background. The reader is encouraged to try this and other examples of overlapping text attributes.

```
// Define attribute set "ugly" and ...
SimpleAttributeSet ugly = new SimpleAttributeSet();

// ... set its attributes to yellow italics
on red StyleConstants.setForeground(ugly, Color.yellow);
StyleConstants.setBackground(ugly, Color.red);
StyleConstants.setItalic(ugly, true);

// Format 32 symbols beginning with 203 using "ugly".
// Any previously assigned attributes are erased.
styledDoc.setCharacterAttributes(203,32,ugly,true);
```

```
// Define attribute set "greenText" and ...
SimpleAttributeSet greenText = new SimpleAttributeSet();

// ... set its attributes to green font
StyleConstants.setForeground(greenText, Color.green);

// Format 15 symbols beginning with 200 using "greenText".
// Any previously assigned attributes except the text colour
// are maintained.
styledDoc.setCharacterAttributes(203,15,greenText,false);
```

When a text range is formatted, position markers are automatically assigned to its beginning and end. These markers – not the values for offset and length specified in setCharacterAttributes – determine the range of the formatting henceforth. Thus, the formatted range will move left or right when text is deleted or inserted before it. Symbols inserted into the formatted range receive the same formatting, thus extending the range.

18.3 ■ Document listeners

When documents are not merely displayed but edited by the user, the application might want to react to changes in the document. One might, for example, want to change the formatting of certain text ranges or protocol the changes made to be able to undo them or to document the development process. In order to react to modifications in the document, one uses a listener, in this case a DocumentListener.

Whenever changes are made to a Document, which has a DocumentListener assigned to it, the listener is informed. The changes include deletions and insertions of text or modifications in the layout. The runtime system then generates an instance of DocumentEvent that contains information on the kind and location of the change. This event is passed to the listener.

To implement the interface DocumentListener, one has to implement the following three methods. They are called by the runtime system when text is inserted, deleted or formatting attributes are changed:

```
public void insertUpdate( DocumentEvent devt)
public void removeUpdate( DocumentEvent devt)
public void changedUpdate(DocumentEvent devt)
```

The instance devt of class DocumentEvent contains information on the event. The class provides the following methods to access this information:

```
Document getDocument()
int getLength()
int getOffset()
DocumentEvent.EventType getType()
DocumentEvent.Element getChange(Element elem)
```

getDocument() returns a reference to the Document that triggered the event. This is useful if the listener monitors more than one document.

getLength() returns the number of symbols affected by the event.

getOffset() returns the offset (position) of the first symbol affected by the event.

getType() returns the type of the event. Using method toString of class Event-Type this can be turned into text; the possible results are CHANGE, INSERT or REMOVE.

getChange(Element elem) – instances of class Element allow access to the text attributes that changed. A number of further classes are involved in this. We do not discuss the mechanism here; refer to the Java documentation.

18.4 ■ Class `DefaultStyledDocument`

As already mentioned in the beginning of the chapter, class DefaultStyled-Document is an implementation of interface Document. Both are found in the javax.swing.text package. We present only a few methods of this powerful class.

```
DefaultStyledDocument()

Position createPosition(int offset)
addDocumentListener(DocumentListener docList)
setCharacterAttributes(int offset, int length,
                    AttributeSet attribSet, boolean replace)

String getText(int offset,int length)
insertString(int offset, Stringtext, AttributeSet attrSet)
remove(int offset,int length)
```

DefaultStyledDocument() is the constructor.

createPosition(int offset) generates a position marker, i.e. an instance of Position, before the symbol currently is at position offset. If the parameters are outside the current size of the document then a BadLocationException will occur.

addDocumentListener(DocumentListener docList) assigns docList as document listener to this document.

setCharacterAttributes – see the discussion in Section 18.2.

String getText(int offset, int length) returns a string consisting of as many symbols as the current value of length, starting at position offset in the document. If the parameters are outside the current size of the document then a BadLocationException will occur.

`insertString(int offset, String text, AttributeSet attrSet)` inserts the symbols in string `text` before the symbol currently at position `offset` in the document. The new text is formatted as specified in `attrSet`. If the parameters are outside the current size of the document then a `Bad-LocationException` will occur.

`remove(int offset,int length)` deletes as many symbols as the current value of `length`, starting with the one currently at position `offset`. If the parameters are outside the current size of the document then a `BadLocationException` will occur.

The text of a document is often read from some file. This is easily done using the utility class `EditorKit`, which is also found in the `javax.swing.text` package. Every Swing component `textComp` that can display documents has an editor kit. It can be accessed by `textComp.getEditorKit()`. We need the following method from `EditorKit`:

```
read(FileReader fReader,Document doc, int offset);
```

The file reader should be assigned to the file whose content we want to insert into the document `doc`. Parameter `offset` specifies that position in the document before which the file content is inserted. For a new document `offset = 0` is used. The following code snippet demonstrates the use. We want to read a file `filename` into `DefaultStyledDocument` called `doc` and then display it in a Swing component `textComp`:

```
DefaultStyledDocument doc = new DefaultStyledDocument();
textComp.setDocument(doc);
EditorKit ediKit = textComp.getEditorKit();
FileReader fReader = new FileReader(filename);
ediKit.read(fReader,doc,0);
```

18.5 ■ An example of using documents

Program `DocumentFrame` demonstrates the features described in the previous sections. The text is administered by an instance `styledDoc` of `DefaultStyled-Document`. We then use a `JTextPane` to display the document. The document content is read from the ASCII file `DocText.txt`. A number of attribute sets is defined in class `DocAtt`. These are then used by `DocumentFrame` to format parts of the document. Also two position markers are placed in the text.

An anonymous document listener is defined in `DocumentFrame` and assigned to `styledDoc`. It monitors the changes made to the document and displays them in a `DocumentStatusPanel` below the document. Every insertion or deletion of text results in a line in the status panel describing what happened. The listener also monitors the two position markers and displays their current positions. We list only class `DocumentFrame`; the other class is on the book's home page. Figure 18.5 shows an example.

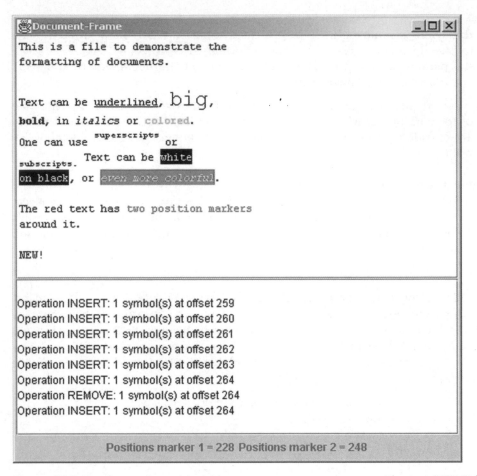

Figure 18.5 The formatting achieved by program `DocumentFrame`. The text 'NEW!' has been added. The status panel displays a protocol of the operations that have been performed

File: `its/Document/DocumentFrame.java`

```
1.   package its.Document;
2.
3.
4.   import its.SimpleFrame.SimpleFrame;
5.   import java.io.FileReader;
6.   import javax.swing.JScrollPane;
7.   import javax.swing.JTextPane;
8.   import java.awt.BorderLayout;
9.   import javax.swing.text.DefaultStyledDocument;
10.  import javax.swing.text.EditorKit;
11.  import javax.swing.text.Position;
```

```
public class DocumentFrame extends SimpleFrame
{
  private JTextPane textPane;
  private DocumentStatusPanel statusBar;
  private DefaultStyledDocument styledDoc;
  private EditorKit ediKit;
  private Position p1,p2;

  private final String filename = "./its/TestData/DocTest.txt";



  public DocumentFrame()
  {
    textPane  = new JTextPane();
    statusBar = new DocumentStatusPanel();
    styledDoc = new DefaultStyledDocument();
    textPane.setDocument(styledDoc);
    ediKit = textPane.getEditorKit();
    JScrollPane sp = new JScrollPane(textPane);
    this.getContentPane().add(sp,BorderLayout.CENTER);
    this.getContentPane().add(statusBar,BorderLayout.SOUTH);
    this.setSize(500,500);
    readFile(filename);
    DocAtt.createAttributes();
    formatText();
    try
    {
      p1 = styledDoc.createPosition(228);
      p2 = styledDoc.createPosition(248);
    }
    catch (Exception ex)
    {
      System.out.println("Problem creating Positions.");
    }
   styledDoc.addDocumentListener(new DocListener(statusBar,p1,p2));
   statusBar.update("",p1.getOffset(),p2.getOffset());


  }

  private void readFile(String filename){
    try
    {
      ediKit.read(new FileReader(filename),styledDoc,0);
    }
    catch (Exception ex)
```

```
12.
13.
14.
15.
16.
17.
18.
19.
20.
21.
22.
23.
24.
25.
26.
27.
28.
29.
30.
31.
32.
33.
34.
35.
36.
37.
38.
39.
40.
41.
42.
43.
44.
45.
46.
47.
48.
49.
50.
51.
52.
53.
54.
55.
56.
57.
58.
```

```
59.      {
60.         System.out.println("Problem reading file "+filename);
61.         ex.printStackTrace();
62.      }
63.   }
64.
65.
66.    // Formats some text ranges using attribute sets defined in
       // class DocAtt
67.    private void formatText(){
68.       styledDoc.setCharacterAttributes
69.           ( 73,10,DocAtt.underlinedText,false);
70.       styledDoc.setCharacterAttributes(85, 3,DocAtt.bigText,false);
71.       styledDoc.setCharacterAttributes(90, 4,DocAtt.boldText,false);
72.       styledDoc.setCharacterAttributes(98, 7,DocAtt.italicText,false);
73.       styledDoc.setCharacterAttributes(110, 7,DocAtt.greenText,false);
74.       styledDoc.setCharacterAttributes
75.           (131,13,DocAtt.superscriptText,false);
76.       styledDoc.setCharacterAttributes
77.           (147,11,DocAtt.subscriptText,false);
78.       styledDoc.setCharacterAttributes
79.           (171,14,DocAtt.whiteOnBlackText,false);
80.       styledDoc.setCharacterAttributes(190,18,DocAtt.ugly,true);
81.       styledDoc.setCharacterAttributes(228,20,DocAtt.redText,false);
82.   }
83.
84.
85.    public static void main(String[] args)
86.    {
87.      DocumentFrame df = new DocumentFrame();
88.      df.showIt("Document-Frame");
89.    }
90.
91.
92.  }
```

Exercises

18.1 Use program DocumentFrame to check the results of inserting or deleting text before, in and after formatted text ranges. Also check what happens to the position markers when text is inserted or deleted at different places.

18.2   Add a menu bar similar to the one in class `Editor` of Chapter 12. Implement the functions for the menu items. Modify the 'Search' function such that all occurrences of the search text are highlighted. Make sure that this also works if the search text is right at the beginning or the end of the text.

18.3   Add a menu item 'Show positions'. When selecting it, all user-added position markers are shown by inserting a blue letter 'M' on yellow background at the marker's position. Selecting the menu entry again makes them disappear.

Printing in Java 19

In this chapter we briefly discuss the printing mechanism of Java. We present an easy way to print graphical components. Finally we implement a generic class that can be used to add print capabilities to other applications.

We shall use classes from the library `java.awt.print`, which we embed by

```
import java.awt.print.*;
```

This library provides classes and methods for adding printing capabilities to graphical interfaces. We do not present all classes nor do we consider all methods. We focus on those necessary to implement an easy way to access a printer. More can be found in Java documentation.

Our example application consists of a frame `PrintFrame` with a menu. The menu has only one item: 'Print'. We define a panel `PrintPanel` with preferred size 300×200. It shows a rectangle, a filled oval and a text. Another rectangle is drawn at the edge of the panel to indicate its margin. This panel is then glued into the content pane of the frame. Figure 19.1 shows how the application looks. The functions of the application are simple: when the menu item 'Print' is selected, the content of the embedded `PrintPanel` is printed.

The general approach to printing a graphical component `printableComp` is as follows:

- The component `printableComp` has to implement the interface `Printable` by defining the method `print`.

- One has to create an instance `printJob` of class `PrinterJob` and pass component `printableComp` to it. This is done by calling the method `print-Job.setPrintable(printableComp)`.

- The `PrinterJob` is then started by `printJob.print()`.

One can specify that a print dialogue appears before the printing is started. This dialogue is the standard print dialogue of the operating system. It normally allows you to select the printer and the pages to be printed and possibly more. The programmer does not have to bother how the graphics is converted into data that the printer understands or how the data are sent to the printer.

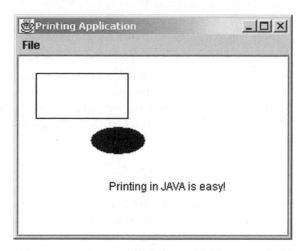

Figure 19.1 A picture of the print application. Note the rectangle at the margins of the panel. This is added to control whether the whole panel is printed

19.1 ■ Interface `Printable`

As mentioned above, a component has to implement the interface `Printable` to become printable. Interface `Printable` demands the implementation of a single method:

```
public int print(Graphics graphics, PageFormat pageFormat,
                 int pageIndex) throws PrinterException
```

This method is called by the runtime system when the component has to be printed. The runtime system also supplies the parameters `graphics`, `pageFormat` and `pageIndex`. This method plays the same role for printing as `paintComponent` does for drawing. In fact, one can think of printing as drawing to another device. The actual printing is started by calling `paint` inside method `print` of the component to be printed. As with `paintComponent` we should not call `print` ourselves. The parameters have the following meaning:

`Graphics graphics` links the application to the platform-specific printer drivers. This is similar to the `Graphics` object in the method `paintComponent` which links to the rendering routines of the operating system. The `Graphics` object is created by the runtime system.

`PageFormat pageFormat` is also created by the runtime system. It contains information on the page size and layout of the selected printer (or the default printer). The class provides `get`-methods to access these parameters.

`int pageIndex` is the number of the page to be printed. The runtime system calls `print` with varying values of `pageIndex`, namely 0, 1, 2, 3, ... If the print command is successful it returns the integer constant `PAGE_EXISTS` (defined in interface `Printable`). Otherwise `print` returns `NO_SUCH_PAGE` and the runtime system will not call `print` again. The programmer has to make sure that the correct value is returned. This way multi-page documents can be printed.

Let us now look at a simple implementation of the interface `Printable`. We implement method `print` such that it prints only one page; our panel is a one-page document. We first check whether the parameter `pageIndex` is 0 (the first page). If so we call the `paint`-method of the panel and return `PAGE_EXISTS`. If `pageIndex` is greater than 0 we return `NO_SUCH_PAGE`. The runtime system will then stop calling `print`.

Let us analyse what is happening in the first case, i.e. when `pageIndex` is 0. By calling the `paint`-method of the panel, a repainting is initiated. The painting is done on some device. Which device this is (the screen or the printer) is determined by the `Graphics` object. In our example we pass the `Graphics` object g which we receive as an argument of `print` on to the `paint` method. This object is generated by the runtime system and refers to some printer. As a result, `paint` draws to the printer and not to the screen. We cannot use `repaint` here because it does not allow a `Graphics` object to be passed as an argument; `repaint` initiates a redrawing of the screen. The skeleton of the implementation then looks like this:

```
public int print(Graphics g, PageFormat pageFormat, int pageIndex) {
    if (pageIndex > 0)
    {
        return(NO_SUCH_PAGE);
    }
    else
    {
        this.paint(g);
        return(PAGE_EXISTS);
    }
}
```

There are, however, some technical precautions to be taken. First of all one should switch off the *double buffering* of the graphics. This feature is important for a nice display when the screen is redrawn but might spoil the printing. After the printing, the double buffering should be switched on again. We therefore surround the `paint` command by some commands as shown below. We do not elaborate on the class `RepaintManager` used here:

```
RepaintManager currentManager = RepaintManager.currentManager(this);
currentManager.setDoubleBufferingEnabled(false);
paint(g);
currentManager.setDoubleBufferingEnabled(true);
```

Another topic to consider when printing is the placement and scaling of the printed image. The origin of the printer coordinate system is normally the upper left corner of the *paper*. Most printers, however, cannot print on some small margin of the paper for technical reasons. Therefore the upper left corner of the *printable area* of the paper is below and to the right of its upper left corner. The `Graphics` object of the `print`-method identifies the upper left corner of the component to be printed with the upper left corner of the paper. Without any correction the image of the component would not show parts outside the printable area. We therefore have to shift the image such that it lies completely in the printable area. Class `Graphics` provides the method `translate` for this purpose. The command

```
g.translate(int xNew, int yNew)
```

moves the origin of the coordinate system of the `Graphics` object g to the point (x_{new}, y_{new}) (in the coordinates before the translation). If $x_{new} > 0$ and $y_{new} > 0$ then the image is shifted to the right and downwards. It remains to determine the amount of the translation. This information is contained in the `PageFormat`-object. The commands

```
double pageFormat.getImageableX()
double pageFormat.getImageableY()
```

return the x- and y-coordinates of the upper left corner of the printable area in the printer coordinates. As these are `double` values, they should be rounded to the next larger integer. Altogether we have the following implementation of the interface `Printable`:

```java
public int print(Graphics g, PageFormat pageFormat, int pageIndex) {
    if (pageIndex > 0)
    {
      return(NO_SUCH_PAGE);
    }
    else
    {
      int  x = (int)pageFormat.getImageableX() + 1;
      int  y = (int)pageFormat.getImageableY() + 1;
      g.translate(x,y);
      RepaintManager currentManager =
          RepaintManager.currentManager(this);
      currentManager.setDoubleBufferingEnabled(false);
      this.paint(g);
      currentManager.setDoubleBufferingEnabled(true);
      return(PAGE_EXISTS);
    }
}
```

19.2 ■ Class `PrinterJob`

Class `PrinterJob` is the Java equivalent of – surprisingly – a printer job, i.e. a request to print the provided data. Class `PrinterJob` has a constructor, which, however, is **not** used. Instead method `getPrinterJob` is applied. A print job is created like this:

```
PrinterJob printJob = PrinterJob.getPrinterJob();
```

The print job is started by calling method `print` of `PrinterJob`:

```
printJob.print();
```

This method throws a `PrinterException` and is therefore embedded into a try-catch block.

To tell the print job which component it has to print we use `setPrintable`. The argument of this method has to be a `Printable` object, i.e. an object that implements the `Printable` interface:

```
setPrintable(Printable printableObject)
```

The print job is sent to the 'default printer' specified on the computer. If one wishes to select another printer, one calls method

```
boolean printDialog()
```

Then a printer selection dialogue similar to the one shown in Figure 19.2 appears. There one can select a number of options, e.g. the printer, the number of copies to print or the paper orientation. On closing the dialogue a boolean value is returned. If the value is `true`, then the print job is processed, otherwise it is cancelled. The following code snippet shows the application of class `PrinterJob` to print `printableComp`:

```
PrinterJob printJob = PrinterJob.getPrinterJob();
printJob.setPrintable(printableComp);
if (printJob.printDialog()){
  try {
    printJob.print();
```

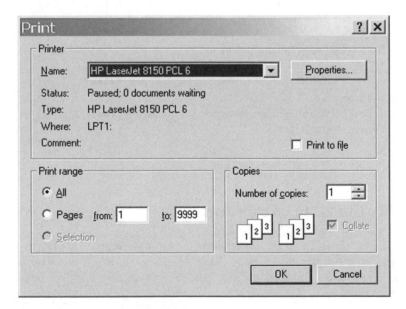

Figure 19.2 A printer selection dialogue

```
    } catch(PrinterException pex) {
      pex.printStackTrace();
    }
  }
```

19.3 ■ An example application

The two classes listed below form an application that allows a panel to be printed.
Class PrintPanel is specified in Figure 19.1. To make PrintPanel printable, we
have to implement interface Printable by defining the print method as described
in Section 19.1.

File: its/Printing/PrintPanel.java

```
package its.Printing;                                                    1.
                                                                         2.
import java.awt.Color;                                                   3.
import java.awt.Dimension;                                               4.
import java.awt.Graphics;                                                5.
import java.awt.print.PageFormat;                                        6.
import java.awt.print.Printable;                                         7.
import javax.swing.JPanel;                                               8.
import javax.swing.RepaintManager;                                       9.
                                                                        10.
public class PrintPanel extends JPanel implements Printable {           11.
                                                                        12.
  public PrintPanel() {                                                 13.
    this.setBackground(Color.white);                                    14.
    this.setPreferredSize(new Dimension(300, 200));                     15.
  }                                                                     16.
                                                                        17.
  public void paintComponent(Graphics g) {                             18.
    super.paintComponent(g);                                           19.
      g.setColor(Color.black);                                         20.
      g.drawRect(20,20,100,50);                                        21.
      g.fillOval(80,80,60,30);                                         22.
      g.drawString("Printing in JAVA is easy!",100,150);              23.
      g.setColor(Color.red);                                           24.
      g.drawRect(0,0,299,199);                                         25.
    }                                                                  26.
                                                                        27.
  public int print(Graphics g, PageFormat pageFormat, int pageIndex) { 28.
    if (pageIndex > 0) {                                               29.
      return(NO_SUCH_PAGE);                                            30.
    } else {                                                           31.
      int  x = (int)pageFormat.getImageableX() + 1;                    32.
```

```
33.        int  y = (int)pageFormat.getImageableY() + 1;
34.        g.translate(x,y);
35.        RepaintManager currentManager =  RepaintManager.currentManager(this);
36.        currentManager.setDoubleBufferingEnabled(false);
37.        this.paint(g);
38.        currentManager.setDoubleBufferingEnabled(true);
39.        return(PAGE_EXISTS);
40.    }
41.  }
42.
43. }
```

Class `PrintFrame` generates a frame that has a `PrintPanel` embedded into its content pane. The frame has a menu with only one item 'Print'. The listener for this item is implemented by defining `actionPerformed`. When the item is selected, a print job for the embedded panel is generated and started as described in Section 19.2. The frame also has `main` method which launches the application.

File: `its/Printing/PrintFrame.java`

```
1. package its.Printing;
2.
3. import its.SimpleFrame.SimpleFrame;
4. import java.awt.event.ActionEvent;
5. import java.awt.event.ActionListener;
6. import java.awt.print.PrinterException;
7. import java.awt.print.PrinterJob;
8. import java.awt.BorderLayout;
9. import javax.swing.*;
10.
11. public class PrintFrame extends SimpleFrame
12.                         implements ActionListener{
13.
14.    private PrintPanel pp;
15.
16.    public PrintFrame() {
17.      this.setTitle("Printing Application");
18.      pp = new PrintPanel();
19.      this.getContentPane().add(pp,BorderLayout.CENTER);
20.
21.      JMenuBar menuBar = new JMenuBar();
22.      JMenu menu = new JMenu("File");
23.      JMenuItem druckItem = new JMenuItem("Print");
24.      menuBar.add(menu);
25.      menu.add(druckItem);
26.      druckItem.addActionListener(this);
```

```
   this.setJMenuBar(menuBar);                              27.
   pack();                                                 28.
 }                                                         29.
                                                           30.
 public void actionPerformed(ActionEvent evt){            31.
   String command = evt.getActionCommand();               32.
   if(command.equals("Print"))                            33.
   {                                                       34.
   PrinterJob printJob = PrinterJob.getPrinterJob();      35.
   printJob.setPrintable(pp);                             36.
   if (printJob.printDialog()){                           37.
     try {                                                38.
       printJob.print();                                  39.
     } catch(PrinterException pe) {                       40.
       System.out.println("Error printing: " + pe);       41.
     }                                                    42.
   }                                                      43.
   }                                                      44.
                                                           45.
 }                                                         46.
 public static void main(String[] args)                   47.
   {                                                       48.
     PrintFrame prfr = new PrintFrame();                   49.
     prfr.showIt();                                        50.
   }                                                       51.
                                                           52.
}                                                          53.
```

19.4 ■ A generic class for printing

To make a component printable as described above needs the `Printable` interface
for that component to be implemented. In our example, we derived a `PrintPanel`
from `JPanel`. Driving a class from another one just in order to print it is quite a
lot of work. We therefore introduce a generic class `PrintSuit` which allows you
to print any component without implementing the `Printable` interface for that
component. In this class we define our own method, called `printComponent`, by

public static void printComponent(Component comp)

The argument `comp` is a graphical component which does not necessarily implement `Printable`. This component is printed as a result of this call. Components
embedded into `comp` are also printed. There is one special case when printing
frames: Only the embedded components of a frame are printed, not the frame itself. The code of `PrintSuit` combines the implementation of interface `Printable`
and the generation of the `PrinterJob` object. Application `PrintSuitTestFrame`

demonstrates the use of `PrintSuit`. As a result the embedded text area and button are printed; the frame itself however, is, not printed.

File: `its/Printing/PrintSuit.java`

```
1.  package its.Printing;
2.
3.  import java.awt.Component;
4.  import java.awt.Graphics;
5.  import java.awt.print.PageFormat;
6.  import java.awt.print.Printable;
7.  import java.awt.print.PrinterException;
8.  import java.awt.print.PrinterJob;
9.  import javax.swing.RepaintManager;
10.
11. public class PrintSuit implements Printable {
12.   private Component compToPrint;
13.
14.   public static void printComponent(Component comp) {
15.     new PrintSuit(comp).print();
16.   }
17.
18.   private PrintSuit(Component comp) {
19.     this.compToPrint = comp;
20.   }
21.
22.   public void print() {
23.     PrinterJob printJob = PrinterJob.getPrinterJob();
24.     printJob.setPrintable(this);
25.     if (printJob.printDialog()){
26.       try {
27.         printJob.print();
28.       } catch(PrinterException pex) {
29.             pex.printStackTrace();
30.       }
31.     }
32.   }
33.
34.   public int print(Graphics g, PageFormat pageFormat, int pageIndex) {
35.     if (pageIndex > 0) {
36.       return(NO_SUCH_PAGE);
37.     } else {
38.       int x = (int)pageFormat.getImageableX() + 1;
39.       int y = (int)pageFormat.getImageableY() + 1;
40.       g.translate(x,y);
41.       RepaintManager currentManager =
                RepaintManager.currentManager(compToPrint)
```

```
        currentManager.setDoubleBufferingEnabled(false);          42.
        compToPrint.paint(g);                                     43.
        currentManager.setDoubleBufferingEnabled(true);           44.
        return(PAGE_EXISTS);                                      45.
    }                                                             46.
  }                                                               47.
                                                                  48.
}                                                                 49.
```

File: its/Printing/PrintSuitTestFrame.java

```
package its.Printing;                                              1.
                                                                  2.
import its.SimpleFrame.SimpleFrame;                               3.
import java.awt.event.ActionEvent;                               4.
import java.awt.event.ActionListener;                            5.
import javax.swing.JButton;                                      6.
import javax.swing.JTextArea;                                    7.
import java.awt.BorderLayout;                                    8.
                                                                  9.
public class PrintSuitTestFrame extends SimpleFrame             10.
                            implements ActionListener            11.
{                                                                12.
  public PrintSuitTestFrame() {                                 13.
    JButton button = new JButton("Print");                      14.
    button.addActionListener(this);                             15.
    this.getContentPane().add(button,BorderLayout.SOUTH);       16.
    JTextArea textPane = new JTextArea();                       17.
    textPane.setText("Test test\n test test\n test test\n test test");  18.
    this.getContentPane().add(textPane,BorderLayout.CENTER);    19.
  }                                                              20.
                                                                 21.
  public void actionPerformed(ActionEvent evt){                 22.
    PrintSuit.printComponent(this);                             23.
  }                                                              24.
                                                                 25.
  static public void main(String[] args) {                      26.
    PrintSuitTestFrame pstf = new PrintSuitTestFrame();         27.
    pstf.showIt();                                              28.
  }                                                              29.
}                                                                30.
```

Swing and threads **20**

Threads are parts of an application which run in parallel. Although most applications in this book seem to be single-threaded, they are not. Any application involving a graphical surface is automatically multi-threaded. A number of threads are generated by the runtime system, and these run in parallel to the program code of the actual application. These threads usually run unnoticed by the user. In some cases, however, this concurrency can cause problems. We want to address the most frequent of these problems in this chapter.

To understand the role of threads in Java applications with graphical user interfaces, let us remember the life cycle of such applications. As mentioned in the introduction, the GUI for the application is created in the start-up phase. Once the GUI is made visible the application is *event driven*. That is, it is steered by events triggered by the user (or by other applications). Such an event is, for example, pressing a button. Events are detected by the runtime system, which informs the appropriate listener of the application. For a button it would be an action listener. This listener then executes a method that contains the code for reacting to the event. For action listeners this is method `actionPerformed`.

The administration of the events is done by a thread that is started unknown to the user, the so-called *event thread*, sometimes also called *event dispatching thread*. We describe this mechanism in the following and then address some problems it might cause. We would like to emphasize that this chapter is not meant as an introduction to concurrent programming with threads in Java. The reader is assumed to know the basics on threads or to look them up in the Java documentation or in tutorials on the web.

20.1 ■ Event thread and event queue

Every Java application starts at least one thread, the *main thread*. Almost all code that the programmer writes is executed in this thread. For an application with a GUI the *event thread* is created and runs in parallel to the main thread. It administers the incoming events. If the events come at a high rate or it takes too long to process them, then a new event might occur before the previous one has been entirely processed. Therefore the event thread uses an *event queue* to temporarily store the events. This is a data structure that handles the events in a first-in-first-out manner.

Any newly incoming event is added at the end of the queue and then gradually moves to the head where older events are taken out and processed. Processing an event means to call a method (e.g. `actionPerformed`) of the appropriate listener. This method then carries out some code as a reaction to the event. The latter happens in the event thread, not the main thread. Besides events that are processed by those listeners defined by the programmer, the queue contains events coming from listeners that are automatically assigned to Swing components. These include requests to repaint a component as a reaction to resizing it or clicking on a menu.

20.2 ■ Blocking a user interface

20.2.1 ☐ How blocking occurs

Our example application `BlockingFrame` shows how a lengthy operation can lead to undesired effects. A `BlockingFrame` has a menu and a label which is glued centrally into the frame's content pane. The label initially contains the text 'Nothing happened'. The menu bar has one menu which contains the single item 'Start'. A listener of type `MenuListener` monitors the menu item. This listener class is defined as an internal class.

When the menu item is selected, the listener's `actionPerformed` method is called. This method performs a lengthy job. We simulate the lengthy job by a for-loop which is executed ten times. Inside the loop, the application waits half a second (500 ms) using the `sleep` command from the class `Thread`. In order to document the work, the text of the label is updated in every execution of the loop. The texts reads 'Working' followed by the number of the loop variable. The same text is also printed to console using `System.out.println`. In addition we print the name of the thread that is currently running. After the last execution of the loop the text is set to 'Done'. We expect that, after selecting 'Start' in the menu, the label will display 'Nothing happened', 'Working 0', ... , 'Working 9', 'Done'.

What we observe is different. After selecting the menu item 'Start' the menu does not retract but remains visible for the duration of a lengthy job – five seconds. The text of the label remains 'Nothing happened'. Clicking on the menu or elsewhere on the frame has no effect. Resizing it will make the text of the label and menu disappear. The GUI is said to be *blocked* as long as the lengthy job is running. After five seconds the menu retracts and the label displays 'Done'. The GUI reacts to the mouse again. On the console we can, however, see the messages 'Working i' to be printed every half second. We can also see that the code for the lengthy work is not performed in the main thread but in the event thread. The output is listed below. `AWT-EventQueue-0` is the name given to the event thread by the runtime system[1]. The first line is printed from inside the `main` method of `BlockingFrame`, which is executed in the thread named `main`.

---

[1] The internal names given to threads by the runtime system might be different on different platforms or in different versions of the SDK.

```
Running in thread main
Working 0
Running in thread AWT-EventQueue-0
Working 1
Running in thread AWT-EventQueue-0
Working 2
Running in thread AWT-EventQueue-0
Working 3
Running in thread AWT-EventQueue-0
Working 4
Running in thread AWT-EventQueue-0
Working 5
Running in thread AWT-EventQueue-0
Working 6
Running in thread AWT-EventQueue-0
Working 7
Running in thread AWT-EventQueue-0
Working 8
Running in thread AWT-EventQueue-0
Working 9
Running in thread AWT-EventQueue-0
```

Let us analyse the observed behaviour. The following list shows what happens in chronological order.

1. When the menu is clicked, a command to repaint the GUI with the rolled-out menu is added at the end of the event queue. Some time after the command has been executed the menu becomes visible. The repaint command is removed from the queue.

2. When the menu item 'Start' is selected, a call to the method `actionPerformed` is added to the event queue.

3. A command to redraw the GUI with the retracted menu is added to the queue, *behind* the call to `actionPerformed`.

4. In every iteration of the `for` loop a command to redraw the label with the updated text is added to the queue, behind the repaint command.

By the first-in-first-out property of the queue the events in 3 and 4 can be processed only after the event in 2 by the event thread. In particular, the lengthy `action-Performed` method is run in the event thread and hinders it from processing the following events. Until `actionPerformed` terminates, the GUI is not updated and shows the rolled-out menu. Also the label and menu bar are not repainted when the frame is resized. The repaint requests are added at the end of the event queue where they wait to come to the head. Further events from the GUI occurring during this time, such as mouse clicks, are added to the event queue. They all have to wait until the previously added requests have been processed, especially the lengthy `actionPerformed` in 2. As no reaction to these events happens during that time,

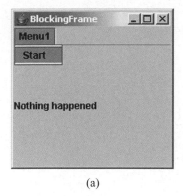
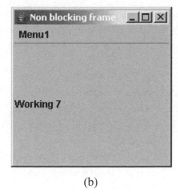

(a)   (b)

Figure 20.1 The results of applications (a) `BlockingFrame` and (b) `NonBlockingFrame`

the GUI appears to be blocked. The console output commands are operations that do not require any graphical components and are not put into the event queue. Therefore they are performed right away and appear as expected. The code for `BlockingFrame` is listed below and the resulting display is shown in Figure 20.1.

File: `its/Blocking/BlockingFrame.java`

```
package its.Blocking;                                          1.
                                                               2.
import its.SimpleFrame.SimpleFrame;                            3.
import java.awt.event.ActionEvent;                             4.
import java.awt.event.ActionListener;                          5.
import javax.swing.JLabel;                                     6.
import javax.swing.JMenu;                                      7.
import javax.swing.JMenuBar;                                   8.
import javax.swing.JMenuItem;                                  9.
                                                              10.
public class BlockingFrame extends SimpleFrame                11.
{                                                             12.
                                                              13.
  private JLabel display;                                     14.
                                                              15.
  public  BlockingFrame(){                                    16.
    display = new JLabel("Nothing happened");                 17.
    this.getContentPane().add(display);                       18.
                                                              19.
    JMenuBar menuBar     = new  JMenuBar();                   20.
    this.setJMenuBar(menuBar);                                21.
    JMenu    menu        = new  JMenu("Menu1");               22.
    menuBar.add(menu);                                        23.
    JMenuItem startItem = new  JMenuItem("Start");            24.
```

```
25.     menu.add(startItem);
26.     MenuListener mListener = new  MenuListener();
27.     startItem.addActionListener(mListener);
28.   }
29.
30.   public static void main(String[] args){
31.       System.out.println("Running in thread "+
                            Thread.currentThread().getName());
32.
33.       BlockingFrame bf = new BlockingFrame();
34.       bf.showIt("BlockingFrame");
35.   }
36.
37.   private void lengthyWork(){
38.       //This is the lengthy work
39.         for(int i = 0; i < 10; i++){
40.           System.out.println("Working "+i);
41.           System.out.println("Running in thread "+
                              Thread.currentThread().getName());
42.           display.setText("Working "+i);
43.           try{
44.             Thread.sleep(500);
45.           }catch(Exception ex){
46.             ex.printStackTrace();
47.           }
48.         }//for i
49.       display.setText("Done");
50.   }
51.
52. //Internal class
53.  class  MenuListener implements ActionListener{
54.
55.    public void actionPerformed(ActionEvent evt){
56.
57.     String command = evt.getActionCommand();
58.     if(command.equals("Start")){
59.        lengthyWork();
60.     }
61.     else
62.     {
63.       System.out.println("Unknown ActionCommand");
64.       System.exit(0);
65.     }
66.   }
67.  }//internal class
68. }
```

20.2.2 ☐ **Avoiding the blocking**

The solution to the above problem is not to run the lengthy `lengthyWork` method in the event thread but in a separate thread. The event thread merely starts this other thread. It then immediately processes the next event in the queue, while the lengthy job is running in the other thread in parallel.

In our example we define an internal class `WorkerThread` which is derived from `Thread`. When a thread is started then its method `run` is executed. Therefore, all the instructions the thread should execute should be placed here[2]. In our example the lengthy job is placed there.

Now, method `actionPerfomed` does not call `lengthyWork` but it creates an instance `worker` of `WorkerThread` and starts it by calling `worker.start()`. After this, `actionPerfomed` finishes. Even though `actionPerfomed` is run in the event thread, it does so only for the time needed to start the worker thread. It does not block the processing of further events. The menu rolls back immediately after we selected the menu item 'Start'. Also the text of the label changes every half second.

On the console we can now see that the lengthy job is performed in neither the main nor the event thread. Instead it runs in a thread called 'Thread-1' which is the internal name for our worker thread. As the lengthy operation now runs in a separate thread, the event thread can process the requests to repaint the frame or label as soon as they come in. Below, a listing of the console output is shown:

```
Running in thread main
WorkerThread1: started as Thread-1
Working 0
Running in thread Thread-1
Working 1
Running in thread Thread-1
Working 2
Running in thread Thread 1
Working 3
Running in thread Thread-1
Working 4
Running in thread Thread-1
Working 5
Running in thread Thread-1
Working 6
Running in thread Thread-1
Working 7
Running in thread Thread-1
Working 8
Running in thread Thread-1
Working 9
```

---

[2] As for listener methods such as `actionPerformed`, this formulation has to be taken with a grain of salt. Some of the code might actually be in other methods, in `lengthyWork` in our case, which are then called from inside `run`.

```
Running in thread Thread-1
WorkerThread1: Done
```

The code for NonBlockingFrame is listed below and the resulting display is shown in Figure 20.1.

File: its/Blocking/NonBlockingFrame.java

```
 1. package its.Blocking;
 2.
 3. import its.SimpleFrame.SimpleFrame;
 4. import java.awt.event.ActionEvent;
 5. import java.awt.event.ActionListener;
 6. import javax.swing.JLabel;
 7. import javax.swing.JMenu;
 8. import javax.swing.JMenuBar;
 9. import javax.swing.JMenuItem;
10.
11. public class NonBlockingFrame extends SimpleFrame
12. {
13.
14.     private JLabel display;
15.     private int nummer;
16.
17.     public  NonBlockingFrame(){
18.         nummer = 0;
19.         this.setTitle("Non blocking frame");
20.         display = new JLabel("Nothing happened");
21.         this.getContentPane().add(display);
22.
23.         JMenuBar menuBar     = new  JMenuBar();
24.         this.setJMenuBar(menuBar);
25.         JMenu    menu        = new  JMenu("Menu1");
26.         menuBar.add(menu);
27.         JMenuItem startItem = new  JMenuItem("Start");
28.         menu.add(startItem);
29.         MenuListener mListener  = new  MenuListener();
30.         startItem.addActionListener(mListener);
31.     }
32.
33.     private void lengthyWork(){
34.             //This is the lengthy work
35.         for(int i = 0; i < 10; i++){
36.             System.out.println("Working "+i);
37.                         System.out.println("Running in thread "+
                                    Thread.currentThread().getName());
```

```
          display.setText("Working "+i);               38.
          try{                                          39.
            Thread.sleep(500);                          40.
          }catch(Exception ex){                         41.
            ex.printStackTrace();                       42.
          }                                             43.
        }//for i                                        44.
      display.setText("Done");                          45.
  }                                                     46.
                                                        47.
  public static void main(String[] args){              48.
      System.out.println("Running in thread "+          49.
                      Thread.currentThread().getName());
      NonBlockingFrame nbf = new NonBlockingFrame();     50.
      nbf.showIt();                                      51.
  }                                                      52.
                                                         53.
  //Internal class                                       54.
                                                         55.
  class  MenuListener implements ActionListener{        56.
                                                         57.
    public void actionPerformed(ActionEvent evt){        58.
                                                         59.
    String command = evt.getActionCommand();            60.
    if(command.equals("Start")){                        61.
      // The worker thread is created and started       62.
      Thread worker = new WorkerThread();               63.
      worker.start();                                   64.
    }                                                   65.
    else                                                66.
    {                                                   67.
      System.out.println("Unknown ActionCommand");      68.
      System.exit(0);                                   69.
    }                                                   70.
  }                                                     71.
                                                        72.
  }//internal class                                     73.
                                                        74.
  //Internal class                                      75.
                                                        76.
  class WorkerThread extends Thread{                    77.
      int num;                                          78.
      public WorkerThread(){                            79.
       nummer++;                                        80.
       num = nummer;                                    81.
      }                                                 82.
                                                        83.
```

```
84.        public void run(){
85.          System.out.println("WorkerThread"+num+": started as "+
86.                    Thread.currentThread().getName());
87.          lengthyWork();
88.          System.out.println("WorkerThread"+num+": Done");
89.          }
90.
91.      }
92.
93. }
```

20.3 ■ Side-effects

! There are some side-effects to be aware of:

■ As the GUI is not blocked after selecting the menu item 'Start', we can immediately select it again, and again. . . . Every time a new WorkerThread is created and started all these threads run in parallel. What happens can best be seen in the console's output. If this is unwanted, one has to check whether there already is a worker thread running before starting the next one. This can be done by setting a 'flag' (e.g. a boolean variable) before starting the thread and have the thread reset it just before it exits (last command in the run method). There are other ways of achieving this which require a deeper knowledge of threads.

■ Sometimes the blocking of the GUI is not that unwanted. If, for example, a large file is read, then one might not want further user commands to be processed before the whole file has been loaded. Here, so-called progress meters might be a more elegant way of solving the problem.

■ If, in our example, a number of threads for the lengthy work are started, all of them are slowed down. They do not finish after five seconds each. The reason is that on one-processor systems – and most computers just have one main processor – the different threads do not really run concurrently. Instead, they have to share the single processor. Each one runs only for a short time and is then interrupted while another thread continues to run for a short time, etc. The different threads receive *time slices*.

20.4 ■ Updating a display at runtime

20.4.1 □ The problem

Consider the situation where a complex drawing is displayed and has to be periodically updated. This is a typical setting when data are continuously received, analysed and displayed. One might experience the problem that the drawing is incompletely displayed. We use a simple example to demonstrate this phenomenon.

We define a class `Drawing` as an abstract representation of the drawing. The drawing shows three parallel lines. Initially the lines are horizontal. Method `flipLines` will change the drawing to three vertical lines. Calling `flipLines` again will make the lines horizontal again. To simulate a complex modification of a drawing, the lines are flipped one after the other with a one second pause after each flip. Class `UpdatePanel` is defined to display a drawing. To this end it has access to an instance of class `Drawing`. We do not list these classes; they can be downloaded from the book's home page.

Class `BadUpdateFrame` is the main class of the application. It has a variable `drawing` of class `Drawing`. It also has an `UpdatePanel` to display this drawing. Initially the lines are horizontal. Then the `BadUpdateFrame` calls the `flipLines` method of the drawing, which flips the lines one after the other in roughly three seconds. This cannot be seen in the display because no event is created to trigger a repaint. Therefore we add a `repaint` command for the panel after the lines have been flipped. Then `flipLines` and `repaint` are called again to flip the lines to horizontal and display this. We only list the program `BadUpdateFrame`; the actual demonstration is placed in method `badDemo`.

File: `its/GraphicsUpdate/BadUpdateFrame.java`

```
package its.GraphicsUpdate;                                       1.
                                                                 2.
import javax.swing.JFrame;                                        3.
import its.SimpleFrame.SimpleFrame;                               4.
                                                                 5.
                                                                 6.
public class BadUpdateFrame extends SimpleFrame{                  7.
                                                                 8.
  private UpdatePanel uppane;                                     9.
  private Drawing drawing;                                       10.
                                                                11.
  public BadUpdateFrame(){                                       12.
    drawing = new Drawing();                                     13.
    uppane  = new UpdatePanel(drawing);                          14.
    getContentPane().add(uppane);                                15.
    pack();                                                      16.
  }                                                              17.
                                                                18.
  public void badDemo(){                                         19.
    uppane.repaint();     // paint the horizontal lines          20.
    drawing.flipLines(); // flip them to vertical                21.
    uppane.repaint();     // paint the vertical lines            22.
    drawing.flipLines(); // flip them back to horizontal         23.
    uppane.repaint ();    // paint the horizontal lines          24.
```

```
25.        drawing.flipLines(); // flip them to vertical
26.
27.    }
28.
29.    public static void main(String[] args){
30.       BadUpdateFrame badFrame = new BadUpdateFrame();
31.       badFrame.showIt("Bad Update");
32.       badFrame.badDemo();
33.       }
34.
35.
36. }
```

This should display a sequence of three drawings. The first has three horizontal lines, the second one three vertical ones and the third one again consists of three horizontal lines:

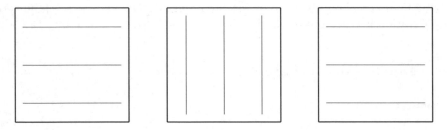

What is really displayed depends on many things: the operation system, the version of the SDK, the current load (number of processes) on the machine and many more things. Also the behaviour might vary from one execution of the application to the next. Most of the time one observes the following sequence of images:

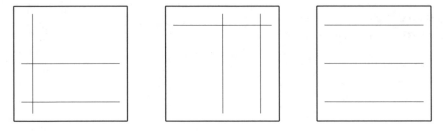

For an explanation let us look at the following three lines of code in BadUpdate-Frame:

```
drawing.flipLines(); // flip them to vertical
uppane.repaint();    // paint the vertical lines
drawing.flipLines(); // flip them back to horizontal
```

Their order suggests that after all three lines are flipped, the new drawing is displayed and only then are they flipped again. The problem comes from the fact that

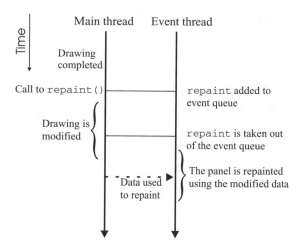

Figure 20.2 The main thread, on the left, modifies the drawing while the `repaint` event proceeds to the head of the event queue. When the repainting is finally performed, the modified drawing is shown

the `flipLine` instructions run in the main thread, while the `repaint` instruction is performed in the event thread. The main thread just adds `repaint` to the event queue to indicate that the GUI should be repainted at some time.

In this case, the order of the code lines in the listing does no longer reflect the order of their execution. It might take some time for the event thread to process the request to repaint. By that time, the main thread has already flipped the first line. The display then shows part of the old and part of the new picture. The temporal order in which things happen is listed below and is also shown in Figure 20.2:

1. All lines are horizontal.

2. The `repaint` command is added to the event queue.

3. The first line is flipped to vertical.

4. The `repaint` command reaches the head of the queue and the panel is re-painted to show the current drawing with the first line already vertical.

5. The other two lines are flipped but the display is not updated.

20.4.2 ☐ A solution by buffering

One way of solving the problem is to use a *buffer* for the drawing. This means that we have two abstract drawings, one of which is displayed and not changed and the other one that is not displayed and modified. When the modifications of the second one are completed, the drawings change their role. To this end the reference to the drawing is changed in the panel. Class `UpdatePanel` provides a method for this purpose (`setDrawing`). Then the new drawing is displayed by calling the `repaint` method of the panel. The content of the currently displayed drawing is copied to the other one. It is important to copy the drawing and not to use an assignment of references such as drawing1 = drawing2. In that case the two drawings would be identified; only one drawing would exist with two references to it. See Section B.1 for a more detailed explanation.

File: `its/GraphicsUpdate/GoodUpdateFrame.java`

```
1.  package its.GraphicsUpdate;
2.
3.  import javax.swing.JFrame;
4.  import its.SimpleFrame.SimpleFrame;
5.
6.
7.  public class GoodUpdateFrame extends SimpleFrame{
8.
9.    private UpdatePanel uppane;
10.   private Drawing drawing1, drawing2;
11.
12.     public GoodUpdateFrame(){
13.       drawing1 = new Drawing();
14.       drawing2 = new Drawing();
15.       uppane = new UpdatePanel(drawing1);
16.       getContentPane().add(uppane);
17.       pack();
18.     }
19.
20.     public void goodDemo(){
21.       uppane.repaint();
22.       drawing2.flipLines();
23.       uppane.setDrawing(drawing2);
24.       uppane.repaint();
25.       drawing1.copy(drawing2);
26.       drawing1.flipLines();
27.       uppane.setDrawing(drawing1);
28.       uppane.repaint ();
29.     }
30.
31.     public static void main(String[] args){
32.       GoodUpdateFrame goodFrame = new GoodUpdateFrame();
33.       goodFrame.showIt("Good Update"); // The drawing contains
34.       goodFrame.goodDemo();
35.     }
36.
37.
38. }
```

A generic graphics **21**
package

In this chapter we combine many techniques from the previous parts of the book to design a generic graphics package for displaying and manipulating drawings. The graphical objects to be displayed are specified in an abstract way and the package may be extended by the user. The package also supports adding and deleting graphical objects through user interaction.

21.1 ■ Specification of the package

The package provides a panel to display a drawing. The panel can be embedded into any GUI that needs to display drawings. The drawing can be changed by an application or by user interaction. The programmer can easily add further graphical objects to the package according to his or her needs. We describe this in more detail below.

- The drawing is composed of *graphical objects*. These can be simple shapes such as lines, circles or triangles but may include much more complex shapes such as polygons or curves. Some of them are defined in the package.

- The programmer can add new graphical objects.

- The graphical objects are specified by coordinates that are real numbers. No knowledge about the display area has to be known.

- The drawing is automatically fitted to the display area such that all of it is visible.

- The programmer can choose whether the scaling is proportional (both *x*- and *y*-axes have the same scale) or not (the drawing is extended horizontally and vertically to fill the panel).

- The colour of every graphical object can be set and changed.

- The display automatically scales when the panel is re-scaled.

- The package provides methods to add or delete graphical objects from the drawing.

21.2 ■ **Structuring the package**

The package is an extension of the interactive application in Chapter 7. It is composed of a number of classes. We now describe the class structure we have selected and explain our choices. From the specification above there are two concepts that obviously play a role in the project: 'graphical objects' and 'drawing'. We shall define two classes to implement these concepts: `GraphicalObject` and `Drawing`. We shall see that it makes sense to define some more helper classes on the way.

21.2.1 ☐ Class `Drawing`

A drawing is composed of graphical objects. Therefore we choose `Drawing` to do the administrative work. This class maintains a data structure that contains all graphical objects currently in the drawing. The data structure allows new graphical objects to be added or existing ones deleted. The class provides a method `draw` which displays the whole drawing. To this end it asks all graphical objects to draw themselves. Some more administrative features will be described later on.

21.2.2 ☐ Class `GraphicalObject`

A graphical object is an abstract description of a geometrical shape. As there are infinitely many kinds of such objects, one cannot define one single class to cover all the possibilities. We therefore define `GraphicalObject` to be an **abstract** class. All features that are common to **all** graphical objects (and that are relevant for our project) are specified in this class. If the programmer needs a new specific shape, then he or she has to derive a class from `GraphicalObject`. In this class those features are implemented that are specific to the shape.

Let us think which features are common to all graphical objects and are also relevant for the task we have in mind. First of all we should know the *place* and *size* of a graphical object. These are specified by the left-most, right-most, top-most, and bottom-most points of the object. This information is important for the project because we have to scale the drawing. Another feature that all graphical objects have is *colour*.

While these features of a graphical object are quite obvious, there are some more that will prove useful. Each graphical object has to be uniquely identifiable. Even if two circles have the same centre, radius and colour they are two different objects. To make graphical objects unique, each one has an integer field called `uid` for 'unique identification number'. If we think of interactively changing a drawing with the mouse, another concept proves useful. Think of a drawing with many graphical objects and suppose we want to select one of them with the mouse. Then one has to link the current mouse position to one of the objects according to some rule. There are many ways to specify which object is closest to the mouse. The methods for finding out which object that is can be quite involved. We therefore define an *anchor point* for every graphical object. Then one can select an object by clicking on its anchor point. Even so, two objects might have the same anchor point, in which case we select one at random. The anchor points are shown in the drawing as little dots.

Another thing we have to consider is the rendering of the graphical objects. As the programmer can add new kinds of shapes, one cannot set up a drawing method in advance that works for all of them. Only the programmer knows what the graphical object has to look like. Therefore, we require that a graphical shape knows how to draw itself. This concept is implemented by an abstract method draw in class GraphicalObject. Every (concrete) class derived from it has to implement this method.

There is, however, a problem here. To actually render the shape, the graphical object has to know the pixel coordinates in the panel where the drawing is displayed. These depend on the panel's current size and the size of the drawing which, in turn, depend on other graphical objects in the drawing. The necessary information is provided by instances of classes DimensionObject and ScaleObject. These classes are discussed later.

As an example, the package has three graphical objects that are implemented, Circle, Line and OpenPolygon. The listing of OpenPolygon is shown below. The constructor receives the corner points of the polygon as an array. It is checked whether the array contains at least two points. If this is the case, the array is traversed to find the extremal coordinates. A DimensionObject with these coordinates is created. The reference point for the object – the *anchor* – is defined to be the first point.

The draw method receives a reference to a Graphics object and a ScaleObject. The latter contains the information on the current size of the display. This information is used to transfer the abstract real coordinates of the polygon into screen (pixel) coordinates. Conversion routines are provided by methods of the utility class Conversions. The pixel coordinates are then used to draw the polygon as a sequence of line segments. Class OpenPolygon provides a method textString which returns a textual description of the polygon.

File: its/GenericDraw/OpenPolygon.java

```
package its.GenericDraw;                                             1.
                                                                    2.
import java.awt.Graphics;                                           3.
                                                                    4.
public class OpenPolygon extends GraphicalObject {                  5.
                                                                    6.
  private RealPoint[] points;                                       7.
                                                                    8.
  public OpenPolygon(RealPoint[] pts) {                             9.
    points = pts;                                                  10.
    if(points.length < 2){                                        11.
      System.out.println("ERROR in OpenPolygon: less than two points.");  12.
    }                                                             13.
    else                                                         14.
    {                                                            15.
      double xmin = points[0].getX();                            16.
      double xmax = points[0].getX();                            17.
```

```
18.      double ymin = points[0].getY();
19.      double ymax = points[0].getY();
20.      for (int i = 1; i < points.length; i++) {
21.        xmin = Math.min(xmin,points[i].getX());
22.        xmax = Math.max(xmax,points[i].getX());
23.        ymin = Math.min(ymin,points[i].getY());
24.        ymax = Math.max(ymax,points[i].getY());
25.      }
26.      dimObj = new DimensionObject(xmin,xmax,ymin,ymax);
27.      anchor = points[0];
28.    }
29.  }
30.
31.  public void draw(Graphics g, ScaleObject scale) {
32.    PixelPoint startPix = Conversions.realToPixelPoint(points[0],scale);
33.    g.setColor(color);
34.    for (int i = 0; i < points.length; i++) {
35.      PixelPoint endPix   = Conversions.realToPixelPoint(points[i],scale);
36.      g.drawLine(startPix.getX(),startPix.getY(),
                  endPix.getX(),endPix.getY());
37.      startPix = endPix;
38.    }
39.  }
40.
41.  public String textString(){
42.    String result = "Open Polygon: "+points[0].toString();
43.    for (int i = 1; i < points.length; i++) {
44.      result += ";"+points[i].toString();
45.    }
46.    return(result);
47.  }
48. }
```

21.2.3 ☐ Class `GenericDrawPanel`

Class `GenericDrawPanel` is derived from `JPanel` and displays the drawing. A programmer who wants to use the `GenericDrawing` package has to know about this class. `GenericDrawPanel` keeps the abstract representation of the drawing in an instance of class `Drawing`. `GenericDrawPanel` also provides methods to add and delete graphical objects. These methods only call the corresponding methods of class `Drawing`. The `paintComponent` method of `GenericDrawPanel` calls the `draw` method of class `Drawing`.

A mouse adapter is implemented as internal class `GenericDrawMouseAdapter`. It supports two operations: if the right mouse button is clicked inside the panel, then the graphical object whose anchor is closest to the mouse position is removed from the drawing. If the left mouse button is clicked once, the mouse position is remembered. If it is clicked a second time, a line between the mouse positions of the two clicks is added to the drawing. The functions of the adapter can be changed or extended by the programmer.

21.3 ■ Helper classes

The helper classes provide data types that support the operations of our project. At first we define two classes for points in the two-dimensional plane. One defines points in coordinates that are real numbers. The other class defines points in pixel coordinates. There are methods to convert real coordinates into pixel coordinates based on the size of the drawing and the panel to display it.

21.3.1 □ Constants

We define a class Constants which contains the definition of some fixed values that are used by one or more classes of the package. These include the width of the margins around the drawing. The class also defines some boolean variables which determine the appearance of the drawing, e.g. whether the anchor points are drawn or whether the drawing is displayed in proportional model.

21.3.2 □ Real and pixel points

The classes RealPoint and PixelPoint each store fields x and y. These are the x- and y-coordinates of the point. The first class uses double and second one int. The constructor of the pixel points checks that the coordinates are non-negative. Both classes provide get-methods to access the fields.

File: its/GenericDraw/PixelPoint.java

```
package its.GenericDraw;                                          1.
                                                                 2.
public class PixelPoint{                                          3.
   private int x, y;                                              4.
                                                                 5.
   public PixelPoint(int xx, int yy){                            6.
     if((xx >= 0) && (yy >= 0)){                                 7.
        x = xx;                                                   8.
        y = yy;                                                   9.
     }                                                            10.
     else                                                         11.
     {                                                            12.
       System.out.println("ERROR: Illegal pixel coordinates.");  13.
     }                                                            14.
   }                                                              15.
                                                                 16.
```

```
17.     public int getX(){
18.       return(x);
19.     }
20.
21.     public int getY(){
22.       return(y);
23.     }
24.
25.     public String toString(){
26.        return("["+x+";"+y+"]");
27.     }
28. }//class
```

File: its/GenericDraw/RealPoint.java

```
1. package its.GenericDraw;
2.
3. public class RealPoint{
4.    private double x, y;
5.
6.    public RealPoint(double xx, double yy){
7.       x = xx;
8.       y = yy;
9.    }
10.
11.   public double getX(){
12.      return(x);
13.    }
14.
15.   public double getY(){
16.      return(y);
17.    }
18.
19.   public double distanceTo(RealPoint p){
20.      return(Math.sqrt(Math.pow((this.x-p.x),2)+Math.pow((this.y-p.y),2)));
21.    }
22.
23.   public String  toString(){
24.      return("("+x+";"+y+")");
25.    }
26. }//class
```

We shall use real points for the abstract specification of geometric objects. Whenever such an object has to be rendered, the real points are converted into pixel coordinates. The pixel coordinates are computed in such a way that the whole drawing fits into the panel. Actually we want to have a small margin around the drawing in the panel. We allow the margin to be different at the four edges. The following data are needed to compute this conversion:

x_{min}	minimal x-coordinate of the drawing	double
x_{max}	maximal x-coordinate of the drawing	double
y_{min}	minimal y-coordinate of the drawing	double
y_{max}	maximal y-coordinate of the drawing	double
w	width of the panel in pixels	int
h	height of the panel in pixels	int
l	width of the left margin around the drawing in pixels	int
r	width of the right margin around the drawing in pixels	int
t	width of the top margin around the drawing in pixels	int
b	width of the bottom margin around the drawing in pixels	int

Then the usable width and height of the panel without the margins are $w_u = w - l - r$ and $h_u = h - t - b$. We now compute the factors f_x and f_y by which the drawing has to be scaled horizontally and vertically to fit into the margins.

$f_x = w_u/(x_{max} - x_{min})$	factor for horizontal scaling	double
$f_y = w_h/(y_{max} - y_{min})$	factor for vertical scaling	double
$f = \min\{f_x, f_y\}$	factor for proportional scaling	double

Then, to convert a real point $P_{real} = (x_{real}, y_{real})$ into the pixel point $P_{pix} = (x_{pix}, y_{pix})$, one uses the following formulas. Note that we have to reflect the y-coordinate because the screen coordinate system is upside down. The L-shaped brackets stand for downward rounding to the nearest integer.

$$x_{pix} = \lfloor (x_{real} - x_{min}) \cdot f_x + l \rfloor$$

$$y_{pix} = \lfloor h - ((y_{real} - y_{min}) \cdot f_y + t) \rfloor$$

In case of a proportional scaling, f is used instead of both f_x and f_y.

21.3.3 □ Dimension objects

Every `GraphicalObject` contains an instance of a `DimensionObject`. The dimension object contains the extremal coordinates of the graphical object. These are the minimal and maximal x- and y-coordinates of the object. For every class derived from `GraphicalObject`, the programmer has to make sure that these values are correctly set. See the listing of class `OpenPolygon` for an example.

The instances of `Drawing` also contain a `DimensionObject` called `extremalDimensions`. It contains the extremal dimension of the whole drawing, e.g. the minimum x-coordinate of any graphical object in the drawing. The values of `extremalDimensions` have to be updated when a new graphical object is added or deleted. When a new shape is added, one only has to check whether one of its dimensions gives a new extremum. Class `DimensionObject` provides a method, combineWith, for doing this. This method compares the minima of this and the DimensionObject given as an argument, and sets the minima to the smaller of the values. The update of the maxima is done in an analogous way. If a graphical object is deleted from the drawing the update of extremalDimensions is more difficult. If one of the values of extremalDimensions, say the minimal x-coordinate, comes from the deleted object, then one has to find that object of the drawing that now has minimal x-coordinate. We do this by re-computing the values of extremalDimensions from scratch. That is, we screen all graphical objects in the drawing to determine the new extremal values. There are more efficient ways of updating the values after a deletion but they require elaborate data structures, the implementation of which would occult the structure of the package.

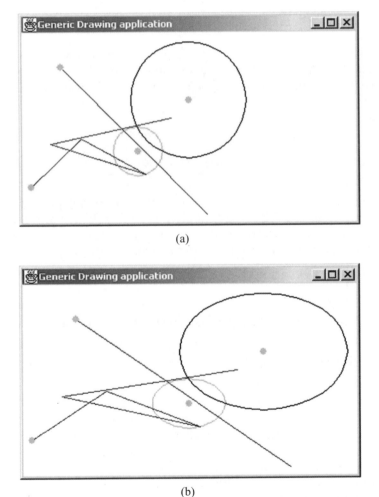

(a)

(b)

Figure 21.1 The test application GenericDrawingDemo. (a) In proportional mode, i.e. both coordinate axes have the same scale – circles appear as circles. (b) In non-proportional mode, i.e. sized to fill the panel – circles might appear as ellipses

21.3.4 ☐ **Conversions and scale objects**

The class `Conversions` provides methods to convert between pixel and real coordinates. To this end the methods have to know the relevant parameters, e.g. the dimensions of the drawing and the size of the panel. These values are supplied in an object of class `ScaleObject`. The conversion methods expect a pixel or real point and a scale object as arguments. They compute the coordinates of the real or pixel point, respectively, from the point they received and return this.

Whenever a re-drawing of the panel is initiated, the parameters of the scale object are set to the current values by class `Drawing`. The `draw`-methods of the classes derived from `GraphicalObject` receive the scale object as a parameter. The coordinates of the graphical objects are real coordinates. With the scale object at hand, the conversions can be used to convert those to the pixel coordinates needed for drawing into the panel.

Two screen shots of a test application `GenericDrawingDemo` are shown in Figure 21.1.

Displaying HTML documents and accessing the web **22**

We now discuss how HTML-formatted text is displayed in Swing components. We shall first show how files containing HTML text can be displayed. Then we show how to make a simple browser which can access and display HTML-formatted web pages.

In Chapters 12 and 18 we saw how ASCII texts can be displayed and edited. Another commonly used text type is HTML (*HyperText Mark-up Language*). Practically all web pages are HTML-formatted and so are many software manuals that are supplied on a CD. Files with HTML-formatted text are ASCII files that contain the text to be displayed and additional formatting instructions. These instructions, called *HTML-tags*, are enclosed in less-than and greater-than signs. For example, the sequence

```
<center>HTML and Swing</center>
```

means that the text 'HTML and Swing' is displayed in a horizontally centred fashion. When loading an HTML file into a Swing component for ASCII text, no formatting is done; the HTML-tags are shown as they appear in the text. The programs that display HTML text in a formatted fashion have to interpret the HTML-tags, and display the remaining text as required by these formatting instructions. Such programs are, for example, web browsers.

We do not have to write an HTML interpreter ourselves to format HTML text. The Swing library contains components with a built-in HTML interpreter, e.g. `JEditorPane`. These components can display most HTML documents in a formatted fashion. One has to be aware that the HTML specification has changed a number of times, in particular new HTML-tags were added which allow more sophisticated formatting. The HTML interpreter of Java knows the tags of a specific version of HTML; newer or non-standardized formatting instructions are ignored. Thus the Swing components might display some new, 'stylish' web pages somewhat differently from a standard web browser.

22.1 ■ Displaying an HTML page

We present a program `SimpleHTMLFrame` which uses a `JEditorPane` to display HTML text. The editor pane receives a *URL* (*uniform resource locator*) in the constructor. A URL is a web address. One can use class URL for this purpose, or one can just pass on the URL as a string. The constructors have the following form:

```
JEditorPane(URL webAddress)
JEditorPane(String webAddressAsString)
```

These constructors have to be embedded into a try-catch block, because generating a URL can throw an exception. To access a local file, the URL has to start with file:/// instead of http://. We use a local file in our example because then the program works without a connection to the Internet. If the computer is connected to the Internet, one can use the following URL:

```
http://www.imm.dtu.dk/swingbook/HTMLTest/test1.html
```

We are only interested in displaying HTML and do not allow the text to be edited using method setEditable(false) of JEditorPane.

File: its/HTML/SimpleHTMLFrame.java

```
package its.HTML;                                                      1.
                                                                      2.
import its.SimpleFrame.SimpleFrame;                                    3.
import javax.swing.JEditorPane;                                        4.
                                                                      5.
public class SimpleHTMLFrame extends SimpleFrame                       6.
{                                                                     7.
  private JEditorPane ediPane;                                        8.
  private static String htmlSource = "/its/TestData/test1.html";      9.
  private static String workingDir;                                   10.
                                                                      11.
  public SimpleHTMLFrame(String URLname)                              12.
  {                                                                   13.
     this.setSize(400,400);                                           14.
     workingDir = System.getProperty("user.dir");                     15.
     // in the following we assume that the program                   16.
     // is run from the parent directory of its.                      17.
     // Use an absolute path if necessary:                            18.
     try{                                                             19.
         ediPane = new JEditorPane("file:///"+workingDir+htmlSource); 20.
       // ediPane = new JEditorPane                                   21.
             ("file:///C:/absolute/path//its/TestData/
         ediPane.setEditable(false);                                  22.
       } catch(Exception e){}                                         23.
     // Later, the code for the link listener will be added here.     24.
       this.getContentPane().add(ediPane);                            25.
     }                                                                26.
                                                                      27.
```

```
28.        public static void main(String[] args){
29.            SimpleHTMLFrame shf = new SimpleHTMLFrame(htmlSource);
30.            shf.showIt("Simple HTML-Display");
31.        }
32.  // Later, the link listener class will be defined here.
33. }
```

Program `SimpleHTMLFrame` displays a single HTML document but it does not use the most important HTML feature: links (*HTML hyperlinks*). When clicking on a link, nothing happens. In the next section we see how links can be followed.

22.2 ■ Using HTML links

In order to trigger a reaction when clicking on a link we need a listener. In Java the interface `HyperlinkListener` is responsible for monitoring HTML hyperlinks. It is found in the `javax.swing.event` library and requires the implementation of a single method:

```
void hyperlinkUpdate(HyperlinkEvent hylevt)
```

The listener is assigned to that component which displays the HTML document, in our case the `JEditorPanel ediPane`. The listener is assigned using the following command:

```
ediPane.addHyperlinkListener(HyperlinkListener hyLis)
```

After the listener is assigned to the panel, it is notified by the runtime system if a link is clicked on, i.e. its `hyperlinkUpdate` method is called. The runtime system also generates a `HyperlinkEvent` object and passes it to `hyperlinkUpdate` as an argument.

The programmer has to insert the code into `hyperlinkUpdate` which is to be executed as a reaction to selecting the link. In our example we want to display that page to which the link refers. We first check whether the event type is ACTIVATED, i.e. whether the link has been selected. Other event types are ENTERED and EXITED. This test is done by inspecting the hyperlink event object `hylevt`

```
if(hylevt.getEventType() == HyperlinkEvent.EventType.ACTIVATED)
```

Next, we extract the URL to which the link is pointing:

```
URL newPage = hylevt.getURL()
```

Then this URL is passed to the editor pane by:

```
ediPanel.setPage(newPage)
```

The new web page is displayed in the editor pane. Methods that access web pages can throw exceptions, therefore calls of such methods have to be embedded into `try-catch` blocks. In our example, we write a message to the console if an exception occurs. In a serious application, an error diagnosis should be performed and a repair should be started.

To enable links, we augment class `SimpleHTMLFrame` to `HTMLViewer` by adding code at two positions indicated by comments in `SimpleHTMLFrame`. At the first position we add

```
LinkLis lili = new LinkLis();
ediPane.addHyperlinkListener(lili);
```

At the second position we add the implementation of the hyperlink listener as an internal class:

```
private class LinkLis implements HyperlinkListener
  {
    public void hyperlinkUpdate(HyperlinkEvent hylevt)
    {
      try
      {
       if (hylevt.getEventType() == HyperlinkEvent.EventType.ACTIVATED)
        {
         URL newPage = hylevt.getURL();
         ediPane.setPage(newPage);
        }
      }
      catch (Exception ex)
      {
        System.out.println("Problems with hyperlink-listener");
      }
    }// method
}// internal class
```

We do not list the resulting program `HTMLViewer`; it can be downloaded from the book's home page. It can, for example, be used to display HTML-formatted help or manual pages. Still, we miss some features when using the viewer. One of them is a 'Back'-function which re-displays the previous HTML page. In the next section we shall extend the viewer to a simple web browser which contains this feature.

22.3 ■ A simple web browser

We now extend the application of the previous section to a simple web browser. Recall that HTML-formatted web pages can be displayed only in the way that is supported by the HTML interpreter of the current Java system. The application lacks a number of security checks that should be added when used for other purposes.

Our application `ITSBrowser` uses a `JEditorPane` to display the web pages. The pane is embedded into a scroll pane, so that large pages can also be displayed. The scroll pane is centrally embedded into a frame. Our browser has some control elements which are arranged in a panel called `ToolPanel`. There is a text field for entering a URL and two buttons labelled 'GO!' and 'Back'. When pressing the first one, the browser loads the web page specified in the text field. One can navigate through the web following links. The browser keeps a record of the previous pages. Pressing the 'Back'-button makes the browser return to the web page from which the currently displayed page had been reached. Going back stops when we get back to the page whose URL had been directly entered into the text field.

The history of recently visited web pages is stored in a *stack*, a data structure which stores data like a stack of paper. New data can be placed on the top of the stack and only the topmost data can be taken from the stack. Assume we first look at web page W_1 which contains a link to page W_2. We use this link to get to W_2. Then the address (URL) of W_1 is put on top of the stack. If W_2 contains a link to page W_3 and we use this link, then the address W_2 is put on the stack. Using the 'Back'-button of our browser will cause the application to remove the top-most address (W_2) from the stack and display the corresponding page. After that, W_1 is the top-most address on the stack. Using the 'Back'-button again will therefore cause the application to remove the address of W_1 from the stack and display it.

The 'GO!'- and 'Back'-buttons of our application are monitored by a `Button-Listener` which implements the interface `ActionListener` and performs the desired actions if one of the buttons is pressed. The hyperlinks are monitored by class `LinkLis` which implements a `HyperlinkListener` like in the previous section.

The application is listed below. It can be tested by using the following URL:

http://www.imm.dtu.dk/swingbook/HTMLTest/test1.html

File: `its/HTML/Browser.java`

```
1.  package its.HTML;
2.
3.  import its.SimpleFrame.SimpleFrame;
4.  import java.awt.*;
5.  import java.awt.event.ActionEvent;
6.  import java.awt.event.ActionListener;
7.  import java.net.URL;
8.  import java.util.Stack;
9.  import javax.swing.*;
10. import javax.swing.event.HyperlinkEvent;
11. import javax.swing.event.HyperlinkListener;
12.
13. public class Browser extends SimpleFrame
14. {
15.    private JEditorPane ediPane;
16.    private static String startURL =
             "http://www.imm.dtu.dk/swingbook/HTMLTest/test1.html";
17.    private ToolPanel tools;
18.    private Stack urlStack;
19.
```

```java
public Browser(String URLname)                                     20.
{                                                                  21.
    this.setSize(600,600);                                         22.
    urlStack = new Stack();                                        23.
    ediPane = new JEditorPane();                                   24.
    ediPane.setEditable(false);                                    25.
    ediPane.setMinimumSize(new Dimension(600,600));                26.
                                                                   27.
    LinkLis lili = new LinkLis();                                  28.
    tools = new ToolPanel(URLname);                                29.
    ediPane.addHyperlinkListener(lili);                            30.
    this.getContentPane().add(tools,BorderLayout.NORTH);           31.
    this.getContentPane().                                         32.
        add(new JScrollPane(ediPane),BorderLayout.CENTER);
    }                                                              33.
public static void main(String[] args)                            34.
{                                                                  35.
  Browser brow = new Browser(startURL);                           36.
  brow.showIt("ITS-Browser");                                     37.
}                                                                  38.
                                                                   39.
private class LinkLis implements HyperlinkListener               40.
{                                                                  41.
  public void hyperlinkUpdate(HyperlinkEvent hyevt)               42.
  {                                                                43.
    try                                                            44.
    {                                                              45.
      if (hyevt.getEventType() == HyperlinkEvent.EventType.ACTIVATED)  46.
      {                                                            47.
       URL t = ediPane.getPage();                                 48.
       urlStack.push(t);                                          49.
       ediPane.setPage(hyevt.getURL());                           50.
      }                                                            51.
    }                                                              52.
    catch (Exception ex)                                          53.
    {                                                              54.
      System.out.println("Problems with hyperlink listener");     55.
    }                                                              56.
  }// method                                                      57.
}// internal class                                                58.
                                                                   59.
private class ToolPanel extends JPanel{                           60.
 private JTextField urlField;                                     61.
 private JButton backButton, goButton;                            62.
                                                                   63.
 public ToolPanel(String URLname){                               64.
   this.setLayout(new FlowLayout());                             65.
```

```
66.        urlField      = new JTextField();
67.        urlField.setText(URLname);
68.        backButton  = new JButton("Back");
69.        goButton    = new JButton("GO!");
70.        JLabel ulab = new JLabel("   URL:");
71.        urlField.setPreferredSize(new Dimension(300,30));
72.        this.add(backButton);
73.        this.add(ulab);
74.        this.add(urlField);
75.        this.add(goButton);
76.        ButtonListener buli = new ButtonListener();
77.        backButton.addActionListener(buli);
78.        goButton.addActionListener(buli);
79.      }//constructor
80.
81.      public String getURL(){
82.        return(urlField.getText().trim());
83.      }
84.    }// internal class
85.
86.    private class ButtonListener implements ActionListener{
87.      public void actionPerformed(ActionEvent actevt){
88.        String command = actevt.getActionCommand();
89.        if (command.equals("Back"))
90.        {
91.          if(urlStack.size() > 0)
92.          {
93.           URL url = (URL)urlStack.pop();
94.           try
95.           {
96.            ediPane.setPage(url);
97.           }
98.           catch (Exception ex)
99.           {
100.             System.out.println("Problem in Back: URL not found.");
101.          }
102.         }
103.       }
104.      else  if (command.equals("GO!"))
105.      {
106.        try
107.        {
108.          URL url = new URL(tools.getURL());
109.          urlStack.removeAllElements();
110.          ediPane.setPage(url);
111.        }
```

```
      catch (Exception ex)                                        112.
      {                                                           113.
        System.out.println("Problem in GO!: URL not found.");    114.
      }                                                           115.
    }//ifelse                                                     116.
  }//method                                                       117.
 }// internal class                                              118.
}                                                                 119.
```

22.4 ■ Reading a web page

In the previous section we saw how HTML pages can displayed in a formatted way. Now we show how the source code of a web page can be read. This is useful if the application has to read and process information from the page. An example for extracting information from the web is given in the next section.

Our non-graphical program ReadURL accesses a web page and writes its source code to the console. We use one of the test pages for this book, namely:

```
http://www.imm.dtu.dk/swingbook/HTMLTest/test1.html
```

In our application we create a URL-object with this address. Then an InputStream for reading from that URL is created. This is done by using method openStream() of class URL. We then use method read() of class InputStream to read the source of the HTML page character by character. Each character is immediately written to the console. The code of ReadURL and the resulting console output are listed below.

File: its/OnlineMonitor/ReadURL.java

```
package its.OnlineMonitor;                                        1.
                                                                  2.
import java.io.InputStream;                                       3.
import java.net.URL;                                              4.
                                                                  5.
public class ReadURL {                                            6.
                                                                  7.
  private static String immURL =                                 8.
    "http://www.imm.dtu.dk/swingbook/HTMLTest/test1.html";
                                                                  9.
  public static void main(String[] args) {                       10.
    readAndPrintTheURL(immURL);                                   11.
  }                                                               12.
                                                                  13.
  public static void readAndPrintTheURL(String urlName){          14.
    // Create a URL                                               15.
```

```
16.      URL urlToRead = null;
17.       try {
18.         urlToRead = new URL(urlName);
19.       }
20.      catch (Exception ex) {
21.            ex.printStackTrace();
22.       }
23.    // Read and the URL characterwise
24.    // and print it to the console.
25.     if(urlToRead != null){
26.      try  { // Open the streams
27.        InputStream inputStream = urlToRead.openStream();
28.        int c = inputStream.read();
29.        while (c != -1) {
30.          System.out.print((char)c);
31.           c = inputStream.read();
32.        }
33.        inputStream.close();
34.      }catch(Exception e){System.out.println("Problem reading from URL");}
35.     }
36.    }
37.  }
```

The source code of the web page that appears on the console looks like this

```
<!DOCTYPE HTML PUBLIC "-//W3C//DTD HTML 3.2 Final//EN">

<HTML>

<HEAD>

<TITLE></TITLE>

<META NAME="Generator" CONTENT="Winedit 2000">
<META NAME="Author" CONTENT="Paul Fischer">

</HEAD>

<BODY BGCOLOR="#FFFFFF" TEXT="#000000" LINK="#FF0000" VLINK="#800000"
ALINK="#FF00FF" BACKGROUND="?">

<H1> TEST HTML-Document</H1>
This is the first page.
<p>
<A HREF="test2.html">Link to the next page</A>.
</BODY>

</HTML>
```

22.5 ■ Harvesting information from the web

Let us now extend the application from the previous section to continuously harvest information from the web. In our example application we want to display stock market information, the German stock index DAX. Such information can be found on many web pages. We use a web page provided by Yahoo. At the time the book was prepared the address was:

```
http://de.finance.yahoo.com/d/quotes.csv
```

It contains the quotes of the DAX and the 30 stocks included in this index. The web address might change, so one has to check this and change it if necessary. The page is formatted as so-called *comma-separated values* (csv). The actual separator, however, is a semicolon. This format is suited to be imported into spreadsheet programs. We use this page because it is easier to analyse than HTML. Every line contains the information on one stock. A line on this page looks like this:

```
^GDAXI;4016,52;1/13/2004;15:58;+20,61;4006,85;4033,67;4003,19;78199616
```

It contains – separated by semicolons – the name of the index, its recent value, date and time of the value and information on the change, highest and lowest values, etc. The page is regularly updated, approximately every 30 seconds. Our application extracts the recent value from the line; in the above example this is 4016.52. In our application we use a so-called web query which allows the line containing the DAX information to be extracted.[1] We do not discuss the HTTP protocol or web queries here. The reader is referred to corresponding manuals and tutorials which are available on the web.

The application reads this web page every five seconds, extracts the current DAX value and updates the display. The quotes are displayed as a graph that is extended to the right. We do not want the display to be blocked while the application waits five seconds before fetching the next value. Therefore, we define a thread for accessing the web. This runs in parallel to the main thread which handles the GUI. Only the thread class `MonitorThread` is listed below.

The `run`-method of `MonitorThread` consists of a while-loop. The condition for the while-loop is a boolean variable `goOn`. This can be set to `false` by calling method `stopThread`. Then, the next time the while condition is checked the loop is terminated, which also terminates the thread. In the loop, the method `getOneQuote` is called and then the thread pauses five seconds. Method `getOneQuote` is a modification of `readAndPrintTheURL` from the previous section. It uses a `BufferedReader` to read the line with the information on the DAX. The private method `getQuoteFromString` parses this line and extracts the recent value of the DAX index as a `double`. This value is then passed to the display panel.

The application consists of three more classes `MonitorData`, `MonitorPanel` and `OnlineMonitor`. The first one implements the data model. It provides methods

---

[1] If the information is contained in an HTML page, we would have to analyse the page and write an appropriate parser to extract the desired information.

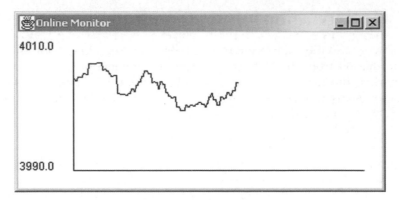

Figure 22.1 The online monitor for the DAX stock index

to add new data, access the present data, and to get information necessary for scaling the data so it fits into the display. The display is implemented in class MonitorPanel which is derived from JPanel. Class OnlineMonitor is derived from JFrame. It has a MonitorPanel embedded and also contains the main-method for starting the application. A screen shot is shown in Figure 22.1.

File: its/OnlineMonitor/MonitorThread.java

```
1.   package its.OnlineMonitor;
2.
3.
4.   import java.io.BufferedReader;
5.   import java.io.InputStreamReader;
6.   import java.net.URL;
7.   import java.util.StringTokenizer;
8.
9.   public class MonitorThread extends Thread{
10.
11.     private static final long delay = 5000;
12.     private String yahooDax =
13.         "http://de.finance.yahoo.com/d/quotes.csv?s=@^GDAXI&"+
            "f=s1l1d1t1c1ohgv&e=.csv";
14.     private MonitorPanel moniPane;
15.     private boolean goOn;
16.
17.     public MonitorThread(MonitorPanel mp){
18.       moniPane = mp;
19.       goOn     = true;
20.     }
21.
```

```
public   void run(){                                                22.
  while(goOn){                                                      23.
    getOneQuote(yahooDax);                                          24.
    try {                                                           25.
      Thread.sleep(delay);                                          26.
    }                                                               27.
    catch (Exception ex) {                                          28.
      ex.printStackTrace();                                         29.
    }//try                                                          30.
  }//while                                                          31.
  System.out.println("Thread stopped");                            32.
}                                                                   33.
                                                                    34.
public void stopThread(){                                           35.
   goOn = false;                                                    36.
}                                                                   37.
                                                                    38.
private double getOneQuote(String urlName)                          39.
 {                                                                  40.
 URL urlToRead = null;                                              41.
   try {                                                            42.
     urlToRead = new URL(urlName);                                  43.
   }                                                                44.
   catch (Exception ex) {                                           45.
       ex.printStackTrace();                                        46.
   }                                                                47.
   try  { // Open the streams                                       48.
     InputStreamReader inputReader =                                49.
         new InputStreamReader(urlToRead.openStream());
     BufferedReader urlReader = new BufferedReader(inputReader);     50.
     String line =  urlReader.readLine();                           51.
     System.out.println(">"+line+"<");                             52.
     double quote = getQuoteFromString(line);                       53.
     moniPane.addData(quote);                                       54.
    }catch(Exception e){System.out.println("Problem in URLReader");}  55.
  return(1.0);                                                      56.
 }                                                                  57.
                                                                    58.
private static double getQuoteFromString(String str){               59.
        String quoteString;                                         60.
        String euro,cent;                                           61.
        StringTokenizer stok = new StringTokenizer(str,";");        62.
        stok.nextToken(); // skip  "^GDAXI"                         63.
        quoteString =  stok.nextToken(); // get quote as "eeee,cc"  64.
        StringTokenizer stok2 = new StringTokenizer(quoteString,",\"");  65.
        euro  = stok2.nextToken();                                  66.
```

```
67.                   cent = stok2.nextToken();
68.             int e = Integer.parseInt(euro);
69.             int c = Integer.parseInt(cent);
70.
71.     return((double)e+(double)c/Math.pow(10,((double)(cent.length()))));
72.
73.   }
74. }
```

Applets

23

Applets are used when a program is designed to run in a browser. Applets replace frames in web applications. The applet is linked to an HTML page. Whenever this HTML page is made visible in a browser, the applet is loaded over the net and runs in the browser.

All the examples we have looked at so far have been based on frames, which are shown on the screen. These programs, running on the local machine, are called *applications*. Applets allow programs to run in a browser. Users everywhere on the web can fetch the applet and run it on their machines. Applets are like frames in that one can embed other graphical components into them. On the other hand one cannot make them visible and run by themselves. They need to be linked to an HTML page. Then if that page is displayed in a browser, the applet is started and can be seen in the browser. Another difference between applications and applets is that applets are not allowed to do certain things. For example an applet may not write or read files on the machine it is running on. This is to protect users who run an applet found on some web page on their computers. We only present a very simple way to use applets. There are more issues the programmer should consider when writing an applet for a serious application.

23.1 ■ Applets in Swing

Class JApplet implements the applet concept in Swing. As mentioned above, applets are similar to frames, because they have a content pane into which other components can be embedded. Thus one uses the following command to embed a component comp into an applet:

```
getContentPane().add(comp)
```

There is a difference between frames and applets. While the embedding is usually done in the constructor of a frame, it is done in method init of the applet. Also, an applet is not directly started by the user. Instead it is externally started by the browser, when the corresponding web page is loaded. An applet has to be linked to the HTML page that displays it. We shall call this page the *master page* of the applet. When the master page is loaded, the browser fetches the code of the applet (its class file) and starts the Java runtime system to execute the code.

Applets are driven by four methods, which we explain below. Even though applets can have a constructor, it should not be used.

```
public void init()
public void start()
public void stop()
public void destroy()
```

init() is automatically called by the browser when the master page is loaded into the browser for the first time after the browser has started. This method replaces the constructor. All the code for embedding other components initializing variables, etc., should go here. This method is only executed once in the applet's life.

start() is automatically called by the browser after the init has finished. It is also called when the user returns to the master page after having looked at other pages without shutting the browser down. The code for resuming interrupted work should go here.

stop() is automatically called by the browser when the user leaves the master page without shutting the browser down. As the applet is paused, all code for interrupting the computations should go here. Some browsers also call destroy at this point. Then the applet is terminated. It is restarted using init when the user returns to this page.

destroy() is automatically called by the browser just before the applet is terminated. All code for the final clean-up should go here.

In our examples we only put real code into the init method. The other three methods contain only print commands. The result of these commands will appear on the *Java console*. The Java console is a program that comes with the Java plug-ins for browsers. How it is activated depends on the browser and the operating system. In recent versions of Windows one can find it in Start -> Settings -> Java Plug-in.

23.1.1 □   A counter applet

In our first example we reuse the CounterPanel from Chapter 3. Such a panel is glued centrally into the applet. No further code is needed, because a CounterPanel supplies all functions of a counter. We list the program below.

File: `its/Applet/CounterApplet.java`

```
1. package its.Applet;
2.
3. import javax.swing.JApplet;
```

```
import its.CounterGUI.CounterPanel;                                      4.
import java.awt.BorderLayout;                                            5.
                                                                         6.
public class CounterApplet extends JApplet {                             7.
                                                                         8.
  public void init(){                                                    9.
   CounterPanel cPane = new CounterPanel();                             10.
   this.getContentPane().add(cPane,BorderLayout.CENTER);               11.
  }                                                                     12.
                                                                        13.
  public void start(){                                                  14.
    System.out.println("Start");                                       15.
  }                                                                     16.
                                                                        17.
  public void stop(){                                                   18.
    System.out.println("Stop");                                        19.
  }                                                                     20.
                                                                        21.
  public void destroy(){                                                22.
    System.out.println("Destroy");                                     23.
  }                                                                     24.
                                                                        25.
                                                                        26.
}                                                                       27.
```

To make the applet run, it must be embedded in an HTML page. This is done by inserting an *applet tag* (<APPLET>) into the page. In the tag one has to specify where the applet's class files are found (CODE), its width (WIDTH) and height (HEIGHT). The value of the CODE parameter is the path to the class files. If packages are used the path has to reflect their structure. Also **all** classes used by the applet have to be there in our example; this includes some classes from the its.CounterGUI package. Here is the directory structure needed for the example:

```
its/Applet/CounterApplet.class
its/CounterGUI/CounterModel.class
its/CounterGUI/CounterPanel.class
its/CounterGUI/CounterListener.class
```

Our HTML page has the minimum structure; HTML-tags have many more formatting capabilities. The page looks like this:

```
<html>
<head>
<title>
Counter Applet
</title>
</head>
```

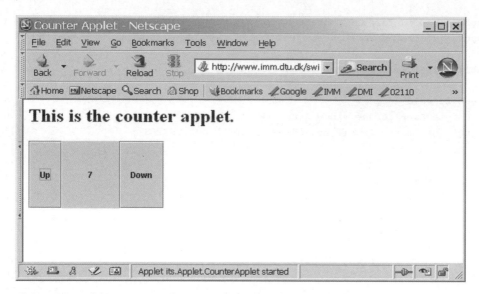

Figure 23.1 The counter applet as it appears in a browser

```
<body>
<h2>This is the counter applet.</h2>
<APPLET CODE="its.Applet.CounterApplet.class" WIDTH="200" HEIGHT="100">
</APPLET>
</body>
</html>
```

The page is placed in the directory right above the its directory which contains the class files. This page can also be reached from the book's home page. You can follow the link to the applet from there or type the following line in your browser to load the page and run the applet. The result is shown in Figure 23.1.

```
http://www.imm.dtu.dk/swingbook/AppletTest/CounterDemo.html
```

23.1.2 ☐ An applet running a thread

The second example is an applet displaying a timer which is incremented every half second. The timer is run in a thread of type TimerThread in order to avoid blocking the applet. A panel (TimerPanel) is used to display the current value of the timer. The thread updates the panel every half second. The applet class is called TimerApplet. The listings are shown below.

File: its/Applet/TimerThread.java

```
1. package its.Applet;
2.
3. public class TimerThread extends Thread {
4.
```

```
private int time;                                                5.
private TimerPanel timerPane;                                    6.
                                                                 7.
public TimerThread(TimerPanel tp) {                              8.
  time = 0;                                                      9.
  timerPane = tp;                                                10.
}                                                                11.
                                                                 12.
public void run(){                                               13.
  while(true){                                                   14.
  try {                                                          15.
    Thread.sleep(500L);                                          16.
    time += 500;                                                 17.
    System.out.println("Running "+time);                        18.
    timerPane.setTime(time);                                     19.
  }                                                              20.
  catch (InterruptedException ex) {                              21.
  }                                                              22.
  }                                                              23.
  }                                                              24.
}                                                                25.
```

File: its/Applet/TimerPanel.java

```
package its.Applet;                                              1.
                                                                 2.
import javax.swing.JPanel;                                       3.
import java.awt.Color;                                           4.
import java.awt.Graphics;                                        5.
                                                                 6.
public class TimerPanel extends JPanel {                         7.
                                                                 8.
  private int time;                                              9.
                                                                 10.
  public TimerPanel() {                                          11.
    this.setBackground(Color.yellow);                            12.
    time = 0;                                                    13.
  }                                                              14.
                                                                 15.
  public void paintComponent(Graphics g){                       16.
    super.paintComponent(g);                                     17.
    g.drawString(Integer.toString(time), 50,50);                18.
  }                                                              19.
                                                                 20.
                                                                 21.
```

```
22.    public void setTime(int t){
23.      time = t;
24.      this.repaint();
25.    }
26.
27.
28.
29. }
```

File: its/Applet/TimerApplet.java

```
1. package its.Applet;
2.
3. import javax.swing.JApplet;
4. import java.awt.BorderLayout;
5.
6. public class TimerApplet extends JApplet {
7.
8.    private TimerThread timer;
9.
10.    public void init(){
11.      TimerPanel timerPane = new TimerPanel();
12.      timer = new TimerThread(timerPane);
13.      this.getContentPane().add(timerPane,BorderLayout.CENTER);
14.      timer.start();
15.      }
16.
17.    public void start(){
18.        System.out.println("Start");
19.    }
20.
21.    public void stop(){
22.        System.out.println("Stop");
23.    }
24.
25.    public void destroy(){
26.        System.out.println("Destroy");
27.    }
28. }
```

23.1.3 ☐ Remarks

The Java SDK contains an *applet viewer*, a program that can display an applet without using a browser. This is helpful when developing and testing an applet.

Sometimes one is making a project which should be used both as an application and as an applet. It is then advisable to use a panel into which all components of the GUI are embedded. One just has to embed this single panel into a frame or an applet to get the desired type of program. The `CounterPanel` is an example of such a *modular design*.

Solutions to selected exercises

A

A.1 ■ Chapter 2

A.1.1 □ 2.1

Both windows close. The reason is that clicking the close button of a `SimpleFrame` results in the command `System.exit(0)`. This terminates the **application**, i.e. the program that contains the `main`-method. In our case this is `SimpleFrameDriver`. As both frames are constructed there, both are terminated.

A.1.2 □ 2.2

The present border components extend to fill the whole area.

A.2 ■ Chapter 4

A.2.1 □ 4.2

The following listings of the package `its.Light` contain a traffic light simulation in a model–view implementation.

File: `its/Light/Constants.java`

```
package its.Light;                                              1.
                                                                2.
                                                                3.
public class Constants {                                        4.
    public static final int LIGHT_RED        = 1;               5.
    public static final int LIGHT_RED_ORANGE = 2;               6.
    public static final int LIGHT_GREEN      = 3;               7.
    public static final int LIGHT_ORANGE     = 4;               8.
}                                                               9.
```

File: `its/Light/LightModel.java`

```
1. package its.Light;
2.
3. public class LightModel {
4.    private int currentColors;
5.
6.
7.    public LightModel() {
8.      currentColors = Constants.LIGHT_RED;
9.    }
10.
11.    public void nextColor(){
12.      switch (currentColors) {
13.        case Constants.LIGHT_RED:
14.          currentColors = Constants.LIGHT_RED_ORANGE;
15.          break;
16.        case  Constants.LIGHT_RED_ORANGE:
17.          currentColors = Constants.LIGHT_GREEN;
18.          break;
19.        case  Constants.LIGHT_GREEN:
20.          currentColors = Constants.LIGHT_ORANGE;
21.          break;
22.        case  Constants.LIGHT_ORANGE:
23.          currentColors = Constants.LIGHT_RED;
24.          break;
25.        default:
26.          System.out.println("ERROR: ILLEGAL COLOR COMBINATION!");
27.          break;
28.      }
29.  }
30.
31.    public int getCurrentColors(){
32.      return(currentColors);
33.    }
34.
35.
36.    public void printColor(){
37.      switch (currentColors) {
38.        case Constants.LIGHT_RED:
39.          System.out.println("RED");
40.          break;
41.        case  Constants.LIGHT_RED_ORANGE:
42.          System.out.println("RED&ORANGE");
43.          break;
44.        case  Constants.LIGHT_GREEN:
```

```
          System.out.println("GREEN");              45.
            break;                                    46.
      case  Constants.LIGHT_ORANGE:                   47.
          System.out.println("ORANGE");              48.
            break;                                    49.
        default:                                      50.
          System.out.println("ERROR: ILLEGAL COLOR COMBINATION!");  51.
            break;                                    52.
      }                                               53.
    }                                                 54.
}                                                     55.
```

File: its/Light/LightTest.java

```
package its.Light;                                    1.
                                                      2.
public class LightTest {                              3.
  public static void main(String[] args) {            4.
    LightModel light = new LightModel();              5.
    for (int i = 0;i < 10 ;i++ ) {                    6.
     light.printColor();                              7.
     light.nextColor();                               8.
    }//for                                            9.
                                                      10.
  }                                                   11.
}                                                     12.
```

File: its/Light/LightFrame.java

```
package its.Light;                                    1.
                                                      2.
import its.SimpleFrame.SimpleFrame;                   3.
import java.awt.Color;                                4.
import java.awt.GridLayout;                           5.
import javax.swing.JButton;                           6.
import javax.swing.JPanel;                            7.
                                                      8.
public class LightFrame extends SimpleFrame {         9.
                                                      10.
  private JPanel redPanel,orangePanel,greenPanel;     11.
  private LightModel light;                           12.
                                                      13.
  public LightFrame(LightModel lm) {                  14.
    light = lm;                                       15.
```

```
16.      this.getContentPane().setLayout(new GridLayout(4,1));
17.      redPanel    = new JPanel();
18.      orangePanel = new JPanel();
19.      greenPanel  = new JPanel();
20.      JButton nextButton = new JButton("Next");
21.      LightListener lightList = new LightListener(this);
22.      nextButton.addActionListener(lightList);
23.
24.
25.      this.getContentPane().add(redPanel);
26.      this.getContentPane().add(orangePanel);
27.      this.getContentPane().add(greenPanel);
28.      this.getContentPane().add(nextButton);
29.      System.out.println("c="+light.getCurrentColors());
30.      setColor(light.getCurrentColors());
31.          this.repaint();
32.   }
33.
34.
35.   private void setColor(int color){
36.     switch (color) {
37.       case Constants.LIGHT_RED:
38.          redPanel.setBackground(Color.red);
39.          orangePanel.setBackground(Color.lightGray);
40.          greenPanel.setBackground(Color.lightGray);
41.        break;
42.       case Constants.LIGHT_RED_ORANGE:
43.          redPanel.setBackground(Color.red);
44.          orangePanel.setBackground(Color.orange);
45.          greenPanel.setBackground(Color.lightGray);
46.        break;
47.       case Constants.LIGHT_GREEN:
48.          redPanel.setBackground(Color.lightGray);
49.          orangePanel.setBackground(Color.lightGray);
50.          greenPanel.setBackground(Color.green);
51.        break;
52.       case Constants.LIGHT_ORANGE:
53.          redPanel.setBackground(Color.lightGray);
54.          orangePanel.setBackground(Color.orange);
55.          greenPanel.setBackground(Color.lightGray);
56.        break;
57.       default:
58.          System.out.println("ERROR: ILLEGAL COLOR COMBINATION!");
59.        break;
60.     }//Switch
61.   }
```

```
                                                              62.
                                                              63.
  public void showNextColors(){                               64.
    light.nextColor();                                        65.
    this.setColor(light.getCurrentColors());                 66.
  }                                                           67.
}                                                             68.
```

File: its/Light/LightListener.java

```
package its.Light;                                           1.
                                                              2.
import java.awt.event.ActionEvent;                           3.
import java.awt.event.ActionListener;                        4.
                                                              5.
public class LightListener implements ActionListener {       6.
                                                              7.
  private LightFrame parentFrame;                            8.
  public LightListener(LightFrame pf) {                      9.
    parentFrame = pf;                                        10.
  }                                                           11.
                                                              12.
                                                              13.
  public void actionPerformed(ActionEvent evt) {             14.
    String actComm = evt.getActionCommand();                 15.
    if(actComm.equals("Next")){                              16.
      parentFrame.showNextColors();                          17.
    }                                                         18.
    else                                                     19.
    {                                                         20.
     System.out.println("ILLEGAL COMMAND SOURCE");           21.
    }                                                         22.
  }                                                           23.
                                                              24.
                                                              25.
  }                                                           26.
```

File: its/Light/LightDriver.java

```
package its.Light;                                           1.
                                                              2.
public class LightDriver {                                   3.
  public static void main(String[] args) {                   4.
    LightModel lm = new LightModel();                        5.
```

```
6.    LightFrame lf = new LightFrame(lm);
7.    lf.showIt();
8.    }
9. }
```

A.2.2 □ 4.3

Here is the code in a non-model–view implementation. It is also in one file and not documented. It works, but one should not program Java like this.

File: `its/ColorSelection/ColorSelectionFrame.java`

```
1. package its.ColorSelection;
2.
3. import javax.swing.*;
4. import java.awt.Color;
5. import java.awt.GridLayout;
6. import its.SimpleFrame.SimpleFrame;
7. import java.awt.event.*;
8.
9.
10.
11.
12. public class ColorSelectionFrame extends SimpleFrame {
13.
14.    private JPanel colPanel;
15.    private JButton redBut, blueBut, yellowBut;
16.
17.
18.    public ColorSelectionFrame() {
19.      blueBut   = new JButton("blue");
20.      redBut    = new JButton("red");
21.      yellowBut = new JButton("yellow");
22.
23.      ColorListener cList = new ColorListener();
24.      blueBut.addActionListener(cList);
25.      redBut.addActionListener(cList);
26.      yellowBut.addActionListener(cList);
27.
28.      colPanel  = new JPanel();
29.      colPanel.setBackground(Color.gray);
30.
31.      GridLayout gLayout = new GridLayout(2,2);
32.      this.getContentPane().setLayout(gLayout);
33.
```

```
      this.getContentPane().add(blueBut);                              34.
      this.getContentPane().add(redBut);                               35.
      this.getContentPane().add(yellowBut);                            36.
      this.getContentPane().add(colPanel);                             37.
                                                                       38.
                                                                       39.
      this.setVisible(true);                                           40.
                                                                       41.
                                                                       42.
                                                                       43.
    }                                                                  44.
                                                                       45.
    // internal class                                                  46.
     class ColorListener implements ActionListener{                    47.
       public void actionPerformed (ActionEvent evt)                   48.
        {                                                              49.
                                                                       50.
           String actComm = evt.getActionCommand();                   51.
           System.out.println(""+actComm);                            52.
           if(actComm.equals("blue")){                                53.
             colPanel.setBackground(Color.blue);                      54.
           } else if(actComm.equals("red")){                          55.
             colPanel.setBackground(Color.red);                       56.
           } else if(actComm.equals("yellow")){                       57.
             colPanel.setBackground(Color.yellow);                    58.
           }                                                          59.
       }//method                                                      60.
     }                                                                 61.
  public static void main(String[] args) {                             62.
    ColorSelectionFrame colorSelectionFrame1 = new ColorSelectionFrame(); 
  }                                                                    63.
}                                                                      64.
```

A.3 ■ Chapter 13

A.3.1 □ 13.1

The following listings of the package its.ResizeJumpDisplay contain the code of a model–view implementation.

File: its/ResizeJumpDisplay/PositionModel.java

```
package its.ResizeJumpDisplay;                                         1.
                                                                       2.
                                                                       3.
public class PositionModel {                                           4.
    //  We allow the positions for the upper                          5.
```

```
6.     //   left corner of the black rectangle to
7.     //   be only at:
8.     //   0/stepNo, 1/stepNo,...,allowedMax/stepNo
9.     //   of the current width or height of the panel.
10.    //   With the choice below this is
11.    //   0/9, 1/9, 2/9, 3/9, 4/9, 5/9, and 6/9.
12.
13.    private static final int stepNo      = 9;
14.    private static final int allowedMax = 6;
15.
16.    //   The next variable specifies the length and
17.    //   height of the black rectangle as a number
18.    //   of steps. Here we take 3.
19.
20.    private static final int blackRectSteps = 3;
21.
22.    //   The next two variables contain the
23.    //   current position of the black rectangle
24.    //   (in fractions of the current width and height
25.    //   of the panel).
26.
27.
28.      private int upperLeftX, upperLeftY;
29.
30.    public PositionModel(int x, int y) {
31.      upperLeftX = x;
32.      upperLeftY = y;
33.    }
34.
35.
36.    public int getXInSteps(){
37.     return(upperLeftX);
38.    }
39.
40.    public int getYInSteps(){
41.     return(upperLeftY);
42.    }
43.
44.    public int getNoOfSteps(){
45.     return(stepNo);
46.    }
47.    public int getBlackSizeInSteps(){
48.     return(blackRectSteps);
49.    }
50.
51.
```

```
  public void moveDown(){                                              52.
    if(upperLeftY < allowedMax){                                       53.
      upperLeftY++;                                                    54.
    }                                                                  55.
  }                                                                    56.
                                                                       57.
                                                                       58.
                                                                       59.
  public void moveUP(){                                                60.
    if(upperLeftY > 0){                                                61.
      upperLeftY--;                                                    62.
    }                                                                  63.
  }                                                                    64.
                                                                       65.
                                                                       66.
  public void moveRight(){                                             67.
    if(upperLeftX < allowedMax){                                       68.
      upperLeftX++;                                                    69.
    }                                                                  70.
  }   public void moveLeft(){                                          71.
    if(upperLeftX > 0){                                                72.
      upperLeftX--;                                                    73.
    }                                                                  74.
  }                                                                    75.
                                                                       76.
                                                                       77.
                                                                       78.

}
```

File: its/ResizeJumpDisplay/ResizeJumpFrame.java

```
package its.ResizeJumpDisplay;                                          1.
                                                                        2.
import its.SimpleFrame.SimpleFrame;                                     3.
import java.awt.BorderLayout;                                           4.
                                                                        5.
public class ResizeJumpFrame extends SimpleFrame{                       6.
                                                                        7.
  public ResizeJumpFrame(){                                             8.
    PositionModel posModel = new PositionModel(3,5);                    9.
    ResizeJumpPanel resizePanel = new ResizeJumpPanel(posModel);       10.
    this.setSize(500,300);                                             11.
                                                                       12.
    this.getContentPane().add(resizePanel,BorderLayout.CENTER);        13.
                                                                       14.
```

```
15.       DirectionPanel dirPanel = new DirectionPanel(posModel,this);
16.       this.getContentPane().add(dirPanel,BorderLayout.SOUTH);
17.    }
18.
19. }
```

File: its/ResizeJumpDisplay/ResizeJumpPanel.java

```
1. package its.ResizeJumpDisplay;
2.
3. import java.awt.Color;
4. import java.awt.Graphics;
5. import javax.swing.JPanel;
6.
7. public class ResizeJumpPanel extends JPanel{
8.
9.
10.    private PositionModel posModel;
11.
12.    public ResizeJumpPanel(PositionModel pm){
13.      posModel = pm;
14.      this.setBackground(Color.yellow);
15.    }
16.
17.    public void paintComponent(Graphics g)
18.    {
19.      super.paintComponent(g);
20.      // get the current dimensions of the panel in pixels
21.      int currentWidth  = this.getWidth();
22.      int currentHeight = this.getHeight();
23.
24.      // compute the current size of a step in pixels
25.      int hStepInPixels = currentWidth/posModel.getNoOfSteps();
26.      int vStepInPixels = currentHeight/posModel.getNoOfSteps();
27.
28.      // compute the pixel positions of the
29.      // upper left corner of the black rectangle
30.      // and its width and height.
31.      int upperLeftX = posModel.getXInSteps() * hStepInPixels;
32.      int upperLeftY = posModel.getYInSteps() * vStepInPixels;
33.      int blackWidth =  hStepInPixels * posModel.getBlackSizeInSteps();
34.      int blackHeight= vStepInPixels * posModel.getBlackSizeInSteps();
35.
36.      //set colour to black
37.      g.setColor(Color.black);
38.
```

```
    //  and draw the rectangle                                          39.
                                                                        40.
    g.fillRect(upperLeftX,upperLeftY,blackWidth,blackHeight);           41.
                                                                        42.
  }                                                                     43.
                                                                        44.
                                                                        45.
}                                                                       46.
```

File: its/ResizeJumpDisplay/DirectionPanel.java

```
package its.ResizeJumpDisplay;                                           1.
                                                                        2.
import java.awt.GridLayout;                                             3.
import javax.swing.JButton;                                             4.
import javax.swing.JPanel;                                              5.
                                                                        6.
public class DirectionPanel extends JPanel {                            7.
                                                                        8.
  public DirectionPanel(PositionModel posMod, ResizeJumpFrame parent) { 9.
    GridLayout gLayout = new GridLayout(1,4);                          10.
    this.setLayout(gLayout);                                           11.
    JButton upBut    = new JButton("Up");                              12.
    JButton downBut  = new JButton("Down");                            13.
    JButton rightBut = new JButton("Right");                           14.
    JButton leftBut  = new JButton("Left");                            15.
    this.add(upBut);                                                   16.
    this.add(leftBut);                                                 17.
    this.add(rightBut);                                                18.
    this.add(downBut);                                                 19.
                                                                       20.
    DirectionListener dirList = new DirectionListener(posMod,parent);  21.
    upBut.addActionListener(dirList);                                  22.
    downBut.addActionListener(dirList);                                23.
    rightBut.addActionListener(dirList);                               24.
    leftBut.addActionListener(dirList);                               25.
                                                                       26.
  }                                                                    27.
                                                                       28.
}                                                                      29.
```

File: its/ResizeJumpDisplay/DirectionListener.java

```java
1. package its.ResizeJumpDisplay;
2.
3. import java.awt.event.ActionListener;
4. import java.awt.event.ActionEvent;
5.
6. public class DirectionListener implements ActionListener{
7.
8.   private PositionModel posModel;
9.   private ResizeJumpFrame parentFrame;
10.
11.   public DirectionListener(PositionModel pm,ResizeJumpFrame rjf) {
12.     posModel = pm;
13.     parentFrame = rjf;
14.   }
15.   public void actionPerformed(ActionEvent evt) {
16.     String actionComm = evt.getActionCommand();
17.     if(actionComm.equals("Up")){
18.       posModel.moveUP();
19.     }
20.     else if(actionComm.equals("Down")){
21.       posModel.moveDown();
22.     }
23.     else if(actionComm.equals("Left")){
24.       posModel.moveLeft();
25.     }
26.     else if(actionComm.equals("Right")){
27.       posModel.moveRight();
28.     }
29.
30.     parentFrame.repaint();
31.   }
32. }
```

File: its/ResizeJumpDisplay/ResizeJumpDriver.java

```java
1. package its.ResizeJumpDisplay;
2.
3. public class ResizeJumpDriver
4. {
5.   public static void main(String[] args){
6.     ResizeJumpFrame rf = new ResizeJumpFrame();
7.     rf.showIt("ResizeJumpFrame");
8.   }
9. }
```

Some general remarks on Java

B

This appendix addresses some problems that frequently appear when one begins to program larger applications in Java.

B.1 ■ Objects, non-objects and references

Java is an object-oriented language. This does not mean that every entity defined in Java is an object. Some basic entities such as integers (`int`), doubles (`double`) or characters (`char`) are not objects. Most of the time it does not matter whether we deal with an object or a basic entity. There are, however, situations where a seemingly equal treatment of objects and non-objects results in essentially different results. These situations occur especially when fields inside an object can be changed.

The fundamental difference between objects and non-objects is that the variable (name) for a non-object is always linked to the **fixed** memory position where this object is created (using the `new`-statement). The name stands for a value. The variable name given to an object is a *reference* to **some** memory position. At creation (using the `new`-statement) it refers to the memory position where the object is created. Later the memory position to which the variable refers can be changed by an assignment to the variable.

Let us look at an example: We create two integers a and b (non-objects) and assign values to them (a = 3 and b = 4). We then assign b to a (a = b) and finally assign a new value to b. After every assignment we print the current values. Below is a listing of the code and output.

Code snippet:

```
int a = 3;
int b = 4;
a = b;
b = 7;
```

Listing of output:

```
Value a = 3
Value b = 4
```

```
Statement a = b  executed.
Value a = 4
Value b = 4
Statement b = 7  executed (new value for b).
Value a = 4
Value b = 7
```

Let us now look at what happens if we use objects. The following code snippet uses arrays of integers instead of integers. Arrays are objects in Java. We use arrays of length two and apply the same operations as above to the elements at array position 1. Below is a listing of the code and output.

Code snippet:

```
int[] A = {1,3};
int[] B = {1,4};
A = B;
B[1] = 7;
```

Listing of output:

```
Value A[1] = 3
Value B[1] = 4
Statement A = B  executed.
Value A[1] = 4
Value B[1] = 4
Statement B[1] = 7  executed (new value for B[1]).
Value A[1] = 7
Value B[1] = 7
```

The behaviour is not as one might have expected. After we set the entry at position 1 in array B to 7, the entry at position 1 in array A is also 7. We would expect A[1] to be 4. The reason for this is that the statements a = b in the first code snippet and A = B in the second one have different semantics and thus different results.

Figure B.1 shows what happens if we use integers. The names a and b always refer to the integer value. Therefore the statement a = b means 'a is assigned the value of b'.

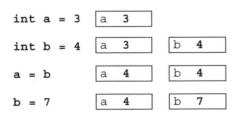

Figure B.1 A visualization of the first code snippet. The Java statements are listed on the left and the results are on the right. A rectangle symbolizes a memory location and the letter inside is the variable name

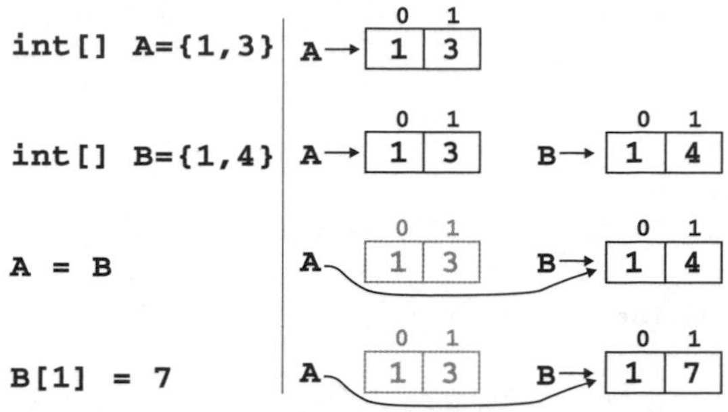

Figure B.2 A visualization of the second code snippet. The Java statements are listed on the left and the results are displayed on the right. A rectangle symbolizes the memory area of an array of length 2. The array indices 0 and 1 are shown above. The arrow from the variable name to the rectangle indicates which array is referenced by the variable name. Here the statement A = B means that A refers to the same array as B. The array to which A originally pointed cannot be accessed any more and is therefore shown in grey

Let us now look at the second program snippet. The statement `int[] A = {1,3}` creates an integer array of length 2. The variable name A is now a reference to the memory location where the array is stored. It does not refer to any integer value. It cannot refer to a value because the array holds two values. Thus the statement A = B means 'A now references the same memory location as B'. Now, changing `B[1]` to 7 has the effect that also `A[1]` is 7. The originally created array with entries 1 and 3 is lost. It cannot be accessed any more because there is no reference pointing to it. Java's automatic garbage collection detects such objects and removes them from the memory. See also Figure B.2.

The full listing of the program can be found in package `its.ReferenceDemo`.

B.2 ■ Declarations and definitions

Consider the following class `FlexArray`. It implements an array of integers where the index is not $0, 1, \ldots, n-1$ but $a, a+1, \ldots, b$ for $a, b \in \mathbb{Z}$, $a \le b$. Class `FlexArrayDriver` shows how to use the class. It is located in package `its.General`.

File: `its/General/FlexArray.java`

```
package its.General;                                    1.
                                                        2.
                                                        3.
public class FlexArray {                                4.
  // Here the variable "data"  is DECLARED              5.
  // NO array is created! Thus data are null            6.
  // at this point. We cannot DEFINE "data"             7.
  // here because we do not know how long the           8.
```

```
 9.     // array should be.
10.     // Variable "data" stores the data.
11.     private int[] data;
12.     // these variables store the start and end index and the
13.     // length of the array
14.     private int startindex, endindex, length;
15.
16.     public FlexArray(int s, int e) {
17.      if(s > e){
18.        System.out.println("ERROR in FlexArray: Start index > end index");
19.      }
20.      else
21.      {
22.        startindex = s;
23.        endindex   = e;
24.        length     = endindex - startindex + 1;
25.        // In the next command the variable "data"
26.        // is defined. We now know how long the
27.        // array has to be. Then "data" is no longer
28.        // null but it references an integer array.
29.        data = new int[length];
30.      }//if
31.     }//constructor
32.
33.
34.
35.      private int indexingFunction(int c){
36.       int result = -1;
37.       if((c < startindex) || (c > endindex)){
38.         System.out.println("ERROR in FlexArray: Illegal index: "+c
39.                           +" not in ["+startindex+","+endindex+"]");
40.       }
41.       else
42.       {
43.         result = c - startindex;
44.       }//if
45.
46.       return(result);
47.      }
48.
49.
50.
51.      public void setValue(int c, int val)
52.      {
53.         if(indexOK(c)){
54.           data[indexingFunction(c)] = val;
55.         }
```

```
  }//method                                                    56.
                                                               57.
                                                               58.
  public int getValue(int c) {                                 59.
    if(indexOK(c)){                                            60.
     return(data[indexingFunction(c)]);                        61.
    }                                                          62.
    else{                                                      63.
      return(0);                                               64.
    }                                                          65.
  }//method                                                    66.
                                                               67.
                                                               68.
  public int size(){                                           69.
    return(length);                                            70.
  }                                                            71.
                                                               72.
  private boolean indexOK(int i){                              73.
    if((i >= startindex) && ( i <= endindex)){                 74.
      return(true);                                            75.
    }                                                          76.
    else{                                                      77.
      System.out.println("ERROR in FlexArray: Index out of bounds.");  78.
      return(false);                                           79.
    }                                                          80.
  }                                                            81.
}                                                              82.
```

File: its/General/FlexArrayDriver.java

```
package its.General;                                           1.
                                                               2.
import javax.swing.JFrame;                                     3.
public class FlexArrayDriver {                                 4.
  public static void main(String[] args) {                     5.
                                                               6.
    // Define a FlexArray with indexing -3,-2,..,2.            7.
    // and fill it with i^3 at position i.                     8.
    FlexArray myArray = new FlexArray(-3,2);                    9.
    for(int i=-3; i <= 2; i++){                                10.
      myArray.setValue(i,i*i*i);                               11.
    }                                                          12.
    //Read a certain value                                     13.
    System.out.println("Value at -2 is "+myArray.getValue(-2)); 14.
    //Read a certain value                                     15.
    System.out.println("Value at 2 is "+myArray.getValue(2));  16.
```

```
17.        //Read an illegal position
18.        System.out.println("Value at -4 is "+myArray.getValue(-4));
19.
20.    }
21. }
```

Here is the result of the test run of `FlexArrayDriver`:

```
Value at -2 is -8
Value at 2 is 8
ERROR in FlexArray: Index out of bounds.
Value at -4 is 0
```

Now let us look at a frequently made mistake. We only add one word in the constructor of `FlexArray`. We replace the line

```
data = new int[length];
```

by

```
int[] data = new int[length];
```

The resulting class is called `WrongFlexArray` and the driver is `WrongFlexArray-Driver`. We do not print the listing, as it differs only in that one line and the fact that `FlexArray` is replaced by `WrongFlexArray` everywhere. Here is the result of the test run:

```
java.lang.NullPointerException
    at its.General.WrongFlexArray.setValue(WrongFlexArray.java:70)
    at its.General.WrongFlexArrayDriver.main(WrongFlexArrayDriver.java:18)
Exception in thread "main"
```

What has happened? Why is there a `NullPointerException` when we want to set a value in the `data` array? Well, the `data` array is not defined. At least not the `data` array we want to use in method `setValue`. The problem lies in the constructor of `WrongFlexArray`. In the line

```
int[] data = new int[length];
```

another **local** integer array by the name 'data' is **defined**. This has nothing to do with the integer array by the name 'data' which is **declared** before the constructor. The local array ceases to exist when the constructor is finished. Then the 'data' array which is **declared** before the constructor is still there, but **not created** by using `new` and thus `null`. When method `setValue` tries to access it a `Null-PointerException` is triggered.

B.3 ■ Accessing variables with get and set

All variables and methods declared and defined in a class are accessible from within that class. The *modifiers* `private`, `public` and `protected` control the *access* from outside the class to variables and methods of the class. Sometimes one talks about the *visibility* of variables and methods instead of access.

A variable or method that is declared `private` cannot be accessed from outside the class. It is not visible outside of the class where it is defined. The `private` modifier is the main tool to implement *data encapsulation*. Private variables are encapsulated in their class and protected against misuse from the outside. Only methods of their class can modify them. Private variables are also not visible in derived classes.

A variable that is declared `public` can be accessed from outside the class. It is visible outside of the class where it is defined. Public variables can be modified by methods of other classes. This bears the risk that the modifications are illegal and corrupt the data. The use of public variables should therefore be avoided as much as possible.

A variable that is declared `protected` can be accessed from the class where it is defined **and** all classes derived from it. One might say that it is private to those classes and is invisible outside them.

In order to access private variables, the classes can provide `set`- and `get`-methods. The `get`-methods are used to return the variable. The `set`-methods are used to set the variable to a specific value. They can in addition check that the new value is legal. For an example, assume that we defined a class for a geometric component. The component has a width and a height which can be set from the outside. We would like to make sure that the component does not become too small. With an appropriate `set`-method we can guarantee this. In the listing below we assume that the width is stored in an integer variable `width`. The method only changes the value if it is at least 50. In addition, the method returns a boolean value indicating whether the value has been changed.

```java
public boolean setWidth(int w){
    if ( w < 50 ){
        return(false);
    }
    else{
        width = w;
        return(true);
    }
}
```

B.4 ■ Passing references

A frequently occurring problem is that one class wants to use methods from another class. To do this it needs a reference to an instance of the other class. We saw examples of this when a listener wanted to update a panel. In the following we describe the mechanism used in this case.

Three classes are defined, AClass, BClass and CClass. AClass has (non-static) method methodA1. Now BClass wants to use that method. CClass is the 'master' class which uses both AClass and BClass. The structure is listed below.

```
1.  class AClass{
2.
3.    public AClass(){
4.    }
5.
6.    public int methodA1(){
7.      // commands
8.    }
9.  }
10.
11. ----------------------------------
12.
13. class BClass{
14.
15.   public BClass(){
16.   }
17.
18.   public void methodB1(){
19.       int n = methodA1();
20.       //methodA1 unknown
21.   }
22.
23.
24. }
25.
26.
27. ----------------------------------
28.
29. class CClass{
30.
31.   public CClass(){
32.   }
33.
34.   public static void main(String[] a){
35.     AClass a = new  AClass();
36.     BClass b = new  BClass();
37.   }
38.
39. }
```

This will result in a compile-time error at the line

```
int n = methodA1();
```

because inside BClass, the methods of AClass are unknown. In order to access the non-static methods of AClass, BClass has to have an instance of AClass. In the listing below we change the constructor of BClass to have an instance of AClass as an argument. Then that can be used to call the methods of AClass. In CClass an instance of AClass is created and then given to BClass.

```
class AClass{                                        1.
                                                     2.
  public AClass(){                                   3.
  }                                                  4.
                                                     5.
  public int methodA1(){   ){                        6.
   // commands                                       7.
  }                                                  8.
                                                     9.
}                                                    10.
                                                     11.
                                                     12.
-----------------------------------                  13.
                                                     13.
class BClass{                                        14.
                                                     15.
  private AClass aClass;                             16.
                                                     17.
  public BClass(AClass ac){                          18.
      aClass = ac;                                   19.
      // now an AClass is known                      20.
  }                                                  21.
                                                     22.
  public void methodB1(){                            23.
      ...                                            24.
      int n = aClass.methodA1();                     25.
      //methodA1() known as a                        26.
      //method of aClass                             27.
  }                                                  28.
}                                                    29.
                                                     30.
-----------------------------------                  31.
                                                     32.
class CClass{                                        33.
                                                     34.
  public CClass{                                     35.
  }                                                  36.
                                                     37.
  public static void main(String[] a){              38.
    AClass ac = new  AClass();                       39.
    // ac is instance of AClass                      40.
                                                     41.
```

```
42.      AClass b = new  BClass(ac);
43.      // ac is given to BClass in the
44.      // constructor.
45.    }
46.
47. }
```

In the `its`-programs, there are examples of this. `AClass` is like `StatusPanel` which provides a method to set the mouse coordinates. `BClass` is like the listener that knows the coordinates and wants to set them in the status panel. The listener gets a reference to a status panel in the constructor, so it can access the method to set the coordinates.

B.5 ■ The classpath

In Java, the classpath points to all directories containing class files to be used by the `javac` and `java` commands. To specify a classpath one uses the `-classpath` option of these commands. For an example, suppose our class files are located in the directories 'D:\Java\Project', in 'C:\Stuff\Java', and in the current working directory, which is denoted by a dot (.). Suppose the main file is called `mymain.java`. In order that the compile command finds the files one uses

```
javac -classpath .;D:\Java\Project;C:\Stuff\Java mymain.java
```

The paths are separated by semicolons and backslashes are used inside the paths. This is correct for Windows systems. On UNIX/Linux systems, colons and slashes are used instead. As a general remark, one should always include the current working directory (dot) in the classpath. When using packages one should include the directory one above the package in the classpath.

As mentioned in the introduction, Chapter 1, one should always run the `javac` and `java` commands from the directory immediately above the root of the package structure used. For the programs of this book that means the directory containing the directory `its`. The syntax then is (for Windows):

```
javac its\[packageName]\[sourceFileName].java
java  its.[packageName].[sourceFileName]
```

Still it might happen that the compiler complains that it cannot find some class files. This usually happens if an *environment variable* is set for the classpath. These are variables that determine the classpath for the whole computer. They might point to directories not containing the classes of the project. Then the compiler looks in the wrong places. One can solve this problem either by including the correct dictionaries into the environment variable or by specifying an explicit class path in the `javac` and `java` commands. For the latter try

```
javac -classpath . its\[packageName]\[sourceFileName].java
java  -classpath . its.[packageName].[sourceFileName]
```

To set the environment variable one uses commands of the operating system, not of the Java development system. Setting these variables differs from one operating system to the next and even from one version to the next of the same operating system. We therefore refer to the manual or online help of the operating system.

Index

Want more on Java?

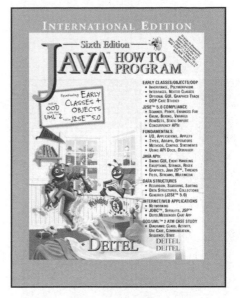

Want more on graphics?

Edward Angel
0321321375
£44.99
Pub Apr 2005

- Bestselling, application-oriented, introductory graphics book with OpenGL - revised for 2005!
- Uses a proven 'top-down', programming-oriented approach to teach core concepts
- Covers all topics required for a fundamental course, including shading, modelling and texture mapping
- Additional student resources include online Source Code
- Lecturer resources include online Solutions, PowerPoint figures, and PowerPoint lecture notes

Visit *www.pearsoned.co.uk/bookshop/*
for more information